SHAYS'S REBELLION

The AMERICAN REVOLUTION'S

Rebellion

FINAL BATTLE

LEONARD L. RICHARDS

PENN *University of Pennsylvania Press, Philadelphia*

10 9 8 7 6 5 4 3 2 1

Published by

University of Pennsylvania Press

Philadelphia, Pennsylvania 19104-4011

Text design by Kristina Kachele

Library of Congress Cataloging-in-Publication Data

Richards, Leonard L.

 Shays's Rebellion : the American Revolution's final battle / Leonard L. Richards.

  p. cm.

 Includes bibliographical references and index.

 ISBN 0-8122-3669-6 (cloth : alk. paper)

 1. Shays's Rebellion, 1786–1787. I. Title.

F69 .R63 2002

974.4'03—dc21   2001058417

For Hazel

CONTENTS

Preface, ix

Prologue, 1

1. Defiance, 4

2. Crackdown, 23

3. Oath Takers and Leaders, 43

4. The Revolutionary Government and Its Beneficiaries, 63

5. Banner Towns and Core Families, 89

6. Reverberations, 117

7. Climax, 139

Notes, 165

Index, 195

PREFACE

THIS BOOK STARTED BY ACCIDENT. FOR TWENTY-FIVE years I rarely gave a thought to Daniel Shays and his followers, even though I lived in the heart of Shays's country and drove down Shays Street every day to work. Like most historians, I thought that as a scholarly topic Shays's Rebellion had been worked to death. I had heard the standard story many times—first as a high school student, then as an undergraduate, then as a graduate. It appeared in every American history textbook as well as scores of scholarly books. I had read it at least two dozen times.

Then, about five years ago, I ran into a classroom problem. Just before the fall classes were to begin, the bookstore phoned with the news that the first book that I had assigned to a class of forty-five students was no longer available. Could I come up with a last-minute replacement? I said "yes" and hurriedly began thumbing through one book after another. In the process, I discovered in a footnote that the Massachusetts Archives had the names of the Shaysites, not just the names of the leaders, but some four thousand names.

That is unusual. With most rebellions, finding out who participated is an impossible task. With Shays's Rebellion, however, the rank and file had the opportunity to avoid harsh punishment by accepting a temporary loss of citizenship and swearing future allegiance to the state and its rulers. Thousands did so. Scores of others were arrested and stood trial.

Why, then, had scholars not studied these men in depth? That puzzled me. Was it worth driving eighty miles to Boston to find out? I procrastinated for months. Then, again by accident, I learned that the university library had the pertinent state archives on microfilm. On taking a peek, I understood immediately what the problem was. The handwriting was awful. Working through it was certain to be arduous, even for someone who had spent years deciphering student blue books.

It was indeed arduous. Once it was done, however, the next step was far more pleasant. I decided to learn something about the men on the list. Here I had the help of town archivists and town historians who always went the extra mile to provide me with the data I needed. Many of these men and women I have thanked in the notes, but of the many who came to my aid I am especially in debt to Bernie Lally of West Springfield. Without his help, I would know next to nothing about his hometown.

From learning about the men on the list, it became obvious that the standard story of Shays's Rebellion did not wash. The notion that the Shaysites were poor farmers hopelessly in debt, a notion that appears in scores of scholarly books as well as every American history textbook, accounted for only a minority of the rebels. What of the majority? And what of men who did not rebel? Many of them were much worse off than the men who took up arms against the state. Why did they not rebel? The standard story made little sense. And with many rebels, it made no sense whatsoever. They did not even come close to fitting the stereotype. So I ended up doing more research and ultimately writing this book.

While writing the book, I received plenty of help from my colleagues at the University of Massachusetts, especially Bruce Laurie, who provided me with a whole stack of pertinent articles as well as much encouragement. I also owe a very large debt to many archivists and librarians, especially those at the University of Massachusetts, the American Antiquarian Society, the Massachusetts Historical Society, and the Massachusetts Archives. Along the way, I also taught three writing seminars on rural rebellions, and the students in those classes undoubtedly taught me more than I taught them. Some of that work I have cited in this book. I also gave a dozen or so lectures on Shays's Rebellion and benefited from the sound criticism I received from members of those audiences. Special thanks are also due to Christopher Clark, who made several suggestions for improving the manuscript, and to Robert Lockhart and Erica Ginsburg, who shepherded the manuscript through publication.

𝒫ROLOGUE

IN THE LATE WINTER OF 1786-87, GEORGE WASHINGTON had to make a decision. The events of the last six months had been maddening. Within weeks mobs ranging from two hundred to one thousand men had shut down the courts in five Massachusetts counties. In January, an army led by three officers of the Massachusetts Line had tried to seize the federal arsenal at Springfield, the storehouse of nearly all of New England's military weapons.

For the retired general, sitting by the fire in his Mount Vernon study, sifting through reports, the news from New England was frightening. Just four years earlier, in 1783, he had said good-bye to war after almost nine years of service. The country had finally won the Revolution, and in a formal ceremony, with much fanfare and tears, he had returned his commission to Congress. Since then, he had been happily retired on the banks of the Potomac. He had never tired of the small details of farming. He loved agricultural experiments, breeding horses and hounds, and especially hoped to produce a superior line of mules. The rhythms of rural life had also rejuvenated him. He no longer felt like a weary traveler who had spent too many days carrying too many heavy burdens on his shoulders. Now, just a few days shy of his fifty-fifth birthday, he had become noticeably more cheerful and far more relaxed.

Yet, according to the reports on Washington's desk, the nation he had done so much to create was falling apart. The newspapers had initially linked the mobs to rural indebtedness. Why else would men shut down the courts if it was not to suspend debt suits? The explanation seemed logical—and later would be embraced by many historians.[1] Yet, if the rebels were just poor debtors trying to stop the courts from foreclosing on their farms, why did they also try to seize the Springfield arsenal? Had they succeeded, they would have been better armed than the state of Massachusetts. Did they also intend to overthrow the Massachusetts government?

Especially troubling to Washington were the reports of his former aide, David Humphreys. Not only was Humphreys someone Washington liked and trusted, but Humphreys was also a New Englander, living in New Haven, just downriver from the troubles. Surely he knew what was going on. Was he to be ignored, then, when he attributed the uprising to the "licentious spirit prevailing among the people"? Or when he characterized the malcontents as "levellers" determined to "annihilate all debts public & private"?[2]

More disturbing yet were the reports from Washington's former artillery commander, General Henry Knox. The three-hundred-pound Knox knew Massachusetts well—did he not? He had been a Boston bookbinder and bookseller before the Revolution. He was now planning a four-story summer place on one of his Maine properties, land that once belonged to his wife Lucy's family. He was a New Englander, through and through. Surely he must understand the strange people who lived around him. He was also Washington's good friend as well as a former subordinate. Would Knox lead his mentor astray? What, then, was one to make of his claim that the real goal of the insurgents was to seize the property of the opulent and redistribute it to the poor and desperate? Had the "levelling principle" truly captured the hearts of the people?[3]

Much in the same vein were the reports from Washington's Virginia correspondents. They too worried about what was to become of their properties. They too had concluded that the whole nation was in danger, that if government in Massachusetts gave way to anarchy, governments throughout the new republic would give way to anarchy. Was Massachusetts not the epitome of sound government and stability? Was its constitution not the best balanced of the new Revolutionary charters? If the people in Massachusetts could erupt in disorder, what lay in store for the other twelve states? After all, every state had its troublemakers. The time had thus come, James Madison suggested, for Washington to come out of retirement, to lead the Virginia delegation at the upcoming convention to be held in Philadelphia, and to help reconstruct the nation that he, more than any other man, had done so much to create.[4]

No more fuel was needed to fire Washington's fears. The hope that "the mischiefs will terminate," he surmised, was probably just wishful thinking. Years ago, "when this spirit first dawned probably it might easily have been checked." But that was no longer the case. There were now "combustibles" in every state just waiting to explode. Thus "it was scarcely within reach of the human ken . . . to say when, where, or how it will end." But the unhappy truth was that the nation's political fabric was probably to be "much tumbled and tossed, and possibly wrecked altogether."[5]

Washington thus made his decision. Remaining in retirement was no longer feasible. He had to attend the Philadelphia convention. He had no choice. Everything he represented, everything he had fought the Revolution for, was at stake. The country desperately needed a stronger national government, one that could maintain order, one that could protect property holders like him, one that could suppress malcontents like those in Massachusetts.[6]

DEFIANCE

out of retirement began the previous summer, two weeks after the tenth anniversary of the Declaration of Independence, July 18, 1786, an unseasonably cool day in much of western Massachusetts.

Worries about the weather, the cold fronts that swept down from Canada and the hot and humid air that came from the southwest, marked the entire region. It was farm country, with the bulk of the population—85 percent or more—eking out a living on small family farms. The state record keepers referred to the owners of these farmsteads as "yeomen," and their adult male workers as "laborers," but the latter was a misnomer. In most cases the laborers were actually the sons of the yeomen, and many in a year or two would come in possession of land themselves and be designated yeomen.

Most of these farm families tried to be self-sufficient but never quite achieved it. Every village thus had a blacksmith with a forge, and in most townships there were also well-traveled paths that led to the dwelling of the tanner who made buckskin out of deerskin, the wheelwright who fashioned carts and wagons, the cooper who combined staves into barrels, and the midwife who came at all hours of the night to help with childbirth.

One of these many specialists was Dr. Nehemiah Hines. In his hometown of Pelham, however, he was not regarded as just a medical man. In 1786 he was also a town leader, the town moderator, an office he had never held before but would hold many times in the coming years. He had been a selectman in the past.[1] Together, the doctor and the selectmen were Pelham's chief administrative officers, with a host of responsibilities, ranging from seeing that the town's children were properly educated to laying out bridges and roads. They were also expected to protect the town against troubles from the outside world. They had been given these responsibilities earlier that spring by the annual town meeting.

In fact, however, they had been selected well before the annual meeting. Every year, at Conkey's Tavern and other Pelham watering holes, men met and discussed who was best suited to run the town. Here most of the politicking took place, and here was where basic decisions were usually made. The annual town meeting, in most instances, just ratified the results. With no nominations, no speeches, no canvassing for votes, the moderator simply called for the secret ballots, and the men of the town stepped forth and gave theirs to the town clerk.

Virtually every town in western Massachusetts had a similar setup. It had been sanctioned long ago by the provincial government in Boston. It was also part of the much-heralded New England tradition which the original settlers had brought with them. In the case of Hines's hometown, most of these founders had come from eastern Massachusetts. In the nearby towns, most had come out of Connecticut. Migrating up the Connecticut River, they had fanned out through the river valley and the surrounding hills, establishing thousands upon thousands of family farms, largely at the expense of the lush stands of oaks, chestnuts, maples, hemlocks, and white pines that had once dominated the region.

All these settlers, in turn, formed town governments that were essentially their own masters. Indeed, ignoring orders from Boston was commonplace. One Massachusetts statute, for example, decreed that all town elections were to be held in March. Some towns followed the rule; others met in February; still others waited until April. Similarly, according to the lawmakers in Boston, only men worth a certain amount of money—£20 in town elections, £40 and then £60 in Massachusetts elections—were eligible to vote. Nearly every town ignored this rule. Indeed, they not only allowed all male inhabitants to attend the annual town meeting and submit a ballot, but fined them if they did not do so. And many towns even elected men who, under the law, were ineligible to vote.

Had Dr. Hines been clairvoyant that July day, he might have stayed at home. Instead, he set off for an emergency meeting of the Pelham town selectmen. The road took him past the farm of Daniel and Abigail Shays.

Hines, at age forty, was one year older than his neighbor. Both men were

Revolutionary veterans, Shays as a captain with five years' service, Hines as a surgeon mate in the Massachusetts Line. Both had served in the same regiment, Woodbridge's Massachusetts, at the outset of the war. Both had been "winter soldiers" who had fought during the "worst of times" as well as the best, the kind of men that Washington had desperately needed to become a national icon. Hines trusted Shays and had lent him money.[2]

Otherwise, the two men had little in common. Daniel and Abigail Shays were relative newcomers to the area, having moved into the adjacent town of Shutesbury just before the war, and their nearest kin lived in the town of Brookfield, many miles away. Daniel was active on the Pelham Committee of Safety, and Abigail was part of a movement to establish a second church. In contrast, the Hineses had deep roots in the community and more family connections. A dozen or so Hineses lived in Pelham and the neighboring town of Greenwich. Scarcely a year passed without one Hines or another being elected selectman or moderator.

The Hineses were also much wealthier than the Shayses. The latter were hardly at the bottom of the economic ladder, as some of their detractors would later claim. They had a farm of over one hundred acres. Only a small portion was in tillage, and they had just enough pasturage for one horse and one cow, but that was common among hill country farmers, who generally strove to be self-sufficient rather than produce bumper crops or livestock for an outside market. Even had the Shayses dreamed of the latter, they would not have had much luck in a place like Pelham. The land was too rocky and too far from navigable water. In this hardscrabble economy, the Shayses' farm was ranked in the second 20 percent of town assessments. In contrast, Hines's holdings put him in the top 5 percent. His economic worth was nearly three times that of Shays. He not only made a living from his medical practice. He also owned a farm and a tavern.[3]

The meeting that Hines attended that July day was triggered primarily by news from Boston. The legislature, ten days earlier, had decided that its work for the year was completed and adjourned until January 31, 1787.[4] That decision, as far as Hines and the selectmen of Pelham were concerned, was the last straw. Once again, the legislature had flouted the will of the people. For the past four years, scores of small communities like Pelham and Greenwich had pleaded with the legislature to address their concerns, and once again the legislature had adjourned without doing so. The communities' petitions had been polite, deferential, sometimes even groveling. But the message was clear: The backcountry economy was in bad shape, and the new state government was just making matters worse.

Daniel and Abigail Shays's Pelham farmhouse, from an old photograph. Reprinted from C. O. Parmenter, *History of Pelham* (Amherst, Mass., 1898), 391. The house, built in the modest Cape style, was standard among hill country farmers. In 1787, it was portrayed as a "stye" by a government supporter who wanted everyone to believe that the former army officer was a "brute" unfit for leadership. Along with the house, Shays owned one hundred acres and was ranked in the top third of town taxpayers.

Woven into the petitions were dozens of tough questions. How, for example, were farmers to pay debts and taxes with hard money when no hard money was available? And why did honest men have to cope with so many layers in the court system? Was it just so well-connected lawyers and court officials could collect fees at every step of the way? And why was there a state senate? Was it not just an unnecessary waste of the taxpayers' money? And did it not just provide another bastion of privilege for the Boston elite? And why was the government in Boston anyway? Why was it not more centrally located as in the other states? Was it so the mercantile elite could pass oppressive laws when distance and bad weather kept the people's representatives from getting to Boston?

Such questions were rarely expressed so boldly, but they had sparked many a complaint about taxes, debts, the shortage of legal tender, and the structure of government. In addition, the legitimacy of the 1780 state constitution had frequently been questioned. So too had the legitimacy of the state's rulers. Was it not the duty of government officials to protect the people rather than oppress them? Were most of the current rulers not just as corrupt as King George's ministers? What then had the Revolution accomplished? Such thoughts clearly circulated in the west, and the town leaders had tried to politely convey the message. Yet, each year the legislature had ignored their complaints and only added to the misery.

The local newspapers out of Springfield and Northampton still counseled patience. So too did the Reverend David Parsons at the First Church in nearby Amherst. Hines and the Pelham selectmen, however, had had it. They had heard the old refrain of "wait until next year" many times before, and each year the legislature had met, ignored their pleas, and caused even more trouble. They decided to write a letter to the selectmen of Amherst, and to eleven other neighboring towns, calling for a meeting on July 31 at John Bruce's inn, which in turn would call for a countywide convention. The goal was to get at the root of the problem, to find "some method" to change the state constitution and thus get a more responsive government.[5]

The town fathers of Pelham were not the only ones to call for countywide conventions that summer. Other towns also set up committees of correspondence and by the end of July several counties had plans for a convention. Bristol County met first at Taunton, on July 23. Then, a month later, Worcester, Hampshire, Middlesex, and Berkshire followed suit. The convention set in motion by the Pelham selectmen, however, was the largest. Held at the Hatfield home of Colonel Seth Murray on August 22, fifty Hampshire towns were represented. Among the delegates were John Hastings, Hatfield's representative to the state legislature; Benjamin Ely, West Springfield's former state representative; and William Pynchon, the eminent voice of Springfield's most powerful family. The delegates, according to the diarist Sylvester Judd, all knew what was coming. That had been made clear to him when the town of Southampton met to select a delegate. The plan, noted Judd, was to set forth a list of grievances and then "break up the Court next Week."[6]

The convention adopted twenty-one articles. Of these, seventeen were grievances, and at least six necessitated a radical change in the state government—indeed, a new state constitution. The delegates wanted the upper house of the state legislature to be abolished, the present mode of representation in the lower house to be radically revised, government officers to be elected annually by the lower house, the salaries of those officers to be determined annually by the lower house, the Courts of Common Pleas and General Sessions of the Peace to be abolished, and the state legislature to be moved out of Boston. The delegates also objected to the state's tax system, the high costs of the state's legal system, the scarcity of legal tender, and various forms of financial favoritism granted by the state to the Boston elite. Finally, they wanted the state legislature to be recalled immediately to address their grievances.[7]

One week later, on the last Tuesday of August, well before daybreak, Captain Joseph Hines led several hundred Greenwich and Pelham men toward Northampton, Massachusetts. A kinsman of the Pelham doctor, Joseph Hines was an old hand at leading men. He had been a captain in the Massachusetts Line during the Revolution. The town fathers of Pelham had wanted Daniel Shays to lead the Pelham men, but he had refused and the task had fallen to Deacon John Thompson, a fifty-year-old militia captain and former town selectman.[8]

At the bottom of Pelham hill, Hines and his men joined forces with a large Amherst contingent led by Captain Joel Billings. A thirty-nine-year-old farmer and the father of eight children, Billings was also an old hand at leading men. He too had commanded troops during the American Revolution. He also had been a town selectman, the same office his father had held for nearly twenty years. With him were many from east Amherst, including most of the large Dickinson clan.

As the men proceeded through the center of Amherst and through Hadley, only a few additional men joined them. Upon crossing the Connecticut River, however, they encountered hundreds of others who had converged on Northampton from the opposite direction, from the hill towns to the northwest and from West Springfield to the south. After daybreak, the combined forces assembled into military formation and with fifes and drums marched on the Northampton courthouse. Some carried muskets, swords, or bludgeons. Others were unarmed.

Several hours later, three justices in full-length black robes and gray wigs, with the sheriff leading them, approached the courthouse. They were blocked at the door. In a face-saving gesture, they decided to hold court at the house of Captain Samuel Clark, a local innkeeper, and to receive a six-man delegation. The delegation, which included Hines and Billings, demanded that the court adjourn without transacting business. The justices then decided to "continue all matters pending" until November and "adjourned without day." They then packed up, untethered their horses, and returned home.[9]

ONCE MEN LIKE Hines and Billings began disrupting the courts, state authorities took notice. To them, it was obvious that the rebels were doing far more than just disrupting debt cases and harassing judges. They were attacking the most visible symbol of state authority in the west, the state judicial system that had been sanctioned by the Constitution of 1780, thus challenging the very legitimacy of the new state government, treating it as no more deserving of their respect than the old royal government. The authorities' first instinct, therefore, was to suppress the rebellion.

At their beck and call, legally at least, were the local militias. Under the law, men in the militia had to respond in the state's time of need. In 1786, over ninety thousand Massachusetts men had this obligation. Theoretically, all ninety thousand were men of substance with deep roots in the community since militia law rather systematically excluded the poor and the transient from service. These local men of property, in turn, were supposed to turn out in times of crisis, largely out of self-interest, to defend the common good. In practice, moreover, whenever the militia turned out in great numbers, it could be effective. That had been the case at Lexington and Concord in 1775, and also at the Battle of Saratoga in 1777, which many patriots regarded as the turning point in the Revolutionary War. But the militia also had plenty of critics, including George Washington, who especially disliked the idea of citizen soldiers electing their own officers. He much preferred an army like the British army, where the officers came from the upper class, the enlisted men from the lower, and the enlisted men did what they were told.

In Massachusetts, the Constitution of 1780 had put curbs on citizen soldiers' electing their own officers. The top officers were all appointed by the governor and the governor's council and so were many of the local officers. Theoretically, then, the state leaders were in control. But, in reality, the authorities were dependent on local men of property turning out in times of crisis, just as they had at Lexington and Concord, just as they had at Saratoga. In the fall of 1786, the authorities learned quickly that they faced an entirely different situation from what the Revolutionary leaders had faced at Lexington and Concord.

That first became clear a few days after the Northampton court had been closed, in early September, when the justices attempted to hold court in Worcester. On the first day of the scheduled court session, the judges encountered an angry crowd of some one hundred men with bayonets blocking the courthouse door. Chief Justice Artemas Ward of Shrewsbury tried to reason with the crowd. He had been a Revolutionary War general and was now speaker of the Massachusetts House of Representatives as well as a judge. He expected to be obeyed. He was heckled instead.

By the second day, the hecklers were joined by another two hundred to three hundred insurgents, most of whom came from the northwestern part of the county. General Jonathan Warner, upon orders from Governor James Bowdoin, called out the Worcester militia. The troops refused the call to action. Many in fact joined the insurgents. Chief Justice Ward and the other judges then decided to postpone all cases, both criminal and civil, until later that fall.[10]

The governor and other state leaders demanded an explanation. What had gone wrong in Worcester? Why had the militia not defended the court? General Warner reported that despite "the most pressing orders," he found the people "universally" reluctant "to turn out for support of the government." In some cases, he had encountered a "flat denial"; in others "evasion or delay which amounted to same thing." Sheriff William Greenleaf attributed the mass disobedience to the insurgents' getting their forces out "much faster and quicker than those for the support of authority." That, he said, "induced a great number of the militia to join them as they appeared most formidable." Artemus Ward simply said that the militia in Worcester were "too generally in favor of the people's measures" to fight for the government.[11]

The news from Worcester shocked the Bowdoin administration into calling an emergency meeting, two days later, with William Phillips, the president of the state's only bank, other financiers, and state officeholders. This group, in turn, agreed to gather a huge crowd for a mass meeting four days later at Faneuil Hall in Boston. The purpose was to endorse a document drafted by the old Revolutionary hero Sam Adams, the merchant Stephen Higginson and his partner Jonathan Jackson, and the insurance underwriter Edward Payne. This document sang the praises of the 1780 state constitution and denounced the insurgents. The crowd, as planned, did what they were told.[12]

If the reports from Worcester dismayed the governor and the state's Boston leadership, what happened the next week was even more alarming. Three courts were due to open—two within forty miles of Boston, the other in the far western end of the state. The first reports trickling into Boston were mixed. In Concord, eighty to one hundred insurgents under Captain Job Shattuck of Groton braved a drenching rain to stop the opening of the Middlesex County Court. They were soon joined by ninety to one hundred reinforcements from Worcester County. The judges expected help from the local militia. They did not get it. Instead, a "convention" of neutrals tried to moderate between the insurgents and the judges. The neutrals finally decided that the situation was hopeless and advised the judges not to hold court. The judges reluctantly agreed and left town without conducting any business.[13]

More upbeat, yet puzzling, was the news from south of Boston. In Taunton, David Cobb, justice of the Bristol County Court of Common Pleas and major general of the militia, had gotten a jump on the insurgents. He had ordered out his own troops and some from nearby Plymouth County well before the court was due to open. Hence, when some 50 armed and 150 unarmed insurgents arrived, they found the court well protected. The judges got inside the courthouse and officially opened court. But they did not transact any business. Instead, they adjourned until December. Cobb claimed that he allowed the adjournment because he did not want to impose any harm on the people. But how was the adjournment to be interpreted? As a defeat for the insurgents? Or a defeat for the state?[14]

What happened in Great Barrington, however, was not open to interpretation. On the evening before the Berkshire County Court was scheduled to open, armed men from the surrounding towns seized the courthouse. The next day, the militia under Major General John Paterson marched into town to protect the court. Paterson had about one thousand men, more than enough to protect the court, or so he thought. But someone suggested a vote, with men in favor of opening the court moving to one side of the highway, men favoring closure to the other. Nearly eight hundred men abandoned Paterson and sided with the rebels. The judges opened court, quickly adjourned sine die, and then retired to the house of Dr. William Whiting. The insurgents followed them and demanded that the judges sign an agreement not to hold court "until the Constitution of the Government shall be revised or a new one made." Of the four judges, only Jahleel Woodbridge of Stockbridge refused to sign.[15]

Two weeks later, the news from Springfield was less dire. In trying to convene the Supreme Judicial Court, the state's highest tribunal, Chief Justice William Cushing and his three associates encountered one thousand farmers who demanded that the court not try men who had broken up debtor courts. The judges had the protection of the militia and hundreds of "respectable gentlemen" assembled by General William Shepard. The two sides paraded back and forth before the court. The court officially opened, but no jurors could be found. Four days later, Cushing and his associates suspended court.[16]

WHAT MADE ALL this doubly maddening to the Massachusetts leadership was that militia units in other states seemed to be far more dependable.

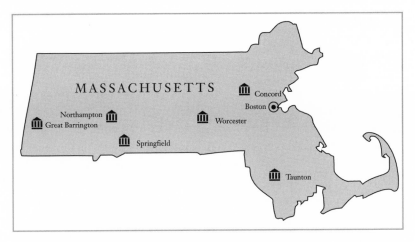

Sites of courts closed by rebels, August–December 1786.

In September, at the same time Massachusetts was having its court troubles, two hundred men surrounded the state house in Exeter, New Hampshire. To get them to disband, Governor John Sullivan promised immediate consideration of their complaints. When they dispersed, Sullivan reneged on his promise and had the Rockingham militia and three companies of light horsemen go after the malcontents. Nearly two thousand militiamen responded to his call. Thirty horsemen galloped across the countryside and seized a bridge to the insurgents' rear, thus cutting off retreat, while a larger force of foot soldiers pummeled the fleeing dissidents. Most of the rebels got away, but to make a point Sullivan forced thirty-nine captives to march with hats in hand twice through government troops, made two rebel leaders beg for their lives, tried six men for rioting, and outlawed all conventions. He then turned to the legislature for approval and got it.[17]

In Vermont, the authorities also enjoyed support from the militia. In October, a band of armed men attempted to close the Windsor County Court. They were dispersed by some six hundred militiamen. In late November, a crowd of one hundred potential rebels, mostly veterans, surrounded the county court in Rutland. They demanded its closure. Local militia companies turned out in droves and defended the court.[18]

Why not the same in Massachusetts? Why was the Massachusetts militia less responsive than Vermont's and New Hampshire's? Conservatives had an answer. In New Hampshire, Governor Sullivan was battling men in the state capital, where dissidents were a minority and where he had the

backing of merchants, shopkeepers, and the coastal militias. He was not trying to suppress an insurgency in the backcountry, as was the case in Massachusetts. And Vermont? Well, Vermont was a special case. It was run by
outlaws, and outlaws controlled both the militia and the courts.

To make matters worse, the leaders of Massachusetts faced sharp criticism from some of their own kind. One such troublemaker was Moses Harvey. A state legislator from the small town of Montague in Hampshire
County, Harvey had been a captain in Brewer's Massachusetts Regiment in
1775, when Boston and the surrounding towns desperately needed help
from the countryside. He and his men had performed bravely, and he had
been honored as a hero of the Revolution. Now a captain in the local militia, he not only refused to back the state's call to arms, but also encouraged
his men to join the rebellion. Moreover, he had characterized the men who
sat with him in the state legislature as "thieves, knaves, robbers, and high-
waymen."[19]

More irritating still was the behavior of Chief Justice William Whiting
of the Berkshire County Court. Like many in the state leadership, the fifty-
six-year-old justice was the scion of a wealthy family. As a youth in Connecticut, he had become a doctor and upon moving to Great Barrington
had become one of the original incorporators of the Massachusetts Medical Society. Regarded as a dependable conservative, he had received a number of appointments from the state leadership, beginning with the post of
justice of the peace in 1775. And, at the urging of Theodore Sedgwick and
other Berkshire conservatives, he had been appointed to the exalted position of chief justice in 1783.

That such a man would now turn on the state leadership caught Sedgwick and his colleagues by surprise. But just days before the Berkshire court
was scheduled to meet, Whiting published a letter justifying the rebellion.
Writing under the name "Gracchus," the chief justice accused the Massachusetts aristocracy of being "overgrown Plunderers." Like the greedy
Roman aristocrats who had outraged the Gracchus brothers in the days of
the Roman republic, they were enriching themselves at the expense of ordinary farmers, and thus they too were enemies of the republican form of
government.[20]

Ordinary citizens, noted Whiting, were also at fault. But their main fault
was their "Inattention to public affairs for Several years past." Had they
exercised their rights under the constitution, electing and instructing good
men, the aristocracy would never have been in a position to plunder them

and the republican form of government would not be in danger. But now that "the people" had discovered these evils, they must act and, if necessary, "disturb government." Indeed, it was not a choice on their part. It was an obligation. In all free republican governments "the People at large" had an "indispensable duty to watch and guard their Liberties, and to crush the very first appearances of incroachments upon it."[21]

Especially incensed by Whiting's behavior was his old comrade Sedgwick. The most prosperous lawyer practicing in Whiting's court, Sedgwick had just built a mansion in Stockbridge, a palace by Berkshire County standards, which had become a symbol of how well lawyers were doing in an otherwise depressed economy. Although the judge never mentioned Squire Sedgwick by name, he saved some of his sharpest barbs for lawyers and state-mandated lawyer's fees. It did not take a genius to figure out whom he had in mind. In private conversations, moreover, Whiting apparently had asserted that Sedgwick was one of the worst plunderers of all, making £1,000 a year because of the state's exorbitant fee schedule. Sedgwick was determined to get even, not by assassinating him as the Roman aristocrats did Tiberius and Gaius Gracchus centuries ago, but by stripping him of his power and reducing him to the level of a convicted criminal.[22]

The troubles that Massachusetts had with its militia also caught the attention of the Continental Congress. On October 20, the congress decided that the Massachusetts elite needed federal help to suppress the insurrection. The state militia just was not up to the job. The federal arsenal in Springfield was also in danger. Congress resolved to add 1,340 soldiers to the nation's 700-man army. Of the new soldiers, Massachusetts was to raise 660 men; the other New England states, 560; the rest of the country, 120.[23]

Congress decided that it was "not expedient," however, to tell the public the real reason "for the raising of such troops." So a phony reason was concocted—that additional troops were needed because of a pending Indian war in the Ohio Valley. The ruse did not work. Most Bostonians, according to General William North, smelled "a rat" as soon as they heard about the need for New England troops against Ohio Indians. In the state legislature, noted Elbridge Gerry, country members found the Indian explanation laughable.[24]

The sharpest critic, however, was probably Baron von Steuben, the Prussian drillmaster who had trained Washington's army. Writing under the name "Bellisarius," the Byzantine general who had suppressed an insurrection in Constantinople and defeated the Vandals and Huns in the 530s, the baron found the whole situation to be a jarring revelation. Had it been Delaware that needed the help of the congress, he argued, it might have been understandable. But Massachusetts, a "state always conducted by superior geniuses," had "on her rolls ninety-two thousand militiamen." Why should it "stand in need of foreign support, in the administration of internal government?" The only plausible reason, suggested von Steuben, was that the "numerous militia" coincided "in sentiment with the malcontents," and that "the present system of administration" had the support of only "a very small number of respected gentlemen." And if that was the case, why "would Congress dare to support such an abominable oligarchy?"[25]

Despite such criticisms, Secretary of War Henry Knox turned the task of expanding the Continental Army over to General Henry Jackson, a close friend. Jackson was bombarded with letters from men who wanted commissions. But he had virtually no luck raising money or recruiting ordinary soldiers. Few men of property were willing to risk gold and silver on a project launched by the Confederation government, and few ordinary men wanted to be privates. Jackson also had to work within certain restrictions. He was to recruit no blacks, no mulattos, no Indians; no man under five feet six inches; no man under age sixteen or over age forty-five. By mid-January, he had only one hundred recruits.[26]

THE COMPLAINTS OF Sedgwick and others forced the governor to reconvene the legislature. Since September, the one-time Revolutionary agitator Sam Adams, along with several Boston conservatives led by the merchant Stephen Higginson and the insurance underwriter Edward Payne, had been publicly calling for harsh measures. Adams in particular insisted that full punishment be meted out, that rebels be strung up and blood be shed. In "monarchies," he argued, "the crime of treason and rebellion may admit of being pardoned or lightly punished, but the man who dares rebel against the laws of a republic ought to suffer death."[27]

In this atmosphere, the Massachusetts legislature passed a series of measures. The new laws were not as draconian as Adams wanted, but rather a mixed bag, reflecting what many regarded as a carrot-and-stick policy. On the carrot side were several bills to ease the tax burden, such as allowing payment in kind for some unpaid back taxes, and extending the due date for current taxes from January 1 to April 1, 1787. To reduce taxes over the long term, plans were made to sell off 1,800 square miles of Maine land and

Samuel Adams, c. 1770–72. Engraving by G. F. Stern after a portrait by John Singleton Copley. Courtesy American Antiquarian Society. The intent of this portrait was to present Adams as an unflinching defender of liberty and of constitutional rights. At the time it was made, Adams was Boston's foremost spokesman against British rule. By the late 1780s, however, he had left the politics of protest far behind him and now insisted that anyone who challenged the government of Massachusetts should be harshly punished.

apply the proceeds to the public debt. Much also was made out of several temporary measures which were supposed to ease some of the pressure on debtors, including one that allowed them to bypass certain legal fees for two years and another that allowed them, for the next eight months, to pay the principal on some private debts in land or personal property.

Also on the carrot side was an act of indemnity, pardoning all those who had obstructed the court between June 1 and publication of the act. The miscreants were given until January 1 to take an oath of allegiance to the state and its rulers. Kindhearted legislators hoped that dozens of militia captains and hundreds of ordinary rioters would take advantage of this act. Instead, only one man did: William Bemis of Spencer.[28]

The sticks tended to reflect Adams's call for blood. One measure, officially labeled the Riot Act, proclaimed that sheriffs and other officials "shall be indemnified and held guiltless" for killing rioters who failed to disperse or resisted capture, and that the rioters "shall forfeit all their lands, tenements, goods and chattels to the Commonwealth . . . and shall be whipped 39 stripes on the naked back, at the public whipping post and suffer imprisonment for a term not exceeding 12 months." While in jail, moreover, the rioters were to receive thirty-nine stripes every three months. Another measure, passed two weeks later, suspended the writ of habeas corpus until

July 1, 1787, and allowed sheriffs and other officials to imprison rioters far away from their home communities—"in any gaol, or other safe place, within the Commonwealth."

Also among the sticks was the Militia Act. Passed in late October, two days before the Riot Act, it was aimed at the likes of Hines and Billings, as well as other militia officers who had taken up arms against the state. It proclaimed that "whosoever officer or soldier shall abandon any post committed to his charge, or shall speak words inducing others to do the like in time of engagement, shall suffer death." Adams wanted them put to death immediately. Most legislators, however, were willing to give them a chance to repent. Clergy across the state were ordered to read the new laws to their congregations.[29]

So, on the following Sunday and the Sunday thereafter, news of the death threat spread. That, however, failed to bring all local militias into full compliance with state law. As before, militia units near Boston generally obeyed the law, those in the backcountry ignored it. The militia in three counties—all in eastern Massachusetts—responded when Governor Bowdoin called upon them to defend the scheduled opening of the Middlesex County Court in Cambridge. This allegedly scared off the insurgents, and the court opened as planned on the last Tuesday of November without a hitch.[30] A week later, however, the governor had trouble for the second time in opening the Worcester court. Both the governor and General Warner, commander of the Worcester militia, knew that trouble was coming. They had heard as much four days before the scheduled opening. But Warner did not trust his men, and the state government was unprepared. After much vacillation, the governor ordered the judges to do something to save face. The judges never got the chance. On Sunday, two days before the court was scheduled to open, some seventy insurgents captured the courthouse. Over the next two days, despite a blinding snowstorm, four hundred more men joined them. On Tuesday, the judges decided to meet in a nearby tavern, dutifully pretended the court to be open, and then promptly adjourned.[31]

The hostility of backcountry militias to state authorities never abated. Again and again, government leaders from eastern Massachusetts went west only to find that they had grossly underestimated the disdain western militias had for state authorities. Especially hostile were Revolutionary veterans. Out of 637 veterans from Northampton and surrounding towns, only 23 volunteered for duty. The captain and senior lieutenant of the Northampton men who responded to the state's call to arms had only fourteen days of Revolutionary service between them.[32] In comparison, all the rebel captains had at least three years of experience.

ESPECIALLY OFFENSIVE TO many old soldiers, and people generally in the west, were the new powers the legislature bestowed on the governor and the governor's council. The act of November 10 gave the governor and his council the authority to imprison "all persons whatsoever" who in their opinion were dangerous to the "safety of the Commonwealth" in any jail in the commonwealth. The law also denied such individuals the right of habeas corpus until July 1, 1787.

On November 28 Governor Bowdoin decided to make use of his new powers. Based on information provided by Oliver Prescott of Groton, a town leader and member of one of the commonwealth's first families, Bowdoin issued a warrant for three Groton men and two Shirley men. All five men were veterans of the Revolution. Two—Oliver Parker of Groton and Nathan Smith of Shirley—had been officers in the Massachusetts Line. One—John Kelsey of Shirley—was currently a town selectman. Four of the five were listed on the indictment as "gentlemen." The only yeoman in the group was Benjamin Page of Groton. He, at age thirty-three, was also the youngest of the five. The other men were either in their late forties or had just reached age fifty. Four of the five had large families, with six to eleven children.

All five men were clearly thorns in the side of the state elite, but the man that Squire Prescott and the governor especially wanted to get was Job Shattuck of Groton. At age fifty, Shattuck did not travel in the same social circles as Prescott, whose family had long enjoyed elite status. But Shattuck was hardly a country bumpkin. He was the largest landowner in town, owning about five hundred acres, much of it bordering the Nashua River. The youngest of eight children, he had benefited from ultimogeniture, the process by which the youngest son inherited the parent's estate, an unusual practice in the English-speaking world, but fairly common in the interior regions of Massachusetts. He had also added to his inheritance and in 1782 had built a three-story house, not a mansion like the Prescotts', but an imposing structure nonetheless. Although he had never been an officer in the Massachusetts Line, he had been a longtime captain of the local militia and had distinguished himself in both the French and Indian War and the American Revolution.[33]

From the standpoint of Squire Prescott and Governor Bowdoin, Shat-

House of Job Shattuck. Reprinted from Virginia May, *Groton Houses* (Groton, Mass., 1978). Courtesy Groton Historical Society. For state leaders who liked to portray the rebel leadership as lowlifes, this house posed a problem, as the owner clearly did not fit the stereotype. Along with this house, which Shattuck built in 1782, he owned five hundred acres of choice farmland and was the wealthiest farmer for miles around.

tuck was an indefatigable troublemaker. As early as October 1781, when Shattuck was a selectman, he had shown his contempt for the new state government and its tax policies. He had first convinced the town meeting to oppose a tax of £840 in silver money that the state had imposed on the town. Then, when that failed to stop the collection process, he, along with Oliver Parker, had led a mob of seventeen Groton men against the two town constables who had accepted the responsibility of collecting the "silver money tax." Two years later, in October 1783, Shattuck had led another mob with "staves and clubs" against other local tax collectors. And in September 1786, he was the leader of the insurgents who had stopped the Concord court from meeting.[34]

Sent to arrest Shattuck and the other four miscreants were three hundred light horsemen commanded by Boston lawyer Benjamin Hichborn and fellow Harvard graduate John Warren. They were joined by the Middlesex County sheriff with about one hundred horsemen. Together, on November 30, they succeeded in seizing the three Groton men—Shattuck, Parker, and Page—but failed in their quest for the two Shirley men. Shattuck resisted, and horseman John Rand slashed him across the knee with a broadsword. Rumor had it that the cavalry also "put out the eye of a woman, and stabbed and cut off the breast of another, and mangled an infant in the cradle." Without question, they injured John Hapsgood, a man not listed on their arrest warrant.

That night, as news of the cavalry raid spread, someone set fire to the potash works of Aaron Brown, a town constable who was instrumental in Shattuck's arrest. Someone also placed incendiary materials under the law office of Ebenezer Champney; these were not lit. Meanwhile, Shattuck, Parker, and Page were whisked off to the Boston jail, some forty miles away, where they remained incommunicado for the rest of the winter, through spring, and into summer.[35]

The suspension of habeas corpus and the jailing of Shattuck, Parker, and Page in a "distant county" set off a storm of protest. More than thirty towns formally protested against the state's action. Held directly responsible was the governor, who had ordered the arrest and had power to pardon and recall troops. His behavior, along with the decisions of the legislature, were likened to "British tyranny," and denounced as "dangerous, if not absolutely destructive to a Republican government."[36]

The state's actions also caused some men to publicly endorse the rebellion. In an address to the "good people of boylston," Sylvanus Billings claimed that in the face of "tirants who are fighting for the promotion and to advance their Intrest wich will Destroy the good people of this Land," there was no other choice but to join the rebels. Also radicalized was Isaac Chenery, a Holden doctor, who proclaimed that living under rulers that "have been cutting and hacking our people" was "not to be suffered," and that he would rather "be under the devil than such a government as this." He now prayed for the overthrow of the government.[37]

Hard-liners among the governing elite, however, had no intention of backing down. They wanted tougher measures than the legislature, especially the lower house, had been willing to authorize. For months they had pressed the legislature to declare a state of rebellion and impose martial law on the western counties. The legislature had refused to go that far.

More receptive had been Governor Bowdoin and his council. Then, in late December, the governor and his men were caught completely by surprise when three hundred insurgents marched on Springfield and forced another court closure. No preparations for the assault had been made. The local sheriff insisted he had no idea that the rebels were coming until the last hour. How could that be? Had the rebels suddenly emerged out of the back alleys of Springfield? No, they had come from towns that were many miles apart, from towns on both sides of the Connecticut River, from towns such as Pelham, Montague, and West Springfield.[38] How could they have organized themselves and marched on Springfield without anyone knowing about it? Only two answers seemed plausible. Either the sheriff was lying, or the government had no friends whatsoever in Hampshire County.[39]

CRACKDOWN

ONCE IT BECAME OBVIOUS THAT WESTERN MASSACHUSETTS was at best indifferent to the plight of the state government, the Bowdoin administration decided to hire an army. On January 4, 1787, without legislative authorization, the call went out for 4,400 men to put down the rebellion. The army was to be under the command of General Benjamin Lincoln.

Just a few days shy of his fifty-fourth birthday, Lincoln was almost as wide as he was tall. He had had a checkered military career. Wounded and something of a hero at the Battle of Saratoga, he had later surrendered an entire army to Sir Henry Clinton at Charleston. Taken prisoner, Lincoln had been paroled home and later exchanged for a British general. Yet, despite this setback, he had survived in military and political circles. Critics said it was only because he had high-level friends. Admirers said it was because he was solid and dependable. Whatever the reason, Washington liked him and had given him the honor of receiving Lord Cornwallis's sword of surrender at Yorktown, and he had later been appointed secretary of war.[1]

Since the legislature had not sanctioned Lincoln's army—much less put up money for it—the governor turned to Boston businessmen for funds. The goal was £6,000. The governor himself subscribed £250. The eminent banker William Phillips contributed £300. But others were slow in parting with their money. Finally, Lincoln himself put the bite on "a club of the first characters of Boston," recommending that they part with a few hundred

Benjamin Lincoln. As portrayed by Henry Sargeant. Courtesy of the Massachusetts His-torical Society. Despite surrendering an entire army at Charleston during the American Revolution, Lincoln had friends in high places and was given the task of crushing the rebellion. Would it change his reputation? When he marched west from Boston, that was still uncertain.

pounds to protect the lion's share of their wealth. That, along with rumors that the insurgents intended to seize the Springfield arsenal, caused sub-scriptions to pick up. Eventually, 153 men contributed to the cause.[2]

Being an officer in Lincoln's army did not appeal to any of the contrib-utors. But to a few members of the Boston aristocracy, it seemed like manna from heaven. Such was the case of Royall Tyler, a Harvard graduate and the heir of a rich Boston merchant. Tyler was technically a lawyer, but he had spent much of his youth dissipating and wasting the family fortune, and was £200 in debt and on the edge of bankruptcy when he heard the call to arms. It "saved" him. A few months later, in April 1787, he produced a play based partly on the characters he met during his brief military career. It was the first American play and as such made Tyler famous.[3]

Only gentlemen like Tyler were offered the rank and privileges of officers. Ordinary soldiers received far fewer enticements. Each was to be supplied with a weapon, a bayonet, a cartridge box, and thirty rounds of ammunition. Each was to get beef, bread, and a half pint of rum per day, as well as £2 for a month's service. Excluded were blacks, even though a month earlier, Prince Hall, head of the Boston African Masons, had pledged seven hundred men. The governor did not want any blacks in Lincoln's army. But "almost all the servants in town" were taken.[4]

Most of the recruits came from the eastern counties. That, however, was not what the authorities had intended. They had counted on the three eastern counties providing two thousand men and the western counties providing twenty-four hundred. Boston exceeded its quota by thirteen men and the other eastern counties met their quotas. This contingent set off for the west in a blinding snowstorm on January 19. As they marched westward, they were to be joined by twelve hundred men from Worcester County. Only six hundred showed up. Then, when they reached Springfield, they were to be joined by twelve hundred Hampshire County men. Only four hundred showed up.[5]

Of these, only a handful were veterans. To Lincoln this was most disappointing. He had expected veterans, officers and privates alike, to turn out in droves. Noteworthy, too, were towns that were especially remiss. Amherst supplied him with just one man—and Pelham supplied him with not a single soldier. Lincoln thus ended up with fourteen hundred fewer men than he anticipated.

The failure of the backcountry to supply troops told just part of the story. The creation of Lincoln's army also radicalized much of the backcountry. Among other things, it tapped the fear of standing armies, a fear that ran deep. In the little town of New Braintree, Joseph Whipple envisioned the army seizing his land, parceling it out among wealthy speculators, and forcing the people to "come under Lordships." James Adams, one of Whipple's neighbors, thought this was a bit optimistic. He forecast state soldiers bringing "us into slavery."[6]

The reaction of the backcountry—and especially the hostility of the backcountry militia—caught Lincoln by surprise. Nonetheless, noted one of his aides, it would have been much worse had it not been for the clergy. Their conservatism and the respect people had for them was all that kept "large numbers of Inhabitants" from taking up arms against the state.[7]

BY THE TIME Lincoln's army began moving west, the state had found a new villain on which to blame its troubles—Dr. Hines's neighbor, Daniel Shays. Shays had been slow in joining the rebellion, rejecting an offer to lead the Pelham contingent in August, but now he commanded the largest insurgent regiment. The authorities insisted that the entire rebellion was also under his direction, that he was the commander-in-chief, the "generalissimo," as the attorney general put it. Some saw him as a potential dictator, others as the tool of King George III.[8] Events would soon prove that they were dead wrong, that there were men who did not follow Shays's directions, but the authorities would continue to depict him as the man in charge and eventually label the entire uprising "Shays's Rebellion."

By this time, moreover, the governor and nearly every newspaper in the state had heard from someone who allegedly had interviewed the newly crowned rebel leader or had served with him in the army. Taken together, these interviews and insider reports made little sense. In one, Shays came across as an aggressive conqueror who intended to burn Boston to the ground; in another, as a hard-luck farmer who worked diligently to prevent all-out violence; in still another, as someone who had been dragooned into the rebellion only because of his military experience.[9] Either the man was a chameleon, mercurial and amazingly deceptive—or half the accounts were fabrications.

A few facts, however, are not in dispute. Shays, like all the other rebel leaders, had been an officer during the Revolution. He differed from the others only in that he worked his way up through the ranks. They had the necessary prestige and connections to begin the war as officers. He had neither and began the war as a common soldier. At the time of the Lexington alarm, he and Abigail were newlyweds trying to carve out a farm in Shutesbury, a hardscrabble hill town some ten miles east of the Connecticut River. When Reuben Dickinson of Amherst called for troops, Shays responded. He fought well, subsequently became a sergeant, then an officer.

The press generally did not dispute Shays's military record. It was clearly distinguished. They just made much of the fact that when the Marquis de Lafayette had honored Shays with a sword, Shays had sold it. To some,

Imaginary portrait of Daniel Shays. Reprinted from John H. Lockwood, *Westfield and Its Historic Influences* (Springfield, Mass., 1922), 2:80. Unlike General Lincoln, the commander of the state forces, Shays never posed for a formal portrait. Yet, in time, he became more famous than his adversary. So what did Shays look like? Most people had no idea, and those who knew him never bothered to fully describe him. But eventually this image caught on and would be reprinted many times.

that proved Shays's poverty. To others, it also proved that he lacked class, that he was at heart a no-account, a poor man who had gained esteem only because of the war—and clearly did not deserve it.

Whatever Shays's true character, he and the other rebel leaders had no intention of submitting meekly to Lincoln's well-armed army. They decided instead to even the odds by seizing the federal arsenal in Springfield. The arsenal, which had been established ten years earlier to supply Revolutionary troops in New England, had the necessary weapons to withstand the invaders. It contained several large field pieces, as well as some seven thousand new muskets with bayonets, several hundred old muskets, thirteen hundred barrels of powder, and over two hundred tons of shot and shells.[10]

Unfortunately for Shays and the other insurgents, twelve hundred militiamen under Major General William Shepard got to the arsenal first. Now in his fiftieth year, Shepard, a gentleman farmer from nearby Westfield, had been a colonel for most of the Revolutionary War. He had a full eight years of military experience. He had expected the insurgents to go after the arsenal. Indeed, he had assumed that their object was to overthrow the government and had wondered why they had not tried to seize the arsenal months earlier "and erect their standard in Springfield."[11]

Drawing of the powder magazine, Springfield arsenal, 1789. Courtesy National Park Service, Springfield Armory NHS, Springfield, Mass. Established during the American Revolution, the Springfield arsenal was the storehouse of most of the military weapons in New England. It therefore was crucial. Had the insurgents gained control of it, they would have been better armed than the state.

Technically, Shepard had no more right to seize the arsenal than did Daniel Shays and his followers. The arsenal did not belong to the state of Massachusetts; it belonged to the federal government. Hence, to use the arsenal and its weapons, Shepard needed written authorization from Secretary of War Henry Knox. He did not have it, yet he knew that Knox was not going to make a fuss if he violated the law. So, without waiting for authorization, Shepard armed his men with arsenal weapons and readied the arsenal's cannons and howitzers to be used against the insurgents.[12]

Against the arsenal's artillery, the insurgents' chances were at best slim. Maybe nonexistent. Most were armed with old muskets, some with only swords or bludgeons. Collectively, they lacked firepower. But that usually is not the way the story is told. Instead the focus is on the chance interception of a message from one rebel leader to another.

The rebels were divided into three regiments, each under a seasoned Revolutionary officer with five or more years of experience. Together, they had more men than Shepard, more than twice as many, but they were not in close contact with one another. Shays's forces were in Palmer, Eli Parsons's in Chicopee, and Luke Day's across the Connecticut River in West Springfield. Miles apart, they had to dispatch messengers back and forth to keep in touch.

The initial plan was for a three-pronged assault on January 25. But just before the scheduled attack, Luke Day unilaterally changed the plan. Claiming to represent "the body of the people assembled in arms," Day sent an ultimatum to General Shepard, giving Shepard and his men twenty-four hours to lay down their arms and return home. If they did not, Day promised "to give nor take no quarter."[13] Simultaneously, Day sent a note to his fellow commanders, Shays and Parsons, telling them that the scheduled attack had been postponed until January 26. The note never reached Shays and Parsons. It was intercepted by Shepard's men.

Hence, late in the afternoon on January 25, two regiments rather than three trod through four feet of snow to attack the arsenal. Leading the onslaught was an advance guard of "about 400 Old Soldiers," eight deep, shoulder to shoulder, commanded by Captain James White, "a brave soldier of the Revolution." To scare them, Shepard had his artillery fire over their heads. But instead of terrifying them, it "only hastened them onward" and accelerated their movement into a trot. To the rear, however, Shays's mounted volunteers panicked, and well over a dozen fell from their horses "through sheer fright." Then Shepard ordered the cannons be fired at "waistband height." At the same instant he had a howitzer concealed on the insurgents' flank spray them with grapeshot. Four men were killed, and many wounded. The rear of Shays's army ran, leaving Captain White and his men alone. White, after "casting a look of scorn behind and before . . . sprang into the bushes at the top of his speed."[14]

Afterward, Eli Parsons blamed the rout on Day. Parsons had expertise. Although now a gentleman farmer from the northwestern corner of the state, he had been an artillery officer during the Revolutionary War. Parsons had been wounded in 1777, and he had wintered with Washington at Valley Forge. He thus knew what it was like to be an underdog in war, short of weapons and supplies, and he also knew the difficulty in assaulting entrenched artillery. Yet he was convinced that there was nothing wrong with the insurgents' original plan. A three-pronged attack on Shepard's artillery, he told a government soldier, would have worked "if their measures had been properly concerted." Only Day's impromptu actions and the errant message, in Parsons's judgment, had "occasioned their failure."[15]

But what if they had succeeded, what if they had taken the arsenal? What then would they have done? On the basis of a purported interview with Shays, the *Massachusetts Centinel* claimed to have inside information. According to the *Centinel*, once the rebels had artillery and were armed to the teeth, they planned "to march directly to Boston, plunder it, and then

William Shepard. Reprinted from John H. Lockwood, *Westfield and Its Historic Influences* (Springfield, Mass., 1922), 2:205. A colonel for most of the Revolutionary War and now a general in the state militia, Shepard became a hero in government circles. He did so, in essence, by violating the law. The Springfield arsenal was federal property, and he had no authority to seize it. But he did so anyway and stopped the insurgents from gaining the weapons they needed.

... to *destroy the nest of devils, who by their influence, make the Court enact what they please*, burn it and lay the town of Boston in ashes." And what was the purpose of all this mayhem? The ultimate goal, Shays allegedly told the interviewer, was to "overthrow the present constitution."[16]

AFTER THE BATTLE at the Springfield arsenal, Shays moved his troops to his hometown of Pelham, Lincoln to the valley town of Hadley. Lincoln still faced backcountry hostility. Even towns like Granby, which produced few rebel soldiers, endorsed Shays's truce terms, which included a pardon for every insurgent, officers as well as privates. Lincoln's army, moreover, had to pay the locals for food and drink, Shays's army did not. "Every exertion," reported Lincoln, was being made by the people in the three western counties "to give Shays succour & aid." Lincoln thus ordered another regiment from eastern Massachusetts to march west "with all possible dispatch."[17]

Despite the grousing, Lincoln still had an enormous advantage in weapons. He had artillery, while Shays had no artillery and less than half of his men were armed.[18] If Lincoln held his forces together, it was only a matter of time. Holding his army together, however, seemed problematic by late January. Further west in Berkshire County, troop commander General John Paterson reported that he could not cope with the "frenzy" against the government and urgently needed reinforcements. In Springfield, cavalry commander Colonel Gideon Burt complained about large-scale desertions, so large that he had stopped sending out patrols, fearing they would run off. In Hadley, Lincoln himself had to court-martial seven men for looting private homes.[19]

Two days later, on Saturday, February 3, Shays moved his ragtag army twenty miles north to the small town of Petersham. Once Lincoln got word, he decided to follow. Leaving Hadley at eight at night, he and his men had to march thirty miles through mostly hostile territory. The first part of the night was "light and the weather clement," but by two or three in the morning the wind shifted westward, and Lincoln's army became trapped in "a very cold and squally" blizzard.[20] By now they were deep into enemy territory, with few if any friendly farms about. They had little choice but to plod on. Had Shays and his men been vigilant, noted one of Lincoln's aides, they could have wreaked havoc on Lincoln's troops, who were stretched out for five miles and moving uphill in narrow lines because of snowdrifts on each side of the road.[21]

But Shays and his men were not alert. They were sound asleep, apparently thinking that no general in his right mind would be out in such a storm. Hence on Sunday morning, at nine o'clock, Lincoln's men, many frostbitten, most in a semistupor, entered Petersham "nearly in the center where Shays had covered his men." They quickly brought two fieldpieces into play and launched their ground attack. Only the steepness of the hill and the depth of the snow stymied them. Had a full-scale surprise attack been possible, noted Lincoln's aide, "we should have arrested very probably one half of his force, for they were so nearly surprised as it was, that they had not time to call in their out parties, or even their guards."[22]

As it was, Shays slipped away, and so did all the other rebel leaders. Most fled north to Athol and then disappeared over the border into New Hampshire and then into Vermont. Most of the rank and file also escaped. They fled in different directions, and then once they were out of harm's way usually headed for home. Lincoln claimed that he captured 150 men. This number, however, is suspect, as not a single officer was captured and only a handful of privates were jailed.

The surprise attack at Petersham made Lincoln's reputation. Years later, a historian or two might attribute his decision to march all night in the teeth of a howling blizzard and his successful assault on Petersham to dumb luck. At the time, however, both the all-night march and the assault were attrib-

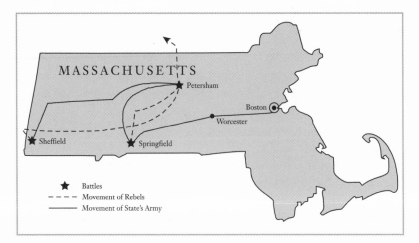

The battles of Springfield, Petersham, and Sheffield, January 25, February 4, and February 17 respectively.

uted to "unbelievable bravery" and superior tactics. And for all practical purposes, Lincoln's "triumph" came to be known as the end of Shays's Rebellion.

AFTER PETERSHAM, THE drive for harsher measures against the rebels reached its peak. For months now, men of Sam Adams's persuasion had been calling for blood. In the eyes of Dr. Jeremy Belknap, soon to be installed as pastor of a prominent Boston church, Lincoln was "too much fettered by his instructions." Having sheriffs read the Riot Act, the eminent clergyman argued, was just a waste of time. The legislature "ought to declare, what everybody knows to be a fact, that a rebellion exists, and then to 'let loose the dogs of war.'"[23]

On the same day that Lincoln and his men seized Petersham, Dr. Belknap got his wish. The legislature declared a state of rebellion and gave the governor power to "exercise martial law, and in every respect treat the citizens in arms against the state and their adherents as open enemies." Within the next two days, the legislature sanctioned an additional 1,500 troops and authorized the state treasurer to borrow £40,000 to meet Lincoln's expenses and to reimburse the Boston merchants who had hired his army. The special loan was to be paid out of impost and excise duties. Governor Bowdoin subscribed £1,763; the banker William Phillips, £2,235; the other merchants, much less.[24]

After receiving news of the battle of Petersham, the Massachusetts elite celebrated General Lincoln as a conquering hero. At the same time, many called for even harsher measures. General Shepard insisted that the rebels be crushed with "much decision and vigour" to "rivet in their minds a compleat conviction of the force of government and the necessity of an entire submission to the laws." General Lincoln himself pressed to have the Supreme Judicial Court sent to the Berkshires "to string up some of the Rebels in the rear of the army."[25]

Echoing these demands was the Boston merchant Stephen Higginson. Even though the rebellion seemed to be "prostrate," declared Higginson, the "disaffection" in the backcountry was so "much more deeply rooted, and extensive, than was apprehended," that once the army was withdrawn, the rebellion might again "erect its daring Standards and openly defy our feeble Government." The insurgents thus had to be crushed, and "every opportunity" had to be "seized" to increase the "energy and stability" of both the state and national government.[26]

Such thinking led to the Disqualification Act. Passed on February 16, just twelve days after the Petersham rout, the bill barred all rebels from serving on juries, holding town or other offices, and voting for civil or military officers for three years. It also barred them from employment as schoolmasters, innkeepers, or retailers of spirituous liquors. Shortly thereafter, Robert Treat Paine, the attorney general, was sent west to prosecute the rebels. A signer of the Declaration of Independence, Paine compiled a "Black List" of the most egregious violators of state law and indicted dozens of men. His methods outraged the Reverend Bezaleel Howard, pastor of the First Church of Springfield. In prosecuting supposed offenders, declared the pastor, Paine "exerted all his Malevolence and Malice." Moreover, the "severe and Tyranical" Disqualification Act was the product of a "wicked and Corrupt Heart." It was designed to "intirely cut off all opposition to Bowdoin" and assure Bowdoin's reelection as governor.[27]

MEANWHILE SHAYS AND his men tried to regroup. On February 13, from Vermont, Eli Parsons issued an appeal to arms:

> Friends and fellow sufferers. Will you now tamely suffer your arms to
> be taken from you, your estates to be confiscated, and even swear to
> support a constitution and form of government, and likewise a code
> of laws, which common sense and your consciences declare to be iniq-
> uitous and cruel? And can you bear to see and hear of the yeomanry

of this commonwealth being patched and cut to pieces by the cruel and merciless tools of tyrannical power, and not resent it even unto relentless bloodshed?

You, as citizens of a republican government [are duty-bound] to support those rights and privileges that the God of nature have entitled you to.

Burgoyne Lincoln and his army.[28]

The rebel leaders also sought support outside Massachusetts. Parsons and Luke Day traveled north to the headquarters of Ethan Allen, the leader of the Green Mountain Boys, to persuade him to take command. Allen had denounced "those who held the reins of government in Massachusetts." He thought that they "were a pack of Damned Rascals and that there was no virtue among them." Nonetheless, the Vermont leader turned down the offer.[29] Five men were also sent to Canada in hopes of getting arms and ammunition. Arriving in Quebec on February 24, they met with the Canadian governor, Lord Dorchester. According to spies for the Massachusetts government, Dorchester wanted to help and promised aid through Joseph Brant, an Indian ally, but the British foreign office under Lord Sidney negated the project as "imprudent."[30]

GENERAL LINCOLN, IN the meantime, had moved to the Berkshires to quell rebellion there.

Privately, the general had little use for the Disqualification Act. To him, it violated republican principles and amounted to an admission that the goals of the American Revolution had failed. He also thought Sam Adams and the others who wanted to lock up everyone in sight had lost touch with reality. Where was the jail space? The jails were already full. Moreover, to lock up everyone in Hampshire County or the Berkshires who opposed the government would require more jail space than existed in all of New England. What Lincoln wanted to do was go easy on rank-and-file rebels, bear down on insurgents who refused to surrender, and get especially tough with insurgents who operated from outside Massachusetts. He also wanted the Supreme Judicial Court to make "a few prompt examples."[31]

For the most part, however, Lincoln did not have the manpower to do much of anything. Stationed in Pittsfield, his command by late February had shrunk to about thirty men. Enlistments for his old troops had expired on February 21. Nearly all the men who had suffered through the march to Petersham had chosen not to reenlist and had gone home. Few troops under the new enlistment had arrived.[32]

THE REBELLION, THEREFORE, just died away with a whimper. There were a number of skirmishes, mainly in the Berkshires, but few of them amounted to much. What they did, mainly, was provide good yarns for later storytellers to embroider.

Each side had its favorites. The rebels particularly liked the story about Mrs. Perry's yarn-beam. Just before Lincoln's dwindling army reached the Berkshires, 250 rebels under Peter Wilcox, Jr., gathered at Lee to prevent the court from sitting. A company of three hundred militiamen under General John Paterson went out to oppose them. The rebels took cover on Perry Hill, got a yarn-beam from the loom of Mrs. Perry and mounted it on a pair of wheels as if it were a cannon. Drawing it back behind a house on the hill, they made all the motions of loading and firing it, flourishing a ramrod and a lighted tar-rope. Paterson's men beat a retreat, and the rebels subsequently negotiated favorable terms, the guarantee of a trial within their own county.[33]

Government supporters, in turn, liked the story of "Mum Bett" and her "old nigger chest." While General Lincoln was in Pittsfield, hoping to somehow get more troops, eighty to ninety rebels under Captain Perez Hamlin entered Massachusetts from New York and pillaged the town of Stockbridge. One party sacked the houses of Squire Jahleel Woodbridge, Deacon Ingersoll, and Ira Seymour. Another ravaged the houses of Captain Jones, Dr. Sergeant, and General Ashley. Still another ransacked the store of Esquire Edwards, the office of Theodore Sedgwick, and the home of Asa Bement. The men who were assigned the task of sacking the Sedgwick mansion, however, got little of value. Sedgwick's faithful black housekeeper, Elizabeth Freeman, better known as "Mum Bett," had hidden the family silverware in her "old nigger chest." She thus became a much-celebrated hero.[34]

The one skirmish that was truly serious occurred right after this incident. In pillaging Stockbridge, Hamlin and his followers made prisoners of thirty-two men, including several leading citizens and two of Theodore Sedgwick's apprentices, Elisha Williams and Henry Hopkins. With their prisoners and booty, they proceeded to Great Barrington, and then in sleighs toward Sheffield, just a few miles north of the Connecticut border.

In the meantime, Colonel John Ashley, the largest landholder in Sheffield, assembled a company of eighty men, largely from those who had fled Great Barrington as well as from his own local militia, and proceeded to the western boundary of Sheffield. There, one of the more deadly encounters of the rebellion took place. Within just six minutes, two rebels, one prisoner, and one government soldier were killed, and thirty insurgents were wounded, one mortally. With the help of reinforcements from Lenox, Ashley and his men routed the rest of Hamlin's insurgents and took 150 prisoners.[35]

The town of Sheffield would later erect a commemorative stone, designating this skirmish as the "last battle of Shays Rebellion." In reality, however, there were dozens of other skirmishes, minor in bodily harm and often botched, in the months to come. At one point even General Lincoln became fair game. In early April, thinking everything was now quiet, Lincoln sought comfort at the hot springs in New Lebanon. Learning of his whereabouts, 120 rebels located just over the New York border decided to go after him. Just ten minutes before their arrival, Lincoln got news of their approach and fled.[36]

Particularly vulnerable were state legislators who had sided with the government against the insurgents. Singled out for attack was Nathaniel Kingsley, who represented the town of Becket. On May 8, a raiding party ransacked his house and took "all the arms in the house, about twenty." He, luckily, was not at home. Less fortunate was his colleague John Starkweather of Lanesboro, who happened to be home on June 13 when the raiding party arrived. They did not kill him, but they roughed him up and scared him "half to death."[37]

ONCE THE REBELLION had simmered down to a whimper, the authorities attempted to put the state back together again. Essentially, they adopted two policies: one for the ordinary rebels, the privates and the sergeants, another for the leaders.

For the ordinary rebels, the peace terms were set forth in the Disqualification Act of February 16. Under this act, a few privates qualified for unconditional pardons. They had to prove that they had deserted the insurgent cause and joined the state militia before February 1, or that they had surrendered and taken an oath of allegiance in response to a proclamation issued by General Lincoln on January 30. All others had to make amends. First, they had to surrender their arms, admit that they had rebelled against the state and its rulers, take an oath of allegiance, and pay a fee of nine pence

Stone tablet, on a back road from Sheffield to South Egremont. From the author's collection. Although a peaceful-looking place, here four men were killed and thirty wounded, one mortally, in just six minutes. The marker commemorating the skirmish as the "last battle of Shays Rebellion" was not erected until a century later, well after all the participants had died.

to a justice of the peace who certified that they had met these conditions. Then, for a period up to three years, they were "disqualified" from voting, holding office, serving on juries, teaching school, working in taverns and inns, and selling liquor. After May 1, 1788, they could have these restrictions lifted if they could prove to the satisfaction of the legislature that they had become good law-abiding citizens loyal to the state and its rulers. In exchange for accepting these punishments, they escaped prosecution by the state, and thus the possibility of being whipped, fined, or hanged. In essence, then, the state offered them what is now called a "plea bargain."

This solution was recommended to Governor Bowdoin by Joseph Henshaw, a sixty-year-old Harvard graduate, who was the justice of the peace of Shrewsbury and a member of the state legislature. Henshaw, along with many others, had already been approached by men who wanted to take an oath of allegiance. It was an old colonial tradition, one that had been used many times before in Massachusetts and elsewhere to cover a multitude of sins. Moreover, the authorities had already offered it as a way to lure some rebels back into the fold. Henshaw, however, had doubted the sincerity of the men who approached him. He had insisted that they turn in their guns before he certified their oaths. Many had refused and then sought out other justices of the peace who were less demanding. Such men, he told the governor, could not be trusted. Their power had to be curtailed. Letting them have a voice in upcoming town meetings was dangerous. So too was letting them have a voice in the militia, in the courts, in schools, in taverns, and in the upcoming spring elections.[38]

Bowdoin bought into this proposal and so did the state legislature. But from the beginning, it struck many as a violation of republican principles and as self-serving. Among the more noteworthy was General Lincoln. Keeping his opposition to himself, the general became part of a legislatively appointed commission that was to seek out the "truly penitent" and grant them full pardons. He and the other two commissioners eventually found 790 men who fit the bill.[39] Also in quiet opposition was the Boston lawyer James Sullivan. The brother of the tough-minded New Hampshire governor, Sullivan hated Bowdoin and suspected everything Bowdoin did. Like his brother, Sullivan wanted to suppress rebels, but from the outset believed that "disqualification" was just a ploy by Bowdoin and his supporters to keep themselves in office.[40]

If that was the case, it did not work. While disqualification kept many men from voting in the April 1787 election, cutting the turnout in towns such as Amherst by half, Bowdoin was trounced at the polls by a three to one margin. The victor was Sullivan's friend John Hancock, who had long been the most popular figure in Massachusetts politics. After Hancock's victory, the new legislature restored suffrage to the some four thousand Shaysites who had taken the oath of allegiance. Subsequently, Hancock proclaimed full indemnification for all but a handful.

The pardons, however, only restored rights of citizenship. The ordinary rebel could still be sued for damages. And such suits took place all over the commonwealth. Attention grabbing was the suit of Dr. David Young. In a melee in the town of New Braintree, he had been shot in the left knee. Now a cripple, he brought suit against nine men. The testimony was long, totaling thirty depositions, and two years later the court awarded Young £2,000 against eight of the defendants. On appeal, they got the total reduced to £900.[41]

Excluded from the pardons, specifically by name, were Daniel Shays and eight other rebel leaders. Also excluded were all insurgents who had held state office or been commissioned officers in the militia, all those who shot at government supporters, all those who reneged on an oath, and all those who had been indicted. Almost all these men lived in the western half of the state. In Essex County, bordering the Atlantic Ocean, only one man was indicted, and in neighboring but more inland Middlesex County, only fifteen to twenty men were indicted. Further west in Worcester County, charges of "high treason," "insurrection," "riot," "sedition," "seditious acts," and the like were filed against some two hundred men. Further west still in Hampshire County, some two hundred Hampshire men were brought to trial in one court, another one hundred Hampshire and Berkshire men in another court.[42]

Toward the end of March, the state's highest court began moving from county to county to hear the most serious charges. Holding court first at Great Barrington in the state's westernmost county, the justices sentenced six men to death, four to lesser penalties. The justices then moved on to Northampton, where they sentenced six men to death, nine to lesser sentences. From there they went to Worcester, where they sentenced one man to death, and then to Concord, where they sentenced one man to death and two to lesser sentences. The whole process took about two months.

Among those sentenced to death were James White, who had led the assault on the Springfield arsenal, and Job Shattuck, who had spent much of the rebellion in a Boston jail. Lesser sentences were imposed on Judge William Whiting and State Representative Moses Harvey. The Bowdoin administration had already taken away Whiting's judgeship. The court added to his woes by fining him £100, sentencing him to seven months in jail, and forcing him to post a bond guaranteeing his good behavior.[43] By the time Harvey appeared in court, a few weeks later, he already had been expelled from the legislature. The court found him guilty of a misdemeanor, fined him £50 plus court costs, and forced him to stand an hour at the Northampton gallows with a rope around his neck. He too had to post a bond guaranteeing his good behavior.[44]

Of the first fourteen men facing the death penalty, none were executed. First, the Bowdoin administration reduced the number to six. The six were clearly scapegoats, chosen largely to make an example. Only one, Job Shattuck, was in any way a leader. The other five just had the bad luck of getting arrested. And of these, only one, Jason Parmenter of Bernardston, had done anything truly noteworthy. In a shoot-out, he had killed a government man.[45]

Then began a series of reprieves, usually not made public until the last minute. After agonizing through several reprieves, Molly Wilcox and Abigail Austin, the wives of two Berkshire scapegoats, took matters into their own hands. They smuggled saws into the Berkshire jail, either in their undergarments or in a loaf of bread, and thus enabled their husbands to break out of jail.[46] The two men who came closest to death were lodged in the Northampton jail. On the day of their execution, they were first taken to church, where the Reverend Moses Baldwin reprimanded them for their lawlessness. Then they were placed in carts along with their coffins and taken to the hanging grounds. There, their arms were pinioned, nooses put around their necks, and their caps drawn over their eyes. Sheriff Elisha Porter, with watch in hand, then announced: "Only one minute." As the crowd hushed, the sheriff waited until the last second. He then pulled out a paper and disclosed that the state "in its mercy" had granted both men a pardon.[47]

Why no hangings? The authorities were clearly afraid of repercussions. Some thought it would lead to more bloodshed, that the rebels would kill an equal number of government men in revenge.[48] All the scapegoats, moreover, were well regarded in their home communities, and scores of their neighbors had signed petitions calling for their release. Also, except for Shattuck, none of the leaders faced death. All had escaped, mostly to Vermont, and while the Vermont governor talked of helping Massachusetts to get them back, this was clearly just talk. Finally, the new Hancock administration had no desire to perpetuate the policies of the Bowdoin administration. The executions, concluded Hancock, "should be avoided for public good."[49]

There was one potential obstacle in all this. The governor's council, under Massachusetts law, had a say in who was pardoned. James Sullivan, a Hancock man, was appointed to the council, and he carried the argument for Jason Parmenter, the Bernardston man who had killed a government supporter in a shoot-out. Reprieving Parmenter, Sullivan had argued, would have a positive effect on the dissidents. It would produce awe at the merciful hand of the administration.[50] But later, when three other men were condemned to death, the council was less forgiving.

The second round of death cases resulted from a second set of trials held in Berkshire County in October 1787. Initially the high court sentenced four more rebels to death. One man was quickly reprieved, but the other three soon were caught up in the pardon system. One of the three, William Manning, had allegedly been one of the ringleaders of the February raid from across the New York border. As time passed, however, it became clear that there were two William Mannings in Berkshire County, and the authorities probably had arrested the less rebellious one. So Manning's sentence was commuted to seven years hard labor at Castle Island.[51]

That left two other men for the council to consider, John Bly and Charles Rose. Both were laborers with few connections. Bly, in fact, was from Connecticut and had only recently moved to Massachusetts. Both had been part of raiding parties that had broken into several homes in May and June. What they had done was clearly part of the rebellion, but with some twisting of the facts could be characterized as simple housebreaking. On November 14 and 15, a majority on the council decided that neither man should be reprieved. Hence, on December 6, Bly and Rose went through many of the same experiences as had the two Hampshire men several months earlier. They were taken to church, where the minister reprimanded them for their lawlessness, and then with their coffins taken by carts to where a large crowd had gathered outside Lenox for the hangings. The sheriff was somber. He had a watch and indicated the time. But he did not pull a piece of paper out of his pocket at the last minute and announce that their lives had been spared. Instead, he went ahead with the hangings.[52]

The day before his execution, John Bly prepared a "last words and dying speech" for publication. He directed it mainly at the men he thought were responsible for the rebellion, namely "DANIEL SHAYS, *and other officers of the militia, and the Selectmen of towns who have been instrumental in raising the opposition to the government of this Commonwealth.*"[53] Of these men, only one, Job Shattuck of Groton, ever came close to sharing Bly's fate. All the others, including Daniel Shays, never faced the gallows. Shays, once he crossed the border into Vermont, was out of harm's way. Eventually, he too was pardoned. In the end, the militia officers joined the privates and the sergeants in taking the oath of allegiance. So too did Dr. Hines and the many selectmen who, in Bly's words, had been instrumental in raising the opposition to the government in the first place.

OATH TAKERS AND LEADERS

sentences, two actual hangings, several hundred indictments, and some four thousand confessions of wrongdoing. Those who were among the latter also took an oath of allegiance to the state and its rulers. Some were "truly penitent," 790 men according to the state's official tally. The remainder presumably took the oath to avoid prosecution and the possibility of being fined, whipped, or hanged for treason.[1]

Among the nonremorseful, a few were singled out by the authorities, usually by a brief notation next to their names. Four insurgents, for example, were black: Moses Sash of Worthington, Tobias Green of Plainfield, and Aaron Carter and Peter Green of Colrain. Sash, who was a veteran of the Revolution, had also been indicted by the attorney general for being one of the more active rebels.[2]

A handful of rebels tried to minimize their participation in the rebellion. One doctor added a note next to his name that he had served as a surgeon mate to the men in arms and had not carried a weapon himself. An Amherst man similarly recorded that he had lent his musket to another man and had not carried it himself. Most oath takers, however, offered no excuses. They simply turned in their weapons, admitted their culpability, grudgingly pledged their allegiance to the state and its rulers, and paid the justice of the peace nine pence for administering the oath.

The oaths, in conjunction with the indictments, provide an unusual opportunity. Usually the participants in uprisings, mobs, riots, and the like remain shadowy figures. A few manage to get their names on the police blotter, but the vast majority get away and disappear from the historical record. And, in most instances, all that is left for scholars to work with are eyewitness accounts and descriptions provided by the authorities. The former are often contradictory, and the latter are often misleading, written by government officials who had a vested interest in disparaging all those who challenged their authority—and in many instances by officials who had no clue about what actually happened and were simply pretending to be on top of the situation.

MANY OFFICIAL REPORTS, to be sure, cite the leaders by name. But that too creates problems. For there is always a temptation to assume that the leaders and the rank and file had much in common. And that can be a fatal mistake.

Consider again the Northampton incident. The leader of the men who came from West Springfield, the first group to arrive in Northampton, was repeatedly identified.[3] In time he became one of the best-known leaders of Shays's Rebellion. Indeed, his failure to take part in the attempted seizure of the Springfield arsenal came to be seen by many as the turning point in the rebellion. Many observers also saw him as more than a leader. They saw him as the embodiment of the rebellion, the personification of the experiences, the hardships, and the desperation of the men he led. His name was Luke Day.

Forty-three years old at the time of the Northampton incident, Day was a member of one of West Springfield's most prominent families.[4] The Day House, now several hundred years old, still stands, a minor tourist attraction and a reminder of the family's one-time influence. Scarcely a year passed without one Day or another holding a town office. In this powerful family, Luke's eminence stemmed largely from his role in the American Revolution.

In April 1775, when the first shots of the Revolution were fired, Luke was a second lieutenant in the local militia. As soon as the Lexington alarm reached West Springfield, he and fifty-two other men marched to Boston and joined the provincial forces that surrounded the city and sieged British forces for nearly a year. In May 1775, Luke was promoted to first lieutenant and assigned to one of the six battalions that the Massachusetts legislature created to drive the British out of Boston. In June, his battalion was selected by the Continental Congress to become part of the Continental Army.

Day house, West Springfield. From the author's collection. The house still stands and is a minor tourist attraction. It also is a witness against all those who claimed that Luke Day, along with the other insurgent leaders, came from the dregs of rural society.

A few months later, Luke along with eleven hundred other men volunteered to take part in Benedict Arnold's expedition against Quebec.

The Quebec expedition was war at its worst. Day and the other volunteers spent weeks marching waist deep up the Kennebec River and hacking their way through dense Maine forests, trying to follow trails that were well known to the Penobscots and Abnakis but not to white men. Dead tired, they soon found themselves running short of provisions and fighting a losing battle against nausea and diarrhea. Sickness and starvation took the lives of 150 men. The shortage of supplies forced one division to turn back. Day and the members of Arnold's other three divisions kept plodding north, to face the heart of the brutal Canadian winter. On the forty-sixth day of their journey, famished and ragged, they reached the St. Lawrence River. A month later, on the last day of December 1775, they joined three hundred soldiers from New York for an assault on Quebec. It was a disaster. Arnold was wounded, the New York commander was killed, almost one hundred other men were killed or wounded, and over three hundred were taken prisoner. Day and the remnant of Arnold's assault force spent the rest of the winter trying to maintain a flimsy cordon around the city of Quebec.

A year and a day after the disastrous assault on Quebec, Day was promoted again, this time to captain of the Seventh Regiment of the Massachusetts Line. He held that rank until the end of the war, experiencing one combat after another, but none so grueling as the Quebec campaign. In the summer of 1781, when Washington began the final assault on Lord Cornwallis, Day and the rest of his regiment were in the first line of battle, under the command of Major General Benjamin Lincoln. They led the rush south that cornered Cornwallis's army at Yorktown and eventually forced his surrender. Twenty months later, in June 1783, Day was mustered out of the army. Overall, he spent a full eight years in the Revolutionary army.[5]

TOWARD WAR'S END, Day became a member of the Society of the Cincinnati, an exclusive organization that was open to officers like him and their firstborn sons. To become a member, he had to donate one month of his military pay. The Massachusetts branch which Day joined was headed by General Benjamin Lincoln. Nationally, George Washington was a member; so was Secretary of War Henry Knox.

Although the society was not officially organized until May 13, 1783, the idea for it was formulated in 1776, at the outset of the Revolutionary War. The chief instigator was Henry Knox, a one-time Boston book dealer who had married into a wealthy Tory family and who would soon gain fame as Washington's chief artillery officer. Always acquisitive, Knox was frustrated by the low pay of American officers. Claiming that it was only one-half that of British officers, Knox convinced Lincoln and others that at the very least American officers should receive the same pension as retired British officers—half pay for life. In April 1778 Washington yielded to Knox's pleas and urged Congress to support a half-pay pension scheme for the sake of the Revolutionary "cause."

By this time, Knox and his cronies had also put together the rudiments of an organization to push their cause. It was blatantly aristocratic. Although there was much talk about old soldiers getting together to perpetuate wartime friendships, not all old soldiers were welcome. Only officers of the Continental Line and their firstborn sons could become members. Membership was also to be hereditary in accordance with the

Membership certificate for the Society of the Cincinnati, signed by Henry Knox and George Washington. To receive such a certificate, Luke Day and hundreds of other officers of the Continental Line gave up a month's pay. In doing so, they had the honor of belonging to the same aristocratic brotherhood as such notables as Washington and Knox. Many also thought that the organization would help them acquire land, titles, and pensions after the war.

dictates of primogeniture, going from firstborn son to firstborn son, generation after generation, down through time. Like many others of the Revolutionary era, the founders tied their cause to a celebrated figure of the ancient world. Their choice was Cincinnatus, the farmer-general who in Roman times left his plow to lead his countrymen to military victory. Like Cincinnatus, they too would go back to their farms after the war, but from time to time get together, renew friendships, tell war stories, elect officers, and wear an eagle badge on a ribbon.

Why Day decided to give up a month's pay to join this organization is not known. But, like other members of the society, he probably liked the idea that he would be rubbing shoulders with the "great men"—with Washington, Knox, and Lincoln. And, like other members of the society, he probably hoped that it would help him get preferential treatment from either the state or national government after the war. Members of the Society of the Cincinnati lobbied extensively for land, titles, and pensions. Even before they officially organized, Washington and the other leaders in October 1780 had talked the Continental Congress into granting them half pay for life.[6]

That settlement created a storm of protest. Ordinary soldiers and non-commissioned officers were to receive much less—a £24 bounty at end of war—equal to private's pay for one year. Why were officers of the Continental Line singled out for such largesse? Such questions not only were raised time and again, but also found support in high places. Henry Laurens of South Carolina, president of Congress, proclaimed that pensions of half pay for life would make retired officers the "drones and incumbrances of society, pointed at by boys and girls—there goes a man who every day robs me of a part of my pittance. . . . This will be the language of republicans." Aedanus Burke, also of South Carolina, wrote a popular pamphlet that was published in Charleston, Philadelphia, New York, Hartford, and Newport. Under the name "Cassius," Burke claimed that the society was a conspiracy of would-be aristocrats to replace republican institutions with a nobility. He also insisted that the mastermind behind this plot was not Knox but Baron von Steuben, the gruff Prussian aristocrat who had trained Washington's army.[7]

Such complaints had little impact on von Steuben and Knox. They deemed the protestations ludicrous. But Washington regarded the backlash as a serious problem, and with his coaxing the society decided to become less blatantly aristocratic and wear the eagle badge and ribbon only at conventions and funerals.

The storm of protest also forced Congress to backtrack on the promised pensions of half pay for life. In March 1783, the pensions were commuted into five years' full pay in government securities bearing 6 percent interest. Getting state support for the commutation settlement, however, proved difficult. And in 1784, when the states finally approved the settlement, the notes had depreciated to about one-eighth of their face value.

BY THIS TIME, Day needed all the financial help he could get. Being an officer in Washington's army had been expensive. Washington wanted his officers to be more like European officers, to dress elegantly, to have an enlisted man as a body servant, to haul around lots of personal baggage, to ride a horse rather than march, to dine in taverns rather than in field messes. All these marks of distinction, Washington contended, showed that an officer was part of a superior order and entitled to the unquestioning obedience of his men.

At first, officers from rural Massachusetts resisted Washington's demands, partly because they wanted to maintain camaraderie with their soldiers and partly because they lacked the income of their Virginia and urban colleagues. But Washington had been persistent. He had insisted that all his officers act and dress like gentlemen, and New England officers had to comply.

For junior officers who brought high social status to their commands, this was easy to do. They had deep purses. They could afford to spend like a gentleman while drawing little or no pay. But for someone from West Springfield, even someone like Luke Day, whose family owned substantially more property than did the families of ordinary soldiers, this was a losing proposition. To live like a gentleman and not get paid meant financial trouble in the long run. Yet, throughout the Revolutionary War, Day had been paid infrequently or in notes that initially had little market value and then quickly depreciated.[8]

Meanwhile, in the face of rising state and local taxes, the farms belonging to Day's immediate family deteriorated. At the beginning of the Revolution, Luke's family had several farms. One legally belonged to Luke, another belonged to his younger brother Thomas, and a much larger one belonged to their father. The father's farm alone put the family in the top 5 percent of town taxpayers. Collectively, in 1775, the father and two sons paid just under £3 in taxes.[9]

With the coming of the Revolution, the two sons went off to war, first Luke, then a year later, Thomas. While they were away, the demand for farm goods skyrocketed, but the family lacked the manpower to take advantage of the soaring prices. Instead, the family properties became less productive as the war progressed. Toward the end of the war, Luke's father turned his holdings over to his sons. The lion's share went to Thomas, who was usually at home rather than off soldiering. The family was still prosperous, but no longer in the top 5 percent of town taxpayers. The land now belonging to Thomas was valued at £290 and ranked in the top 20 percent of property holdings. The property in Luke's name was valued at £120 and ranked in the second 20 percent. Collectively, the two brothers now paid nearly £12 in taxes, four times as much as the family had paid before the war.[10]

To restock his deteriorating farm and keep the tax collector at bay, Luke incurred more and more debt. Within two years of his discharge, his financial affairs were in a shambles. Among other obligations he owed some £25 to Nathaniel Lee and Jonathan Tracy of Newburyport and nearly £10 to

John Kirkland. In July 1785 both parties had him imprisoned for debt at the Northampton jail.[11]

WITH HIS INCARCERATION, Day undoubtedly learned more about imprisonment for debt than he cared to know. By the time he was committed, imprisonment for debt had been practiced throughout Massachusetts for over one hundred years. An outgrowth of English common law, it had been incorporated by the Puritans into the Massachusetts General Laws in 1654.

Generally speaking, Puritan lawmakers had associated debt with high living, frivolous spending, and other bad habits. They thus had little sympathy for debtors and worried instead about making creditors whole. Accordingly, they gave creditors the right to go to a justice of the peace and get a writ to attach the person or property of the debtor. For years, the right was uncertain, subject to legislative tinkering. Then, after numerous statutory amendments and clarifications, the creditor obtained the right to arrest the body of his debtor and keep him imprisoned until the judgment was paid.

The main intent of this legislation was to make an example of the debtor so that others would not follow in his footsteps. But imprisonment for debt was also supposed to stop the debtor from fleeing the jurisdiction, deter him from hiding assets, and force his relatives to pay off the debt. For the most part, it only benefited the creditor who took his debtor to court and won a judgment.

Such a creditor usually had a year and a day to act on the court's ruling. Essentially, he had three options. He could have his debtor's property appraised at "fair and just value" and seize the appropriate amount. In hard times, however, the appraised value was likely to be much higher than the current market value. So, to offset this problem, Massachusetts gave the judgment creditor the option of having the debtor's property sold at auction and obtaining the appropriate amount of cash from the sale. The third option was to have the debtor imprisoned on the presumption that he was hiding assets or that well-heeled relatives would pay off his debt.

What about the insolvent debtor? He had neither any assets nor any well-heeled relatives. Was he to rot in jail? And who was to pay for his keep? That problem was partly solved with the "Poor Debtor's Oath." Based on the importance of oaths in Puritan society, whereby lying under oath was considered a grave sin, the impoverished debtor was given the right to have the justice of the peace look at his circumstances and administer an oath to him in which he swore that he was insolvent. Although the creditor was expected to honor the oath, he legally had the right to prove the oath false, but he had to do so within a certain prescribed time, within a month if he lived nearby, and up to a maximum of fifty days if he lived in a distant community. The creditor also could keep his debtor in jail by paying jail costs or swearing out another writ and beginning the process all over again. Otherwise, the debtor was released by "order of law."

In practice, penniless debtors escaped the horrors of debtor's prison. Keeping a penniless debtor in jail was thought foolhardy. The minimum cost in the 1780s was four shillings, sixpence a week. And if the man was married, the cost was prohibitive, since the town was expected to take care of the man's family. An unmarried debtor could legally be sold into servitude, but by the 1780s selling a white man into bondage no longer had community support. In contrast, jailing a man whom creditors thought had valuable assets was deemed sensible and just. Gentlemen like Day thus comprised a far larger portion of the jail population—about a fifth—than they did of the general population.

The prevailing system was injurious not only to the debtor, but also to a creditor who had no desire to go to court or was slow in doing so. Oftentimes, he was left with nothing, as the law did not provide for the equal distribution of a debtor's property. The process of attachment favored the creditor who went to court, especially the creditor who filed the first suit. This, in turn, was a bonanza for lawyers and court officials, who convinced many a worried creditor to act quickly and take his debtor to court, even if the creditor was certain that the debtor was honorable and intended to pay the debt.

In the 1780s, rural communities across the state denounced the entire process. Too many picayune matters, they insisted, necessitated going to court, the lower courts could not make a binding decision, and thus appeals of even the most trivial cases were common. No one, they claimed, benefited from this "bloodsucking" legal system except the lawyers, judges, and court officials who collected fees at every step of the way. Strident voices demanded that one entire level of courts be abolished. They also clamored for a change in the laws so that honorable creditors would get their rightful due and honorable debtors would not be dragged into court. They bombarded the state legislature with petitions.

The legislature, in response, passed only temporary measures. The Confession Act of 1782 permitted a debtor to go before a justice of the peace, acknowledge his debt and his creditor's right to take his property on the debt's due date, thus avoiding court and court costs. Another temporary measure passed in 1782 allowed a debtor to pay off his debt in personal property at appraised value rather than in specie. Four years later, still another temporary law allowed a debtor to satisfy his debt in real and personal property at appraised value rather than in specie. This act was later amended so that a creditor could choose to wait and receive specie at a later date.[12]

AT THE TIME Day was incarcerated, the Northampton jail housed six other debtors. Two were subsequently released upon payment of their debts. The other four were released after taking the oath or by order of the court.

Two of Day's cellmates were fellow gentlemen: Silas Wright of Northampton, who would be released a week later because of an oath he had taken, and John Morgan of Springfield, who would be released by his creditor in early September. The other four were yeoman farmers: Edmund Burgess of Conway; Micah Pratt of Pelham; Joseph Patterson of Ware; and Isaiah Johnston of Belchertown. Like Day, both Pratt and Johnston had several judgments against them. Pratt had four, and Johnston eventually had five.[13]

Statewide, according to one study, most men who were imprisoned for debt before 1800 were released within two weeks.[14] That was not the case with Day and his fellow Northampton inmates. Of the seven men, not one got out in two weeks. Edmund Burgess of Conway served the shortest term, about six weeks. The longest by far was that of Isaiah Johnston of Belchertown, who entered the jail just a few days before Day and did not get out until eleven months later, in late May 1786.

None of these men were treated like felons. They were confined to the jail only at night. During the day they were expected to earn their keep out in the "Yard," which in practice meant all of downtown Northampton. If they wandered to the outskirts of town, they were clearly out of bounds, but as long as they remained within easy walking distance of the jail they were abiding by the terms of their confinement. At night they had to return to the jail, to the same building as the felons, but they slept in different quarters.

Day spent most of July, all of August, and half of September in Northampton, working in town by day and sleeping in the jail at night. Meanwhile his wife and five children in West Springfield had to make do without him, and the family farm continued to deteriorate. Finally, on September 13, he was released "by order of law" for his first debt. For the second he "Broke his Bond & made his Escape." He was the second runaway that year. And like his predecessor, he did not flee to the hills or hide out in the woods. Instead, he went home to West Springfield and helped harvest the crop.

WAS DAY A typical rebel? In most respects, not in the least. First of all, he was a "gentleman." The authorities sometimes portrayed him as a disreputable dirt farmer, but they knew better. Even the Northampton jailer acknowledged his status as a "gentleman." To the embarrassment of the authorities, he was not the only gentleman who challenged their supremacy. Scores of other gentlemen also took up arms against the government, and the authorities eventually indicted fifty-four of them for crimes against the state. Yet, as gentlemen, all were atypical. The vast majority of rebels were "yeoman" farmers—and their sons—who, for want of a better term, were usually listed in the records as "laborers."

Day's war record was also atypical. Again, to the embarrassment of the authorities, he was not the only war hero who sided with the rebels. At least thirty officers of the Massachusetts Line took up arms against the government, and the authorities arrested nineteen of them. Most were junior officers like Day, but two had reached the rank of major before being mustered out of the army, and one now held the rank of full colonel in the state militia. Nor was Day the only member of the Society of the Cincinnati to participate in Shays's Rebellion. At least two other society men were also involved.

But, in reality, only a handful of men in all of Massachusetts could match Day's service record. The typical Massachusetts soldier spent only a few months in arms—and then returned to the farm. Men like Day who spent a full eight years in the Revolutionary army were exceptional.

Day also had been imprisoned for debt. That was not only unusual for men in Hampshire County but also most unusual for the rebels. In 1785 and 1786 only ninety men in all of Hampshire County were imprisoned for debt, while some eighteen hundred Hampshire men participated in Shays's Rebellion. Of these, only Day and Perez Bardwell of Williamsburg spent time in the Northampton jail for debt.[15]

Bardwell was also listed by the jailer as a "gentleman." Jailed by six different creditors, Bardwell had been released months before Day was imprisoned. Nonetheless, Day probably knew him. Like Day, Bardwell had been a militia lieutenant at the time of the Lexington alarm in 1775. He too had responded immediately to the call to arms and marched to Boston. And subsequently, he too had become an officer in the Massachusetts Line. If anything, he was more of a malcontent than Day. He had been one of the leading participants in the Ely Rebellion four years earlier, had been imprisoned as a result, and had subsequently been broken out of jail by a regiment of men led by Captain Reuben Dickinson of Amherst.[16]

None of the other eighty-eight men who were imprisoned in the Northampton jail for debt in 1785 and 1786 participated in Shays's Rebellion.[17] And in some cases, that is surprising. Micah Pratt of Pelham, for example, lived within a mile of Daniel Shays's farm and in a town that supported the rebellion. He was jailed by four different creditors the same summer that Day was imprisoned. Yet, neither Micah nor his brother Sylvanus, who was jailed the following spring by two creditors, joined their neighbors in taking up arms against the state.

Of the other eighteen hundred Hampshire men who participated in the rebellion, some undoubtedly were like Day in being heavily in debt. And some, even though they had not been imprisoned for debt, had been sued for debt. Daniel Shays was the most famous example.

Often pictured as "destitute," Shays nonetheless had had no trouble borrowing money. Upon marrying Abigail Gilbert in 1772, he had started acquiring land, first in Shutesbury and then in Pelham, two rock-infested hill towns ten to fifteen miles east of the Connecticut River. By 1786 he had bought five parcels totaling 251 acres and sold four parcels totaling 147 acres. He had also mortgaged 98 acres to his wife's kinsman Daniel Gilbert of Brookfield and had paid him off. But, like many New England officers during the Revolution, he ran up a number of small debts that he had trouble paying off. Needing cash, he sold a sword given to him by his commander, the eminent Marquis de Lafayette. He was sued by John Johnson of Pelham for £12 in 1784 and then, two years later, by the estate of Jeduthan Baldwin, Esquire, of Brookfield for £4. At the time of the rebellion, he owed money to at least ten men. After he fled the state, they would sue him, hoping to get a legal claim on the landed property he left behind.[18]

But even Shays was atypical. Most of the eighteen hundred Hampshire County rebels never were hauled into court for debt. Indeed, for every Shaysite who appeared in court as a debtor, another Shaysite went to court as a creditor. Of the ten men who filed suit against Daniel Shays after he fled the state, for example, three were fellow rebel leaders. Indeed, they were under indictment by the state when they took Shays to court. One, Timothy Hines of Greenwich, had been charged with high treason. And another was Shays's neighbor, Dr. Nehemiah Hines.[19]

OVERALL, THEN, LUKE DAY was an atypical rebel. In one respect, however, he had much in common with the oath takers. He came from a town that provided far more than its share of insurgents.

In acknowledging that they had borne arms against the state, the oath takers usually listed their hometowns and sometimes their occupations. From that data emerge a number of curious facts. The one that stands out most prominently is that the western counties as a whole did not rebel against the state government. Nor did the vast majority of poor farmers. In the five-county area in which courts were shut down, 72 of the 187 towns produced not a single rebel, and 34 others only one to four rebels. At the other extreme, 5 towns produced more than 100 rebels, 12 towns between 51 and 100, and 28 towns between 21 and 50. These 45 towns made Shays's Rebellion possible. They provided nearly four-fifths of the rebels. Luke Day's West Springfield was one of the banner towns, yielding 141 rebels, 10 of whom were indicted by the state for treason.[20]

Of the five counties embroiled in the court closings, the two nearest Boston scarcely deserve the name "rebel counties." They were essentially neutral throughout the rebellion. Only a handful of towns in either county came to the state's aid in its time of need, and similarly only a handful provided men for the rebellion. In Bristol County, southwest of Boston, nearly all the men who took up arms against the state lived in Rehoboth or within a few miles of Rehoboth. In Middlesex County, nearly all the insurgents hailed from just four towns in the northwest corner of the county—Shirley, Townsend, Groton, and Pepperell. And except for these isolated pockets of rebellion, the vast majority of people in both counties were just onlookers, perhaps critical of the state, but largely doing nothing to hinder or help the rebellion.

In contrast was Hampshire County, which at that time extended from the top of the state to the bottom, from the Vermont and New Hampshire borders to the Connecticut border. Support for the rebellion was more widespread in Hampshire County, and the county as a whole was by far the most rebellious. It produced nearly half the insurgents, almost as many as the other four counties combined. On its flanks were the two runners-up, Worcester County to the east and sparsely populated Berkshire County to the west. It turned out twice as many men as Worcester and nearly five times as many as Berkshire.

Within Hampshire County, however, the turnout was anything but even. Eight towns produced not a single rebel, five produced over one hundred. The banner town was Colrain, one of the northernmost towns in the county, lying just a few miles west of the Connecticut River and bordering Vermont. A small town, which had been founded only fifteen years before Shays's Rebellion, Colrain had 234 males sixteen years of age and older in 1785. Two-thirds of them bore arms against the state in 1786.[21] In contrast were Heath and Rowe, just a few miles west of Colrain and also bordering Vermont. Incorporated as towns in 1785, just a year before Shays's Rebellion, both were tiny farm communities with a combined population of 144 males sixteen or older. Not a single resident took up arms against the state. Also in contrast was Granville, another farm community west of the Connecticut River but at the southern border of the state. Made a town eleven years before the rebellion, Granville had 375 males sixteen years of age and older in 1785. Only one man took up arms against the state.

Overall, half of the towns in Hampshire County were like Granville, Heath, and Rowe, providing little or no help at all for Luke Day and other rebel leaders. It was a handful of towns like Colrain that made Shays's Rebellion possible. They provided three-fourths of the county's eighteen hundred rebels.

Were the authorities aware of this uneven distribution of rebels? In one sense General William Shepard, who sent a report to the governor on the number of insurgents in Hampshire County, was well aware of this fact. In estimating the number of Hampshire men who would march under the direction of Daniel Shays, he knew that West Springfield would provide more men than neighboring Granville, and that Colrain would provide more men than neighboring Heath and Rowe. But he was way off in his numbers. He thought little Colrain would turn out about twenty-five men. And he thought the folks in West Springfield, who lived only a few miles from his farm, would turn out about sixty men. Never did he imagine that the two towns would turn out close to three hundred men.[22]

Shepard was deemed to be the local expert on Hampshire County. Both the governor and General Lincoln depended on his estimates when they put together an army to suppress the rebellion. Shepard, however, underestimated the total by nearly half. That he grossly underestimated the rebelliousness of the people of Colrain is understandable. After all, they lived at the other end of the county. He probably knew next to nothing about them. That he also underestimated the rebelliousness of such towns as Amherst, Pelham, Greenwich, Wendell, and Ware is also understandable. Those folks lived on the other side of the Connecticut River and a long day's journey from his Westfield home. That he underestimated the

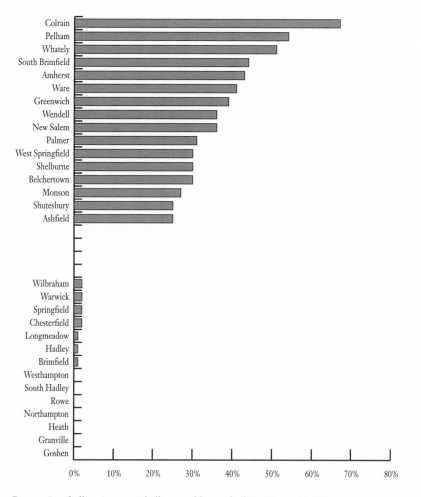

Percent in rebellion in most rebellious and least rebellious Hampshire County towns.

rebelliousness of West Springfield, however, makes one wonder. They were, after all, his neighbors.

In the long run, not knowing his neighbors proved costly to Shepard. He won the battle at the Springfield arsenal, but the way he won was never forgotten. He later maintained that he acted with restraint, and his biographers have argued that he was a kind and decent man. But men in his own unit heard him order that the cannons be aimed at "waist height." He thus became widely hated as the "murderer of brethren." Within months of his arsenal victory, a band of nine men made their way to his Westfield farm, burned his fences and woodlands "beyond recovery for many years," and cut off the ears and gouged out the eyes of his prize horses. For the rest of his life, he lived as a marked man, harassed by angry neighbors who never stopped seeking revenge. The harassment took its toll. He received honor after honor, was hailed as Westfield's most distinguished citizen, yet died in poverty.[23]

THE UNEVEN DISTRIBUTION of rebels undermines the standard explanation of Shays's Rebellion. For many years now we have been told that the rebels were "destitute farmers," "debt-ridden farmers," "hopeless poor farmers," and the like, who were victimized by the postwar Massachusetts economy.

At the end of the American Revolution, so the story goes, wholesalers in Boston and other New England port cities imported huge quantities of English goods, thus draining the region of specie and taking on immense debt. The wholesalers then sold the goods on credit to retailers in the interior, in towns such as Springfield and Northampton, who in turn sold them on credit to backcountry farmers. Thus a "chain of debt" was created. For a while it presented only minor problems, but then the British closed their West Indian islands to American shipping. Once that happened, the wholesale merchants suddenly had no way to trade their way out of debt. The wholesalers accordingly sued the backcountry merchants, who in turn sued the farmers. By 1785 and 1786, so the story concludes, nearly one-third of all the men in western Massachusetts had been hauled into court as defendants in debt suits, and it was to prevent those trials that Luke Day and his fellow rebels closed the courts in the summer and fall of 1786.[24]

There are a number of problems with this account. First of all, when it came to private indebtedness, western Massachusetts farmers were hardly unique. Heavy debt was common throughout the backcountry, in the Carolinas as well as in New England, in New Hampshire and Vermont as well as in Connecticut, the much-heralded land of "steady habits." During 1786, for example, Connecticut creditors filed more than six thousand court actions. According to one estimate, they took over 20 percent of the state's taxpayers to court.[25] Why, then, did the "chain of debt" not lead to a full-scale revolt in Connecticut? Why did the whole backcountry not explode? Why only western Massachusetts?

Second of all, the men who sent the Northampton judges packing in August 1786 were hardly doing something new and bold. Members of their families had been doing the same thing, off and on, since 1774. In that year, when British authorities shut down the Massachusetts legislature, a convention in nearby Hadley had split into two camps over whether they should take similar action against the county court. Impatient of debate, some three thousand men had gathered in Springfield, closed the court, and forced all the king's appointees to resign their posts in writing. In the same summer, further west in Great Barrington, a crowd of fifteen hundred had shut down the Berkshire County Court. These actions had been applauded by patriot leaders as responses to British high-handedness. But opposition to the courts continued long after the patriots gained control of the Massachusetts government. Throughout much of the Revolutionary War, state-appointed justices found it impossible to hold court in western Massachusetts, in Hampshire County until 1778 and in Berkshire County until 1781.

The excuse for shutting down the courts during these years was that Massachusetts did not have a proper constitution. The Revolutionary leaders of Massachusetts, so the argument went, were trying to rule the commonwealth without the consent of the governed. Elsewhere, in nearby New Hampshire and faraway South Carolina, Revolutionary leaders had appealed directly to the people for guidance in establishing new governments. Why did the Revolutionary leaders of Massachusetts not do the same? Why were they trying instead to build a new government on the rotten and crumbling foundation of the old colonial charter? The old charter, said the "constitutionalists," may have been fit for a people dependent on Great Britain. For a free and independent people, however, it was totally inadequate. Until the state had a proper constitution sanctioned by the people, the "constitutionalists" promised never to allow the state courts to open. At one point they even threatened to secede from Massachusetts and join Vermont, which had constitutional government.[26]

Even when the leaders of Massachusetts wrote a constitution and got it approved in 1780, there was still much hostility to the state courts. The most famous incident occurred in Northampton in the spring of 1782. By this time, about two-thirds of western Massachusetts had concluded that the "great men" were taking advantage of them and costing them too much, even more than the king's favorites had in the days of George III. The new constitution, many contended, made a mockery out of the Revolution. Under it, the eastern elite had too much power, many good men lacked the right to vote, the senate was beyond the control of the people, the governor had too much salary, the judges and justices of the peace were not answerable to the people.

Into this discontent stepped the Reverend Samuel Ely, who although educated at Yale had become a spokesman for the downtrodden, first in Connecticut, now in Massachusetts. All the complaints were valid, said Ely at one town meeting after another. The people thus must assert their authority. They must overthrow the new constitution and reestablish republican government. They must stop the courts, the representatives of this odious constitution, from sitting. He had, so he said, a better constitution in his pocket, "one that even the Angel Gabriel could not find fault with."

In April, at Northampton, Ely raised a mob against the court. He called for violence, telling his "brave boys" to "go to the woodpile and get clubs enough to knock their Grey Wiggs off and send them out of the World in an Instant." For this and other offenses he was subsequently arrested and brought to trial in Springfield, where he was convicted and sentenced to jail for six months. In June, hundreds of men, many dressed in military array, broke Ely out of jail. Ely got away but some of his rescuers were run down by the sheriff's posse. They agreed to return Ely to jail and as surety allowed the sheriff to lock up three of their men, all distinguished Revolutionary War veterans, in the Northampton jail. The governor then ordered that the three prisoners be transferred to Boston. Shortly thereafter, a regiment of men under Captain Reuben Dickinson of Amherst forced the sheriff to release the three prisoners. Nothing was done to bring Dickinson and his men to justice.[27]

THERE IS STILL another problem with the old story that the fear of debt suits led to the court closings. While it is easy to prove that the number of debt suits skyrocketed in the 1780s, there is no correlation—none whatsoever—between debt and rebel towns.

Consider, for example, a table that Van Beck Hall compiled years ago in a fine book entitled *Politics Without Parties*. Hall traced the number of "recognizance" cases that made their way to the Supreme Judicial Court. These were cases in which a debtor, in trying to buy time and delay payment of his debt, appealed a lower court decision to the higher court and then failed to follow it up. What this did was force his creditor to file a "recognizance" so that the higher court could affirm the lower court's judgment. Statewide, the number of "recognizances" shot up by about 50 percent between 1782 and 1784. In Worcester County, the number of yearly filings doubled and by 1784 exceeded the state average by more than two times. In Berkshire, the annual filings rose from way below the state average in 1782 to equal the state average in 1784. But in Hampshire, the most rebellious county, the annual filings were initially well below the state average and never rose at all, thus dropping to about half the state average by 1784.[28]

It is possible, of course, to explain away the Hampshire numbers. One could argue, for example, that the rebellious Hampshire towns were over their heads in debt, even worse off than the folks in Worcester County, while the nonrebellious Hampshire towns were debt-free. That, however, was not the way things were. Only two of the most rebellious towns—Belchertown and West Springfield—were among the top ten towns in suits for debt. On the other hand, three of the least rebellious—Granville, Northampton, and Worthington—were also among the top ten.[29]

THEN THERE IS a problem with the details. Consider again the "banner town" of Colrain. In 1785 and 1786, the Hampshire courts handled nineteen debt suits against Colrain men, which was about "average" for Hampshire County. Only thirteen men, however, were actually sued.[30] On six occasions the court heard charges against Abner Rockwell, twice against Joshua Hunt, and twice against Josiah Newell, once with his brother Oliver. Rockwell and Oliver Newell subsequently took up arms against the state. So did one other debtor, and two sons of still another debtor. Altogether, then, of the twelve families involved in debt proceedings, four provided men for the rebellion. Yet Colrain supplied 156 men. And the leader of those men, singled out by the state and convicted of high treason, was James White, the "brave soldier of the Revolution" who led the assault on the Springfield arsenal. He, too, had been in court, but as one of the two creditors who filed suit against Joshua Hunt.

Or consider again the non-rebellious town of Granville. In 1785 and 1786, Granville residents were hauled into court forty-two times as defendants in debt cases. This was an extremely high number, fourth highest in the county. In addition, Granville creditors filed twenty-eight debt suits. Of these, sixteen were against neighbors. This was even more unusual. In small towns, nearly everyone was in debt to someone who lived nearby. Often, these debts were circular. That is, one farmer owed two days of labor to his neighbor, who in turn owed three cords of wood to the minister, who in turn owed the wife of the first farmer for her services as a midwife. Eventually, all these debts were expected to be settled, but not by insistent dunning of the midwife's husband or taking the neighbor to court. The whole local economy relied on a chain of trust, and creditors were expected to go to great lengths to settle neighborly problems out of court. There were always exceptions, as in the case of James White and Joshua Hunt of Colrain, but generally neighbors did not sue neighbors. As a result, even though most people never borrowed from anyone outside their own community, only one case out of four was between neighbors. So Granville, in at least two respects, had serious financial troubles. Yet Granville residents never got involved in Shays's Rebellion.

Granville and Colrain illustrate another problem with the chain of debt thesis. Supposedly, Boston merchants were putting pressure on local merchants, who in turn were putting the screws on local farmers. Yet Abner Rockwell, the Colrain farmer who was hauled into court on six different occasions, was not being harassed by local merchants. His problem was a New York farmer named Thomas McGee, from whom he had bought land. And no one in Colrain, or the neighboring towns, had been sued by a Boston merchant. In Granville, a family named the Tillotsons was being hard pressed by William Phillips, one of Boston's premier merchants and the president of the state's only bank. Yet most of Granville's outside debts were to Connecticut merchants.

And this was true not only of Granville, but the entire Connecticut Valley. In a sense Hampshire County was an extension of Connecticut. Most of the towns had been founded by families who came out of Connecticut, by men and women who had followed the Connecticut River north and still had family and business ties with Connecticut residents. The county's storekeepers were no different. They too dealt largely with men who lived farther down the river. And the court cases clearly reflected this dynamic. In 1785 and 1786, Hartford creditors filed four times as many suits in the Hampshire court as Boston merchants, 160 suits as compared to 38 suits. And in terms of money value, the ratio was the same, four to one.

Was there, then, no "chain of debt" running from hard-pressed western farmers back to Boston and beyond? In Boston, merchants were undoubtedly heavily in debt. They had greatly overimported in 1783 and 1784. They had well over £100,000 of unsold goods on their shelves. Every newspaper talked of the need to expand the Boston market. One Danish observer reported that Boston merchants had an "amazing Superfluity of all kinds of European goods." The reason, he said, was because they had "no Back Country to consume their goods."[31] That was clearly an overstatement. Boston merchants were reaching as far west as Worcester. But most of them had not reached as far west as Hampshire County. And farther west in Berkshire County, trade with Boston was virtually nonexistent.

4

THE REVOLUTIONARY GOVERNMENT AND ITS BENEFICIARIES

WHAT, THEN, TRIGGERED SHAYS'S REBELLION? HEAVY private debt might account for the behavior of Luke Day, but it hardly explains the behavior of James White and scores of other rebel leaders. What does? The answer is twofold: the new state government—and its attempt to enrich the few at the expense of the many.

That was made clear from the beginning in the words that the insurgents chose to describe themselves. They never depicted themselves as dissident debtors. Nor did they refer to themselves as rebels, insurgents, or Shaysites. Those were words pinned on them by their enemies. They saw themselves instead as "Regulators" and made that explicit to all recruits. "We do Each one of us," read a typical muster form, "acknowledge our Selves to be Inlisted . . . in Colo Hazeltons Regiment of Regulators . . . for the Suppressing of tyrannical government in the Massachusetts State."[1]

THE WORDS "REGULATORS" and "tyrannical government" were key. They conveyed a message in the backcountry, a message that put the insurgents in the same tradition as men who had risen up elsewhere to chasten the governing elite and restore communal order. Used in England as far back as the 1680s for men who sought to revise borough constitutions and thus gain more control over parliamentary elections and their elected leaders,[2] the term "Regulators" had gained usage in the British colonies in the late 1760s, thanks largely to two events, one in North Carolina, the other in South Carolina.

In backcountry North Carolina, middling farmers proclaimed in March 1768 that they had no choice but to join together as "Regulators," because they were "determined to have the officers of this county under a better and honester regulation." The land, they contended, had once been theirs. Then in the mid-1760s swarms of land speculators and lawyers moved into the area and quickly took over the county courts. The new courthouse rings fleeced would-be homesteaders, imposed heavy taxes and fees on old settlers, and seized the land of nonpayers. Corruption was blatant. The new sheriffs, according to the provincial governor, embezzled "more than one-half of the public money."

Yet neither the governor nor the provincial assembly did much about it, and the homesteaders soon became convinced that the courthouse rings enjoyed the full support of the coastal elite. The aggrieved farmers thus took the law into their own hands, drove the judges from the bench, whipped obnoxious lawyers, and terrorized corrupt sheriffs. In 1770 they seized the Orange County Court at Hillsborough and tried cases on the docket themselves. A few weeks later, they burned down the presiding judge's house and set fire to his barns and stables.

This so alarmed the provincial assembly that they passed a riot act, and the following year the governor led twelve hundred militiamen against the rebels and overpowered them at the Battle of Alamance. One Regulator leader was executed on the battlefield, and six were subsequently hanged. The rank and file were forced to take oaths of allegiance to the province and its rulers. Hundreds abandoned their homes and left the province. The whole movement soon became widely known throughout the backcountry, celebrated in an outpouring of songs, poems, and folk stories.[3]

In South Carolina, "ambitious and enterprising" backcountry farmers adopted the name "Regulators" shortly after the North Carolinians. They published a "Plan of Regulation" in June 1768. They too had been plagued by thieves, but the thieves were not judges, sheriffs, and lawyers. Instead they were outlaw gangs, which had come to dominate much of the Piedmont after the Cherokee War. Besides robbing everyone in sight, the gangs had also tortured planters, raped their wives, and abducted young girls to serve as "paramours." In response, the distraught planters had turned to the authorities in Charleston for help. Getting none, they took the law into their own hands.

The South Carolina Regulators, in sharp contrast to the North Carolinians, generally prevailed. At first, they focused mainly on the outlaws, burning their homes, whipping them unmercifully to the accompaniment of drums and fiddles, forcing hundreds to flee for their lives, and (with the tacit support of the authorities) hanging sixteen men. Gradually, they broadened their activities, flogging "whores" and forcing the idle to work on their plantations.

In the process, they sealed off the backcountry from Charleston interference, stopped the ordinary legal system from operating, and broke their own members out of jail when provincial officials tried to curb their vigilantism. They also threatened to march on Charleston. They created a backlash, a major counteraction according to some accounts, but the authorities generally left them alone, and they emerged largely triumphant. They finally disbanded in 1769 when the provincial assembly passed the Circuit Court Act, giving them the courts, jails, and sheriffs they wanted, plus additional representation in the legislature. Many of them did well. Of the known Regulators, one-quarter later became justices of the peace, and about one-fifth became militia officers and prosperous slaveholders.[4]

The New England press first learned about "the people called regulators" in July 1768. Various reports from the Carolinas made their way from one newspaper to another.[5] Some portrayed the Regulators as slothful and ignorant and ignored their complaints about predatory land speculators, unscrupulous lawyers, and crooked officials. Countering these accounts, however, were the many Regulator ballads and tales that accompanied the North Carolina Regulators who fled north after the Battle of Alamance. How many of these songs and stories reached as far north as western Massachusetts is uncertain. So too is their impact. But New Englanders did not need to look to the Carolinas to learn about attempts to maintain communal order. There were nearby examples, and they involved fellow Yankees. As in the South, one had ended in failure, while the other seemed to be a rousing success.

The failure had taken place in New York, just a year or two before the Carolina incidents. It had grown out of widespread hostility toward the great landlords who dominated the eastern shore of the Hudson River. For years there had been much grousing about how a few families through political connections, fraud, bribery, and other shenanigans acquired vast manors. The Livingstons had 160,000 acres; the Van Rensselaers, 1,000,000 acres; the Cortlandts, 86,000; and the Philipses, 205,000. These families, moreover, refused to offer their lands for sale. Instead, they leased their lands and behaved much like feudal barons.

At first most of their tenants were of Dutch descent, but as New Englanders began pushing west, the great landlords had to deal more and more with Yankee farmers. The Yankees, by all accounts, never tired of denouncing the system. Some dutifully paid rent, others just squatted on manor land. Nearly all apparently thought it abominable that a few rich and powerful families had the power to withhold from the market several million acres of prime land, and nearly all clamored for the establishment of New England–style towns where middling farmers owned farms in fee simple.

Trouble broke out in 1766 when farmers on the great Philipse estate in Westchester County refused to acknowledge the Philipses as the true owners of the property. Instead the farmers claimed that the land belonged to a local tribe, and that the tribe had granted them favorable terms. The Philipses began a series of lawsuits to eject these farmers, and the courts backed the Philipses. Other farmers led by William Prendergast of Dutchess County joined the fight, vowing to reinstate the ejected farmers and to pay "no rent" until the battle was won. Soon they organized themselves into militias and began harassing tenants loyal to the Philipses, burning barns, fomenting rebellion on other proprietorships, and battling sheriffs and British soldiers. In response, the governor called out the troops, the militia as well as British regulars, and eventually quelled the rebellion. Prendergast was captured, tried for treason, sentenced to death, but subsequently pardoned. Most of the defeated rebels took off for less fertile lands to the north and the west—or accepted the landlords' terms.[6]

While the New York debacle in 1766 hardly served as an encouraging example to aggrieved farmers in western Massachusetts, what happened a few years later certainly did. The Vermont insurgency in the 1770s was a major success story, and it was well known throughout the hill country of western Massachusetts. Again the battle was against New York aristocrats, this time against land speculators who claimed to hold title to land settled by Yankees. The Yankees, who for the most part had migrated up the Connecticut River into Vermont, had settled on land where nearly all land titles were in dispute. Both New York and New Hampshire had at one time claimed Vermont, and both had granted land to favorites. While some Yankee settlers had purchased land from New York speculators, most had titles that could be traced back to land grants made by New Hampshire governor William Benning.

Spearheaded by a "paramilitary protective association" of Bennington farmers led by Seth Warner, settlers on the Hampshire grants literally went to war against the New York speculators and their representatives. They burned out New York sympathizers, stopped courts with a New York bias from sitting, and terrorized surveyors sent out by the speculators. Later, under the flashier leadership of Ethan Allen, the Green Mountain Boys established the independent republic of Vermont and wrote a very democratic constitution. As citizens of an independent republic, moreover, Vermonters did not have to help pay off the huge national debt that the United States had acquired in fighting the American Revolution. This alone enticed thousands of young couples in nearby states to pack up their belongings and head for Vermont.[7]

All these events were well known in western Massachusetts. Ethan Allen not only waged war on the ground, but also waged a war of words and wit with the New Yorkers. He published broadsides, newspaper articles in Hartford, which were picked up by the press elsewhere. The articles characterized the struggle as between "poor honest men of the land and the princes of privilege." When the governor of New York placed a bounty of £150 on Allen's head, Allen responded by placing a bounty of a measly £5 on the head of John Kemp, the attorney general of New York, and advertising it in several New England newspapers.[8] His actions delighted all those who held a dim view of the "great men" and their agents.

At the time of Shays's Rebellion, the state of New York and its speculators were still pushing New York land titles. They were hoping that New York, or the combined forces of New York and other states, would crush the "outlaw" leaders of Vermont. The gentry of Massachusetts and conservatives everywhere undoubtedly had the same hope. But bringing Vermont to heel was at best a long shot. And to dissidents in western Massachusetts, Vermont was anything but an outlaw republic. It was a model society, a possible homeland despite its long winters, a place where ordinary men ruled and the grasping elite were held at bay.

THUS, THROUGHOUT THE backcountry, "regulation" had been common for decades. It was not always successful and sometimes resulted in humiliating defeat. But there was a tradition that whenever distant authorities got out of hand, or whenever outsiders threatened a bona fide settler's landholdings, the people had an obligation to rise up and restore communal order. This way of thinking, moreover, had been strengthened by the actions and the rhetoric of the American Revolution. The Declaration of Independence, especially, was unequivocal:

> Governments are instituted among Men, deriving their just Powers from the Consent of the Governed, that whenever any Form of Gov-

ernment becomes destructive of these Ends, it is the Right of the People to alter or to abolish it, and to institute new Government . . . it is their Right, it is their Duty, to throw off such Government, and to provide new Guards for their future Security.

Washington, Knox, and Bowdoin may not have taken these words seriously. But others did. To them, the people's obligation to "throw off" destructive and tyrannical government not only was clear, but it had been further sanctified by the thousands who fought and died for the Revolution. It had become a sacred trust, a moral imperative, an "indispensable duty" as Judge William Whiting put it.[9]

BUT WHY WAS there, in the words of the enlistment form, "tyrannical government in the Massachusetts State?" How had the authorities in Massachusetts got out of hand? For one thing, the state constitution had increased their power and their ability to do mischief. It was an "aristocratic" document both by backcountry standards and by the standards of the day. It was even a "reactionary" document given the sequence of events.

Massachusetts had been slow in writing a constitution. By the time the gentry got around to the task, most of the other states had already set examples. The worst example in the eyes of the gentry was that of Pennsylvania, where in the summer of 1776 "radical" forces had gained control and fashioned a document without any system of "checks and balances." Written by Revolutionaries, it discriminated against all those who opposed taking up arms against the king, Quaker pacifists as well as Tories. Yet, in its treatment of those who supported the war effort, it was remarkably "democratic," empowering poor men as well as rich men, privates as well as generals.[10]

In so doing, the authors of the Pennsylvania constitution had rejected the concept of "checks and balances." Tom Paine, the leading patriot voice in Pennsylvania, had spoken against any complicated system of government that balanced one social interest against another. In a republic, he had insisted, government should be simple and in the hands of the people. In keeping, the new Pennsylvania constitution established a single, all-powerful legislature, elected annually by taxpaying males over the age of twenty-one. There were no property qualifications for holding office. And instead of a powerful governor with a veto, there was a plural executive consisting of a president and a council, whose job was to simply carry out the will of the legislature.

A year later Vermont took the Pennsylvania model one step further. In

Tom Paine. From an engraving by William Sharp. Courtesy American Antiquarian Society. Best known for his pamphlet *Common Sense*, in which he attacked the British monarchy and everything it stood for, Paine was widely regarded as the voice of the American Revolution. But Paine had little support among the Massachusetts gentry. In their eyes, his campaign for simple republican governments that put all power in the hands of single-chamber legislatures was monstrous. So too was his insistence that ordinary farmers and artisans would make "the best governors."

just six days the Green Mountain Boys drafted a constitution that largely copied the Pennsylvania document, except that it also banned slavery and enhanced the power of local governments, even allowing towns to decide such matters as legal fees. In the eyes of many in western Massachusetts, Vermont was an example to be followed. Strengthening town government, enhancing the power of town meetings, was clearly the direction in which to move. In the eyes of the Massachusetts gentry, however, Vermont was an outlaw state and its constitution was an abomination.[11]

The Pennsylvania example also reinforced Rhode Island's decision not to write a new constitution. Rhode Island, which in the eyes of the Massachusetts elite was also a state of ne'er-do-wells, simply deleted all references to the British crown from its old colonial charter. After the deletions, the charter was much like the Pennsylvania and Vermont constitutions. It also placed power in the hands of an all-powerful legislature, with both the executive and the judiciary being at the mercy of the legislature. It too made it possible for "democratic" forces to gain control of the state by simply winning a majority of the assembly seats.[12]

Horrified by these democratic possibilities, the Massachusetts gentry wanted no part of such constitutions. More to their liking were the recommendations of John Adams, who although born and raised in rural Braintree had gone to Harvard and become a full-fledged member of the professional elite. To Adams, as ardent a patriot as Tom Paine or any other Pennsylvania democrat, it was folly to put all power in the hands of a single chamber legislature. No one could "live" under such a government. It was necessary instead to have "balanced" government, and especially to have an upper legislative chamber that represented the interests of the rich.[13]

Maryland came close to satisfying Adams and the Massachusetts gentry, with stiff property requirements for voting, and even stiffer ones for holding office. The Maryland constitution excluded all men worth less than £1,000 from the upper house, and all those worth less than £500 from the lower house. It also established longer intervals between elections. Also more satisfying to the Massachusetts elite was the New York constitution, which created a state senate that essentially represented the rich. And both states established strong governorships, whose holders were independent of the legislature rather than servants to it.

Only in Massachusetts, however, did Adams and other supporters of "balanced" political institutions fully get their way. They had two tries at it, submitting one constitution to the voters in 1778, another in 1780. The first constitution was actually more "democratic" and less "aristocratic" than the second. Although it established "balanced" government and excluded from the body politic women, blacks, mulattos, Indians, and white paupers, it allowed all free white male taxpayers to vote for the lower house, and those worth £60 to vote for the senate and governor.[14]

The exclusion of blacks, mulattos, and Indians from the electorate irritated some voters. The absence of a bill of rights upset many more. But it was the ratification process itself that virtually guaranteed the defeat of the 1778 constitution. To become law, the document needed the unqualified support of a two-thirds majority. The key word was "unqualified." Objection to details meant rejection of the whole document. Many towns missed that point, and as a rule the people of a town voted as one, all in favor or all against. Several towns clearly supported the overall scheme but thought they still could suggest amendments without killing the entire document. They were wrong. Their objections were counted as "no" votes. The document thus did not come close to passing and was defeated by a five to one margin.[15]

In rejecting the proposed constitution, some towns submitted detailed criticisms. Of these the most influential was the "Essex Result." Written

John Adams, c. 1783. Reprinted from Daniel Munro Wilson, *Where Independence Began: Quincy* (Boston, 1902), frontispiece. A native of rural Braintree, Adams became the chief spokesman against the simple republicanism preached by Tom Paine. To put all power in the hands of a single-chamber legislature, Adams contended, was foolhardy. There had to be checks on the power of the lower house. There had to be a strong governor with a veto, and there had to be an upper legislative chamber that essentially represented the interests of the rich.

largely by a staunch conservative, a Newburyport lawyer named Theophilus Parsons, it allegedly represented the "considered opinion" of the towns of Essex County. The "Result" essentially attacked the 1778 constitution for lacking a bill of rights and being too democratic. It called for more representation of property, the separation of powers, a veto power for the governor, higher property qualifications for officeholders and especially the governor, an independent judiciary, and the indirect election of representatives and senators through county conventions.[16]

How did these proposals sit with westerners? Most western towns never expressed their opinion one way or another. The few that did, however, largely rejected the thinking of the Essex Result. Fourteen towns protested against property qualifications for voting, and twelve insisted that all civil and military officers be elected directly by the people.[17]

The following year the leaders of Revolutionary Massachusetts made another concerted attempt to write a constitution. In the fall, 247 towns sent representatives to a statewide convention. Meeting in Boston, the delegates assigned the hard work of composing a new document to a committee consisting of John Adams, Sam Adams, and James Bowdoin. All three were from eastern Massachusetts. John Adams did most of the writing. Once he finished drafting the document, he left for France on a diplo-matic mission. That winter, constitutional delegates were to gather again in Boston to approve, disapprove, or modify his handiwork.

Westerners could not get there. It was one of the worst winters in Mass-achusetts history, worse even than the winter of 1717, and probably as bad as the disastrous winter of 1740. Boston Harbor froze solid, and for over a month no vessel left or entered the port. Only one major road was open in the west, the road from Hartford to Boston. Elsewhere travel was pos-sible only by snowshoes. The convention had to wait weeks before there was a quorum, and in the end only forty-seven towns were represented. Nearly all were within ten or fifteen miles of Boston, or near the seacoast. This rump group made the final decisions that became the Constitution of 1780.[18]

The new document was much in keeping with the Essex Result. It included a bill of rights, and overall it enhanced the power of the rich and well-born, more so than the rejected constitution of 1778, and more so than the old colonial charter. It established two legislative chambers, with the upper house based on taxes paid rather than population, and the lower house weighted in favor of the eastern mercantile towns. It also created a strong governor with extensive veto and appointive powers, provided for an independent judiciary that was beyond the control of ordinary people, and raised the property requirements for voting and holding office. No longer could a man worth £500 be elected governor; he now had to have a £1,000 freehold. Nor could a man with a £200 freehold and £400 total wealth still serve in the senate; he now had to have a £300 freehold and £600 total wealth. Gone, too, was the suffrage clause of the rejected 1778 con-stitution allowing all white male taxpayers to vote for the lower house. Now to vote for any state office a man had to be worth at least £60, which was £20 more than under the old colonial charter. And finally, there was a clause for-bidding any amendments to the new constitution for at least fifteen years.[19]

This time the constitution makers formulated a ratification process that virtually guaranteed approval of their handiwork. Instead of requiring unqualified support, this time a town might suggest scores of amendments and still be counted as a "yes" vote. Every town was to vote on the consti-tution, clause by clause, and state objections to any clause that did not obtain a majority. Then the adjourned constitutional convention was to look at the results, and if there appeared to be a two-thirds majority for each clause to declare the constitution ratified, and if there did not appear to be a two-thirds majority to make alterations "in accord with the popular will."

What if there was no popular will? What if sixty towns objected to a provision for one reason, and another sixty for the opposite reason? Such was the case when it came to the relationship of church to state. And what if a town never took a vote on an article it objected to? If it had just suggested an amendment and voted on the amendment? Should the votes for the amendment be counted as votes against the original article? That might seem logical, but that is not what happened. In fact, most towns never took a vote on an article that the majority clearly opposed, just on the substituted amendment, and these votes were not counted as votes against the original article. Often, in one way or another, they were counted as votes in favor of the original article. Similarly, the vote counters decided other ticklish issues in behalf of their creation. Every article thus passed by a landslide.[20]

Some of the provisions, however, had little support in towns which later became the nucleus of Shays's Rebellion. In one way or another, many of these towns complained that power was being taken out of their hands and given to the Boston elite. They much preferred, it was clear, to be ruled by men who were answerable to them rather than to the governor or the governor's council. Rather than endorsing judicial independence, twenty-nine towns wanted superior court judges to be either elected or appointed annually, and thirty-one wanted justices of the peace to be elected. And rather than supporting property qualifications for voting, thirty towns insisted that any man who was respected in the community, or who served in the militia and defended the commonwealth, should have the right to vote.[21]

Not every town explained its position. Those that did often reminded the constitution's authors of the goals of the Revolution. The explanation of Colrain for rejecting property qualifications for voting by a thirty-eight to four margin was succinct: "Taxation without Representation we Consider unreasonable." Equally terse was Colrain's explanation for voting twenty-seven to zero against property qualifications for holding elective office: "we Consider money no Qualification in this Matter."[22] Similarly, Belchertown rejected property qualifications for voting because it "denied that Liberty and Freedom which we are this Day Contending for"; Greenwich because it violated "Natural Rights"; New Salem because it was "both unfair and unjust to Tax Men without their Consent"; Petersham because "Riches and Dignity Neither Makes the Head Wiser nor the Heart Better."[23]

Twenty-two towns also censured the new constitution for allowing the house to do business when only sixty members were present. This, they argued, was especially biased in favor of the mercantile elite and the eastern part of the state. It ensured that eastern Massachusetts could pass laws even when delegates from western Massachusetts could not get to Boston. Finally, many western towns complained about the fact that this untried constitution could not be amended for fifteen years. What if the new government proved to be unjust? Why was the governing elite afraid of change?[24]

IN AT LEAST one major respect, these complaints were justified. The Constitution of 1780 undoubtedly consolidated power in the hands of the mercantile elite and the eastern part of the state. It shifted power from the rural backcountry to Boston, from the poor to the rich, and from town meetings to the state senate and the governor's office.

That, to be sure, might not have mattered if the change in power relations had only been on paper. Before the American Revolution, the royal governor and the governor's council also had great power over the backcountry. But for the most part that was only on paper. Apart from the appointment of judges and justices of the peace, decisions made in Boston rarely had much impact on men and women living in Amherst, Colrain, Whately, and other Shaysite communities. What happened in their town meetings mattered. What happened in Boston rarely did. They were largely ruled by men they knew, not by men who lived eighty or one hundred miles away.[25]

That was not the case after 1780. Now what happened in Boston, as never before, came to have a decisive impact on life in towns that had seldom been bothered by distant authorities. That fact was magnified by a number of distressing decisions the legislature made after 1780. Of these the most costly involved the Massachusetts debt.

THE BAY STATE had a heavy war debt, heavier than states that were away from the war zone, but its basic problem was hardly unique. Nearly every battle-tested government faced the same problem: It had issued notes that it could not honor, and the question was what to do with the outstanding notes.

One answer was to consolidate the notes and hope to pay them off sometime in the future. But consolidate at what value? What, for example, should be done with the notes Massachusetts issued in April 1778? These notes initially traded at about one-fourth of their face value. By 1781 they had plummeted to about one-fortieth of their face value.[26] Should they be consolidated at their value when issued? Or at their current market value? Or at some other value?

Faced with the same problem, other states generally sank their currency at full depreciation, Virginia as much as a thousand to one. So did the central government, at forty to one.[27] But not Massachusetts. When the mercantile-dominated state legislature took up the matter of consolidation, it ignored what the notes were actually worth and promised to pay what the notes were worth on the day of issue. This decision had enormous consequences. First of all, it was incredibly expensive, obliging the state to pay out at least twice the amount that was necessary for the state to become creditworthy. Of this amount, £1,250,000 was earmarked for the holders of "Consolidated Notes" and £270,000 for the holders of notes originally given to officers and soldiers of the Massachusetts Line in compensation for the depreciation of their wages. The state also owed an equally large sum of money as its share of the continental debt.

The consolidation was a bonanza for speculators. Most of the soldiers had been in no position to hold onto their notes. Their personal affairs generally deteriorated as the war dragged on. They needed nails to repair barns and fences, hard money to pay taxes, and salt and other necessities for their families. Most therefore had long parted with their notes, often for one-eighth or one-tenth of their original value. So too had most people who had received promissory notes or purchased bonds in support of the war effort. Not all of these transactions can be traced, and hence who traded what to whom is often a mystery. But some £600,000 can be traced, and if these transactions are at all typical the overall story is fairly clear: Nearly 80 percent of the state debt made its way into the hands of speculators who lived in or near Boston, and nearly 40 percent into the hands of just thirty-five men.

These men claimed that they had come to the government's aid in its time of need. But that was true of only a handful. The vast majority had seldom obtained notes directly from the government—and hence had rarely paid top dollar for their notes. Instead the typical big operator, with £7,500 or more in notes, had acquired 91 percent of his holdings on the open market and often at rock-bottom prices. At one end of the spectrum was John Sprague, a Dedham physician. He was the original purchaser of £2,575 of the £20,400 traceable notes in his possession. In contrast was John Peck, a Boston broker, who bought directly from the government just £14 of the £15,600 in his possession.

Commonwealth of MASSACHUSETTS.

[Handwritten note: dated January 1st A.D. 1782, borrowed and received of Wm Farnsworth the Sum of Twenty-five pounds four shillings & nine pence]

which Sum I promise for Myself and Succeſſors in the Office of TREASURER of this *Commonwealth* to pay to the ſaid *William Farnsworth* or Bearer on or before the *firſt* Day of *January* A. D. *1785* with Intereſt, at Six *per Cent. per Annum* ; the Intereſt to be paid ANNUALLY : Both Principal and Intereſt to be paid in the ſeveral Speçies of *Coined SILVER and GOLD*, enumerated in an *ACT* made and paſſed in the Year of our LORD, *One Thouſand ſeven Hundred and Forty-Nine*, entitled, "*An ACT for aſcertaining the Rates at which Coined Silver and* "*Gold, Engliſh Half Pence* and *Farthings, may paſs within this* "*Government, according to the Rates therein mentioned.*"

WITNESS MY HAND,

£25..4..9   *Thomas Davis* Treaſurer.

Wm Dawes } COMMITTEE.

A 6 percent note for consolidating the state debt. Courtesy American Antiquarian Society. Issued in 1782, this note was one of the thousands that were given out in exchange for a motley assortment of unpaid notes that the state had previously issued. For the recipient, the question was whether this piece of paper was any better than what he turned in. The government had yet to make good on any of its promises. Would the future be any different? Such worries were common in 1782, and as a result speculators found it easy to buy up the new notes for almost nothing.

All these speculators of course were gambling on the future. Only a few, however, had put themselves in a position where they could lose "everything." Many were market-timers, buying and selling as the volatile securities market dipped one week, rose the next. Some were involved in complicated land speculations whereby they could swap securities for government land. And some bought only from the truly desperate. Jonathan

Portrait of William Phillips. With permission of the Trustees of Phillips Academy. Phillips was a mover and shaker in Boston politics, not only as a major political figure but also as the president of the state's only bank. One of Boston's biggest speculators, he eventually accumulated some £28,000 in state notes. He contributed £300 in hard cash in support of General Lincoln's army. No man contributed more.

Mason, for example, gradually accumulated £16,500 in traceable notes. All but six shillings was acquired from soldiers and other noteholders. Mason also amassed an additional £13,500 in untraceable notes. Most of these, one suspects, also came from soldiers and other noteholders. His business partner William Phillips also speculated heavily in notes, obtaining eventually some £28,000 worth. So did Mason's son Jonathan, Jr., with over £6,000, and his son-in-law, William Phillips, Jr., with nearly £15,000. Altogether, these four men had obtained about 5 percent of the Massachusetts state debt.[28]

All these men, moreover, had political influence. Mason's partner William Phillips, for example, was a key figure both in the Boston financial community and in Boston politics. Aged sixty-four at the time of the Regulation, Phillips was the youngest son of a prominent Andover minister. His two older brothers had gone to Harvard and gained fame as the founders of the two prestigious academies that bear the family's name, Phillips Andover and Phillips Exeter. Instead of following in their footsteps, William, at age fifteen, had gone to Boston and become an apprentice of Edward Bromfield, one of the port's foremost merchants. At the end of his apprenticeship, Phillips had become Bromfield's partner and subsequently married Bromfield's daughter. Thanks to the Bromfield connection and his own acumen, Phillips gradually amassed a huge fortune and became Boston's most prominent financier. At the time of the Regulation, he was the president of the state's only bank.

For the past twenty years, Phillips had also been a leading figure in Boston politics. In the decade leading up to the American Revolution, he had served on numerous committees, was elected town selectman and provincial representative, and, along with Sam Adams and John Hancock, was a stalwart member of the Revolutionary North End caucus. On the outbreak of the war, Phillips moved his family to Norwich, Connecticut, and was largely out of Boston politics for as long as the British had possession of the city. Then in 1779, when the war shifted to the South, he was back in Boston and again a major player, serving as a member of the convention that framed the Massachusetts constitution, and then during the 1780s as either a state representative, a state senator, or a member of the governor's council. At the time of the Regulation, he was one of the most powerful members of the state senate.[29]

Similarly, of the thirty-five men who held over 40 percent of the state debt, all of them during the 1780s either served in the state house themselves or had a close relative in the state house. They thus had a big hand in writing law, although never a free hand, as they always needed the acquiescence of other Boston merchants who held few securities and had less interest in paying off speculators.

All these men, furthermore, had a vested interest in maintaining the existing government. No other state government had passed laws that were so favorable to public creditors. No other government, in fact, had even come close to passing such laws. And everyone knew it. Thus, when General Lincoln went looking for money to hire an army, he knew exactly where to go. He went to William Phillips and his associates at the Massachusetts Bank. He also sought out other Boston merchants and professionals.[30] With some he had no luck at all. Even such an eminent merchant as John Hancock refused to contribute.

But speculators and bankers like Phillips were a different story. Of the 153 men who dug into their purses to hire Lincoln's army, over half were speculators, and many undoubtedly had high hopes of making a killing on state notes. Forty-one of these men, including eight of the eleven biggest contributors, were part owners of the Massachusetts Bank. From bank president William Phillips, who had at least £28,000 in state notes, Lincoln obtained the biggest contribution, £300, enough to hire 150 soldiers for a month. Phillips's partner Jonathan Mason, who had almost as many notes as Phillips, contributed £150, enough to hire another 75 soldiers. Along with Phillips and Mason, nine other men donated over £100 to the cause. Collectively, these nine men provided Lincoln with enough money to hire still another 1,655 soldiers. Of these nine donors, at least seven speculated heavily in state securities. Only one, the merchant and bank director Samuel Breeck, held more notes than Phillips and Mason. The holdings of the others were much less, about £13,000 on average.[31]

HOW WIDESPREAD WAS the knowledge of this bonanza? Did men and women who lived miles from Boston have the same knowledge that an insider like Lincoln had? Did they understand how the new state debt—and its accompanying tax system—benefited Boston speculators? Or did they accept the legislative argument that the chief beneficiaries were "worthy patriots" who had come to the aid of the state in its time of need?

The answer is clear. Knowledge was widespread. What was going on in Boston was hard to hide. Brokers like Joshua Eaton advertised for "Publick Securities of every denomination," and the Boston market in securities was large enough to produce quotable prices from time to time.[32] Also, thousands of backcountry soldiers and farmers had sold notes to speculators at rock-bottom prices. They had stories to tell. Cries of injustice were thus common.

Especially angry were veterans. Their tales of woe were printed, and reprinted, across the commonwealth. The lament of the "Old Soldier," for example, first appeared in the *Hampshire Herald* and then a month later in the *Massachusetts Gazette*. He, like most veterans, had received part of his army pay in notes. He had tried to pawn them off on merchants and his hired hands, but neither would accept them at par. Finally, the "necessities" of his family had obligated him "to alienate them at one quarter part of their original value." Now he was to be taxed to redeem the notes at a much higher value. Was that just, he asked, especially with three-fourths of the money going to "the man who has sauntered at home during the war, enjoying the smiles of fortune, wallowing in affluence, and fattening in the sunshine of ease and prosperity?" "No," he contended, "if these securities are to be made good, let the hardy soldier, who has withstood the vicissitudes of the war, receive what is no more than in fact his due."[33]

The lament of the "Old Soldier" was unusual in only one respect. He claimed that he got one-quarter of the value for his notes. Others insisted that they got much less. Thomas Grover, a rebel leader from Montague, pointed out to the readers of the *Hampshire Herald* that securities had commonly been sold for a pittance—"two shillings, three shillings, four shillings, and the highest for six shillings eight pence on the pound."[34]

Nonrebels often agreed with these numbers. Joseph Hawley, one of Northampton's wealthiest and most influential citizens, reported on the situation in the Connecticut Valley. The "old Continental men" could not get money for their notes, said Hawley. Nor could they use them for taxes. Hence they had been forced to "put off" their notes "for almost nothing to Sharpers." Further south, in Springfield, the Reverend Bezaleel Howard, pastor of the First Church, fully agreed with Hawley's appraisal. Howard was anything but a rebel. He denounced the Regulators from his pulpit. Yet he insisted that all the soldiers got for their notes was two shillings, sixpence on the pound, and he attributed the rebellion to "the venality and Exorbitant Demand" of the state legislature.[35]

Several newspaper commentators agreed with Howard. Writing under pen names, they berated lawmakers for enriching at taxpayer expense speculators who had "amassed an immense hoard of Public Securities for a mere song." They insisted that these "harpies," once interest had accumulated, had already received 18 percent on their original investment and to give them any more for their "cheap-bought wealth" was outrageous. Justice, they argued, demanded that the state debt be reduced to its market value and that the interest be paid off in paper indents. "Public Faith" told the readers of the *Massachusetts Centinel* that the legislature's decision to redeem the notes at their original value, rather than at the going rate, was so blatantly biased in favor of the speculators that it endangered the commonwealth. Similarly, one delegate at the Hatfield convention insisted that "15/16ths of the present holders" had no right to be paid the original value for their notes. As it was, they were going to "draw three times as much interest as in justice they ought to."[36]

Even Noah Webster, soon to become famous for his *Blue-Backed Speller*, chastised the legislature. "To pay the debt to the men who now hold the evidences of it," wrote Webster, "appears to me the most iniquitous measure that a legislature can adopt—a violation of their own engagements as well as of the compact by which society exists." It was especially unconscionable, argued Webster, to pay the speculator his gain at the expense of the poor man who out of necessity had to sell his notes at depreciated value. More outrageous yet was the legislature's claim "'that the original creditors may now re-purchase their certificates with the same or a less sum of money than they received for them.'" That was obviously "fallacious reasoning." Did the Massachusetts legislature "suppose that the poorest of the public creditors have grown rich since the war?"[37]

Once the Massachusetts legislature made the crucial decision to redeem the notes at the original value, rather than at the going rate, a number of towns over the next several years tried to get the law changed. None of these attempts came close to succeeding, but the calls for change continued. In September 1785, Pittsfield instructed its state legislators to work to modify the law so that speculators would get no more for their notes than what they paid for them. In June 1786, the town of Groton issued the same orders to its representative. Two months later, the fifty Hampshire towns that met at the Hatfield home of Colonel Seth Murray also demanded that the law be changed. A month later, the Worcester County convention followed suit.[38]

At the same time, out in Berkshire County, Judge William Whiting summed up the discontent about the legislature's decision to transfer wealth from ordinary citizens to wealthy speculators living in Boston, Salem, and other port cities. It was, wrote the chief justice, the most alarming breech of "our free republican form of government." Not only had these speculators purchased the notes at five or six shillings on the pound, or "more likely" two shillings and sixpence to three shillings on the pound, these same men out of "toryism or avarice" had opposed the exertions made against Great Britain. To expect ordinary citizens "under their present distress'd circumstances" to pay twenty shillings for every two shillings and sixpence that these speculators had invested was thus outrageous. And it was even worse that the "poor soldier" now had to pay these sums for what had been given to him in wages. "It would certainly have been much better for him to have received no wages at all."[39]

HAVING MANAGED TO consolidate the state debt at twice what was necessary, the mercantile-dominated legislature in the early 1780s also made a number of crucial decisions on how to pay the debt. One was to redeem all the £270,000 in "army notes" by 1786, and one-third of the £1,250,000 in "Consolidated Notes" later in the same year. That meant that Massachusetts somehow had to come up with several hundred thousand in taxes and come up with the money quickly. It also meant that Massachusetts had to increase the tax burden by five or six times. But this was not all. The legislature also decided to pay interest on the notes at 6 percent annually in specie. This meant that from July 1782 to October 1786 the state somehow had to come up with over £265,000 in hard money. Then there was the question of what to do for the years when the state paid no interest. Here it was decided to compound the amounts due along with the principal, and add another 4 percent as a bounty for not being paid on time. All this was supposed to stop the new notes from depreciating as fast as the old notes.

To retain any creditability at all, the state legislature had to make good on the interest payments that were almost immediately due, and these payments had to be made in hard money. The hard money requirement, by itself, was pernicious. Not everyone dealt in hard money, and this was especially true in the backcountry, where goods, livestock, and labor had usually sufficed in payment of debts. Even well-established rural storekeepers, like Oliver Dickinson in Amherst, dealt in cash transactions only about one-fourth of the time. The rest was in barter. Now, thanks to the legislature, the demand for hard money soared.[40] But how was it to be acquired? By refusing payment in goods, livestock, and labor—and accepting only hard currency? That might work for the short term, but in time every Spanish dollar and every British shilling would be squeezed out of the backcountry. What then?

Initially, the legislature eased some of the tension by turning mainly to impost and excise duties. Goods coming into Boston and smaller port cities were to be taxed, and so were wine, tea, rum, brandy, and carriages, with the latter taxes allegedly having the fringe benefit of suppressing "immorality, luxury, and extravagance."[41] All these monies, it was decided, would be used for nothing but interest payments on the notes. This continued for the next four years, with every year the legislature juggling the figures and toying with the list of items to be taxed. State notes still continued to depreciate, not as quickly as in the past, but to the dismay of worried speculators.

Just paying the interest, however, was not what the legislature had in mind. It was determined to pay off the entire state debt by the end of the decade—and to pay off the debt in hard money. The army debt was to be paid off in three annual specie payments beginning in 1784, and the consolidated debt was to be redeemed in four annual installments beginning in 1785. That meant heavy taxes, payable in hard money, and the legislature decided to rely on two ways that Massachusetts had raised money in the past. One was a poll tax, a tax on males sixteen years and older; the other was a property tax. Town authorities were told to provide detailed data. How many polls were in each family? Did the family own a house? A barn? Any other buildings? How many horses did the family own? Oxen? Milch cows? How many acres did the family have in tillage? In pasture? What was the size of the family's woodlot? Unimproved land?[42]

Thus the news that the tax man was coming spread into every nook and cranny in the backcountry. No one thought for a moment that the assessor's questions were meaningless. Every farmer knew that he was going to have to pay for every son sixteen years or older, every horse he owned, every cow, every barn, every acre in tillage. Everyone also knew that the tax bite was going to be regressive. Only about 10 percent of the taxes were to come from import duties and excises, which fell mainly on people who were most able to pay. The other 90 percent was direct taxes on property, with land bearing a disproportionate share, and on polls. The latter was especially regressive, since it mattered not a whit if a male sixteen years of age or older had any property or not. Rich or poor, he was going to have to pay the same amount, and altogether polls were going to pay at least one-third of all taxes.[43]

NOT ONLY WAS the tax bite going to be heavy, then, it was biased against farm families with grown sons, and the chief beneficiaries were to be Boston speculators. These were inflammable ingredients, and what made them more flammable was what was happening in nearby Rhode Island. Indeed, the Boston elite blamed Shays's Rebellion on the Rhode Island "virus."

In Rhode Island, "democratic" forces in 1786 finally achieved what John Adams and other devotees of balanced government had long feared. They won control of the legislature and thus the whip hand in the state government. As late as February 1786, they had been on the outside looking in. The conservative Mercantile Party was in control, and the legislature had just repudiated paper money by a two-to-one vote. Then, in the spring elections, the Country Party, led by sea captain John Collins and blacksmith Daniel Owens, waged a fierce campaign under the slogan "To Relieve the Distressed." To the joy of backcountry farmers, the Country men defeated the long-dominant Mercantile Party at the polls. Newcomers won nearly two-thirds of the seats in the assembly, half the seats in the upper house.

With both the executive and the judiciary being at the mercy of the legislature, the Country men quickly rammed through a program that amounted to a sea change in Rhode Island politics. In May, the legislature enacted the emission of £100,000 in paper money, based on a land-bank scheme, for the payment of all debts. In June and August, the legislature passed penalty acts, which included a £100 fine for creditors who refused to accept the new currency and disfranchisement for second offenders.

The judiciary fought back. In September, Newport butcher John Weeden refused to accept paper from cabinetmaker John Trevett. Trevett took him to court. Four of the five superior court judges, in defiance of the new state laws, ruled that they had no jurisdiction, threw Trevett out of court, and declared the penalty act unconstitutional. Two weeks later, the legislature, which appointed the judges and was the state's highest judicial body, not only overruled the superior court but hauled in the judges to face possible criminal charges. The judges escaped criminal indictments, but the four who defied the new state laws were not reappointed.[44]

Simultaneously, Rhode Island also began to discharge its state debts by means of a forced payment. Just like neighboring Massachusetts, Rhode Island had issued notes to pay the army and for supplies during the Revolutionary War. Since these notes were neither legal tender nor receivable for taxes, soldiers and other ordinary folk had sold their notes to speculators. John Brown, a major Providence merchant who profited from the war, bought up a huge quantity of soldier notes. His spiraling wealth created resentment, so much resentment that when he went riding in his handsome new carriage a workman yelled at him: "Soldiers' blood makes good varnish."[45] In defense, he and other speculators argued that they had done the soldiers a favor. The soldiers would have been much worse off if speculators had not come to their rescue. Rather than blaming the speculators, the soldiers should blame the state, which left them in the lurch in the first place.

For years, the Mercantile Party had endorsed this logic and worked diligently to make sure that Brown and the others like him were paid handsomely for their notes. Now, in 1786, the Country Party inaugurated a sharply different policy. All state creditors, with few exceptions, were ordered to present their securities and receive one-quarter of the principal in paper money. When state creditors balked, the state legislature fixed a time limit after which the creditors would forfeit their entire payment. Within months, public creditors were forced to accept paper money that had depreciated to one-eighth of its face value. The creditors howled, but the legislature insisted that it was just, indeed that the speculators were still profiting, because they had rarely paid more than one-tenth of face value for their soldier notes.[46]

All this horrified the Boston elite. One newspaper called for seizing "Fool's-Island" and giving it to another state "for care and protection." Merchant and diplomat Francis Dana thought the only solution was to divide Rhode Island between Massachusetts and Connecticut. Such a division, he maintained, would have the support of the "commercial part" of Rhode Island and save the state from ruin. The lawyer Rufus King was more optimistic. He predicted that Rhode Island paper money would soon destroy itself and leave "an useful Lesson to the neighbouring States before the first of February. The sober part of the community will prevail over those turbulent characters who are now moving the people for Convention, Reform, &c, &c."[47]

THERE WAS ANOTHER development coincidental with the Rhode Island "virus" that turned Massachusetts into a tinderbox. For several years the inflammable ingredients in the Massachusetts tax system had remained in check because the state's perennial governor, John Hancock, had little interest in activating the collection process.

While still in his twenties, Hancock had inherited the mercantile firm of his uncle, which in turn had made him one of the richest men in Boston. But very early he had deliberately decided to build a public career based on popularity, and he had worked hard to create a following, both among his own employees in Boston and in the countryside, where he provided impoverished churches with free Bibles. When hard times came, Hancock added to his popularity by insisting that only his wealthy debtors pay him in silver and that his poor debtors pay him in depreciated paper notes. His enemies accused him of grandstanding and setting a bad example. They also accused him of not enforcing the tax law. Hancock ignored them. With little of his own money invested in state notes, he had no interest in jeopardizing his great popularity by energizing the cumbersome Massachusetts collection system. Taxes fell in arrears, and by 1786 some £279,000 was delinquent.[48]

In the previous year Hancock declared that he was suffering from an acute attack of gout and would not stand for reelection. In his place was chosen James Bowdoin, who like Hancock had inherited a large estate and added to it. But Bowdoin, although listed as a Boston merchant, spent little time in trade. He was a major landlord and far more interested in land and note speculation. He held at least £3,290 in state notes. More significant were his extensive landholdings in Boston and his huge land claims in Maine. To his dismay, squatters on his Maine lands repeatedly challenged his proprietorship and from his perspective caused him serious financial injury. He had a low opinion of them—and of people generally who lived in the backcountry.[49]

Bowdoin's primary supporters were conservative merchants and fellow

John Hancock. Reprinted from John R. Musick, *John Hancock: A Character Sketch* (Dansville, N.Y., 1898), frontispiece. Although one of the richest men in Boston, Hancock was never trusted by many wealthy Bostonians. To them, he was a traitor to his class, a demagogue who catered to the masses. Getting rid of him, however, was not easy. He was incredibly popular and won every election by a landslide. In 1785, to the joy of the wealthy, he decided to take himself out of the next gubernatorial race and let someone else serve as governor.

James Bowdoin. Reprinted from John Fiske, *The Critical Period of American History, 1783–1789* (Boston, 1888), 201. Unlike Hancock, Bowdoin had the support of Boston speculators. Not only was he one of them, he was also determined to enforce the laws in their behalf. Electing him, however, was uphill work. He lacked the popular support that Hancock enjoyed, and he never attained it.

speculators. In their eyes he was far more trustworthy than Hancock and had long been their mainstay in Massachusetts politics. He had been the president of the convention that drafted the 1780 constitution and chairman of the committee that did the actual writing. Although the document itself was largely the work of John Adams, Bowdoin was given credit for many of its more conservative features. Yet, even though conservatives gave him high marks, electing him was no easy task. Not only did Bowdoin lack Hancock's popularity and Hancock's reputation as an ardent patriot, but Bowdoin's only daughter had married a high-level British official who was in line to become a baron. The election was bitter and so close that no one emerged with a majority. Thrown into the legislature, the senate insisted on Bowdoin, and the house at first backed his opponent but eventually gave way to the senate.

Bowdoin, as his backers anticipated, was no Hancock. A public creditor himself, he waxed eloquent in his inaugural address on the state's need to fully honor its debts. The new governor also cared far less about public support and far more about enforcing the state's laws. To his way of thinking, the only support he needed was the backing of the "better sort." Under his prodding, the "better sort" in the legislature enacted new taxes and exerted pressure to collect overdue taxes.

The results were disastrous. The combined load of overdue taxes and current taxes was more than many residents could pay in a year, five years, or even a decade. Taxes levied by the state were now much more oppressive—indeed, many times more oppressive—than those that had been levied by the British on the eve of the American Revolution. Even Massachusetts conservatives, men like Rufus King and John Adams, thought the tax bite was now "heavier than the People could bear."[50]

*B*ANNER TOWNS AND

CORE FAMILIES

THE RESULT WAS THE EXPLOSION IN THE BACKCOUNTRY
that came to be known as Shays's Rebellion. But, as we already noted, only
one out of three backcountry towns actually participated. What was it about
these rebellious towns? Why did 121 men turn out in Amherst and just 2 in
neighboring Hadley? Why did 156 men turn out in Colrain and none in
neighboring Heath?

In each instance, the Regulators had the support of prominent families
as well as hard-pressed families. The men who followed Daniel Shays and
Luke Day into battle were not just a motley assortment of penniless farmers. Nor were they just men who were one step ahead of the sheriff and
debtors' prison. Like almost everything else in the eighteenth-century
backcountry, the Regulation was largely a family affair.

IN THIS RESPECT, Daniel Shays, the man who came to symbolize the
insurrection, was atypical. Shays was not part of a huge extended family. His
Pelham family consisted only of him, his wife, and their children. None of
their kin, near or distant, lived nearby. When his wife Abigail set off for
church, she did not encounter aunts, nieces, and nephews. Similarly, when
Daniel took up arms against the state, he was not joined by a brother, an
uncle, or an in-law.

More typical was Job Shattuck, whom the state also designated a leader of
the rebellion. Shattuck was surrounded by relatives, both in his hometown

Representation of Daniel Shays and Job Shattuck. Reprinted from *Bickerstaff's Boston Almanac for 1787*, 3d ed. This woodcut carried a mixed message. At first glance it did not appear to be derogatory. It depicted Shays and Shattuck as officers and gentlemen, equipped with swords and dressed according to rank. Yet it used the same terms that the attorney general and other government officials were using to belittle the two men— "Generalissimo" Shays and "Colonel" Shattuck.

of Groton and in the neighboring town of Pepperell. When he went to war against the state, he had considerable family support. Three Shattucks from Groton joined him, as did twelve from Pepperell. His second in command, Oliver Parker, also had family support. He was joined by six Parkers from Groton and eight from Pepperell. The Parkers and the Shattucks, in turn, were joined by sixteen members of the Blood family. Together, these three families formed the nucleus for the insurgency in the Groton area.[1]

Just as men like Shays who took up arms largely on their own were the exceptions rather than the rule, so too were young men who bucked the will of their families. Notable was Moses Cook of Amherst, a thirty-five-year-old Revolutionary War veteran. His father, also named Moses, had been one of the town's leading Tories. After the war, both men had financial problems, and both had been sued for debt. Then came Shays's Rebellion. The senior Moses, the former Tory, conspicuously sided with the state. In September 1786, he formed a militia unit of eleven Amherst men and marched to Springfield to defend the state court. His namesake Moses not only refused to go along but became a Regulator. Moses's brothers, Levy and Martin, followed their father. They served as privates in his unit, marched to Springfield with him, and earned seven days' pay from the state.[2]

The behavior of Levy and Martin was the norm throughout the backcountry. Sons usually acted in concert with their fathers. Brothers often went off to battle with brothers.

Many also went off to battle with uncles, cousins, and in-laws. Just as families usually stuck together, so too did kinship groups. Today, obligations to aunts and uncles, cousins, and in-laws are commonly of secondary importance, voluntary in many cases, selective at best. Two centuries ago, family and kinship ties were central. Prominent New England families such as the Hutchinsons and the Winthrops built trading networks by turning to relatives in England and the British West Indies. Ordinary merchants and artisans kept craft and business skills within their own families by apprenticing exclusively their own sons and nephews.

Inbreeding was also common. At least one-fourth of all marriages were between couples with the same surname.[3] Some families even encouraged marriages between first cousins to cement political alliances and to keep property within the family. Similarly, entire families paired off, with the children in one family marrying the children in the other. Thanks partly to such inbreeding, seven interrelated families in the Connecticut River Valley, known popularly as the "River Gods," had gained control of the county courts, the local militia, the regional associations of Congregational ministers, and the local market economy.

According to one popular notion, the American Revolution had undermined the importance of family and kinship ties.[4] That may have been true in long-settled communities, but in backcountry New England family and kin still played a critical role in every aspect of community life. And more than anything else, family and kinship ties explain the large turnout of insurgents in towns like Amherst, Pelham, Colrain, and West Springfield. That is not the way historians have told the story, to be sure, but that definitely was the way it was.

IN AMHERST THE key family was the Dickinsons. Nineteen Dickinson men took up arms against the government. So too did seven men who were married to Dickinson women, two who were sons of Dickinson women, and two who were courting Dickinson daughters. All told, one-fourth of all the Amherst rebels were connected in one way or another with the Dickinson family.

The Dickinsons were anything but down-and-outers. They were one of the town's premier families. The top six men on the Amherst tax list were Dickinsons. Five of the six took up arms against the state. Of the next four men on the tax list, three joined the Regulation. One, Oliver Cowls, was married to a Dickinson. Other well-off Amherst farmers also sided with the Regulation. Along with their sons, they provided the lion's share of rebel soldiers:[5]

Tax List	Dickinsons	Other rebel families
Top 20%	12	14
2d 20%	3	15
3d 20%	4	12
4th 20%	4	8
Bottom 20%	2	4

The Dickinsons, in keeping with their affluence, had considerable political power in Amherst. They held far more than their share of town offices. Of the nineteen Dickinsons who took up arms against the state, ten held the office of selectman or state representative at one time or another, and three were sons of selectmen.[6] This was hardly unusual. Traditionally, in both large and tiny Massachusetts towns, selectmen and state representatives came from the wealthiest 20 percent of the population.

Among these wealthier rebel leaders was Moses Dickinson, who ranked in the top 5 percent in taxable wealth. Over the years, he had been elected selectman, town moderator, and state representative more times than most townsfolk could remember. He was nearly seventy years old at the time of the Regulation. He was slowing down. Nonetheless, he took up arms against the state. So too did his sons, Elijah and Medad. In subsequent years, they would follow in their father's political footsteps. Scarcely a year passed when one or the other would not be elected selectman, town moderator, or state representative. Participation in the insurrection, contrary to what state leaders wanted people to believe, hardly hurt their reputations.

Equally prominent in town affairs was Nathan Dickinson, Jr. The great-grandfather of the renowned poet Emily Dickinson, he marched against the state along with three of his brothers, two of his sons, and two of his sons-in-law. At the time, Nathan, Jr., was a prosperous farmer, not as wealthy as Moses Dickinson, but ranked in the top 20 percent of all property holders. In his early fifties, he had been continually involved for over a decade in virtually every aspect of town affairs. He had represented the town in the

Nathan Dickinson house. Reprinted from Carpenter & Morehouse, *History of the Town of Amherst* (Amherst, Mass., 1896), 135. Built sometime before 1745, this was the house in which Nathan Dickinson, Jr., lived for much of his life. His family had always been one of the most prominent in town, and would remain so long after his death. Being a rebel family, despite what state officials later claimed, was never detrimental to their social standing.

state legislature for nine years, served as town clerk for twelve years, as town treasurer for nine years, and as town moderator for two years. He held most of these offices simultaneously and, hence, for the entire decade preceding the Regulation had had a huge impact on town governance.

Nathan, Jr., along with Moses Dickinson and the rest of the large Dickinson clan, were mainstays in the Second Congregational Church. This church had just come into being a few years before the rebellion. At one time, the entire Dickinson clan, as well as nearly everyone else in town, attended the First Church. Then, over the years, a number of grievances developed. One was simply the result of population growth. By 1773, the meetinghouse could no longer accommodate the town's growing population. The town faced a choice: enlarge the old meetinghouse or build a second church. It proved divisive. Many parishioners, complaining of the distance that they had to walk to get to the First Church, called for a second church. They were voted down. Instead of accepting defeat, many resented it.

Other grievances were triggered largely by the conduct of two ministers, both named David Parsons, father and son. They dominated the First

Church in Amherst for eighty-two years, from roughly forty-five years before Shays's Rebellion to thirty-five years after. The elder Parsons came to Amherst in the 1730s, soon after he graduated from Harvard, when the town was still part of Hadley and looking for a "Learned orthodox Minister." Even though Parsons was only twenty-three years old at the time, he drove a hard bargain, getting the town to grant him two lots of land, £175 toward building a parsonage, £100 salary to be soon raised to £160, and sixty wagon loads of wood per year.

The wood allowance, especially, struck many as excessive. For most farmers, it meant a lot of additional work. They had to cut down several more trees each winter, chop them up into firewood, let the wood dry, and move it by sled to the parsonage the following winter. Over the next twenty-five years, the minister and his flock bickered over his salary and wood supply, but he usually got what he wanted. His wood allowance was increased to 80 loads in 1744, to 90 loads in 1749, to 100 in 1751, and 120 in 1763. Noted the local chronicler Sylvester Judd: "I never found in any records, a minister who consumed as much wood as Mr. Parsons."[7]

Then came the American Revolution. The Dickinsons became the town's leading patriot family, and the Reverend Parsons the most vocal Tory. At one point the Tory pastor was supposed to read a proclamation that ended with "God save the Commonwealth of Massachusetts." He added: "But I say, God save the king." A voice from the congregation then responded: "And I say, Sir, that you're a rogue." In an effort to suppress Toryism, the patriots in Amherst imprisoned nine of the most prominent men in town and got the town to vote "That the conduct of the Rev'd David Parsons is not friendly to the Common Cause." They also shorted him on his wood supply and let his salary fall into arrears.

Then in 1781, after forty-five years in the pulpit, Parsons died. None other than his son David, also an adamant Tory, was invited to take his place. He had to accept less wood, twenty-five cords initially, to be raised to forty cords. Of the seven neighboring ministers who took part in the ordination service, four were fellow Tories. This was too much for many patriots to swallow, especially Nathaniel Dickinson, Jr., a classmate of Parsons's at Harvard. Breaking completely with the First Church, the "aggrieved brethren" petitioned the state legislature for separation, citing by name Parsons's Tory backers. Within a month they received permission to form a Second Church. It was organized at the home of a prominent Dickinson in-law, Ebenezer Mattoon, Jr. The members then erected a meetinghouse and hired Ichabod Draper, a thirty-one-year-old Harvard graduate, to be their minister. Just months before the rebellion, in January 1786, he was formally ordained.[8]

Not every Dickinson joined the Second Church. Nor did every patriot. But there was a noticeable difference between the two congregations. The First Church included both patriots and loyalists, but not the Second Church. In the new congregation, Tories were clearly not welcome.[9] Meanwhile, the younger Parsons and the other executor of his father's estate sued the town for the elder Parsons's back pay. They claimed that the town had shorted the former minister £399. They wanted that amount plus £39 interest.[10]

The Dickinsons were not just vocally at odds with Parsons and other Amherst Tories. They also provided far more than their share of fighting men for the Revolution. Of the thirty Shaysites who were Dickinsons by blood or marriage, twenty-three were of fighting age at the time of the Revolution. All but two fought in the war. Also qualifying for the sobriquet "Old Soldier" were many other Amherst rebels:[11]

	Dickinsons	Other insurgents
Veterans	21	40
Nonveterans	2	26
Youths	7	25

Half of the 121 Amherst men who joined the Regulation, then, were Revolutionary veterans. Of these 61 men, most had been recruited by Reuben Dickinson. The son of an original settler, Reuben was forty-six years old at the time of the Lexington alarm. He was already a veteran, having fought in the French and Indian War as a young man in his twenties. He had been part of the 1755 expedition against Crown Point to seize the French fortress on Lake Champlain. A sergeant at the time, he had subsequently risen to the rank of militia captain. By the 1770s, he was also prominent in town affairs, repeatedly elected selectman, and recruited by the county elite to be a member of the Hampshire County grand jury.

As soon as the Lexington alarm reached Amherst, town patriots turned to Reuben Dickinson to raise a company of sixty men and lead them into battle. Among the men he recruited was Daniel Shays of Shutesbury. Less than two weeks later, this company disbanded. Dickinson immediately formed a new company, which included Shays and many other men from his previous unit, and led them at the Battle of Bunker Hill. Several months later, this company also disbanded. In the meantime, Dickinson had been selected to be a captain in the Massachusetts Line. In January 1776 he enlisted for three years and formed a third company of eighty-six men from Amherst and the surrounding towns. This unit marched west and north into New York, fought in the Ticonderoga and Saratoga campaigns, and witnessed the surrender of General John Burgoyne's army of fifty-seven hundred redcoats and Indian allies.

After the war shifted south, Reuben Dickinson was again involved in town affairs. At this time he also conspicuously challenged the new state government. In 1782, the authorities took into custody three former Revolutionary officers who had been part of a mob that broke the Reverend Samuel Ely out of the Springfield jail. The officers were to be held in the Northampton jail as sureties for Ely's return. Learning of a plan to ship the three hostages to Boston, Dickinson gathered three hundred men and sought a meeting with the high sheriff, Colonel Elisha Porter, under whom he had served during the war. When Porter would not cooperate, Dickinson doubled the size of his regiment, marched on Northampton, and forced the sheriff to release the hostages.[12]

Like Luke Day and several other former officers of the Massachusetts Line, Reuben Dickinson was in deep financial trouble by war's end. The war was hard on all Amherst farmers. With the workforce depleted, one farm after another had to reduce the number of acres in tillage. Grain production dropped precipitously, from eighty-five bushels per taxpayer in 1771 to twenty-six bushels in 1782.[13] In the case of Dickinson, who spent several years away from the farm, the toll was devastating. Although he still ranked in the top 5 percent of Amherst taxpayers in August 1786, the month the rebellion started, the ranking hid a crucial fact. He was heavily in debt to Martin Cooley and Nathaniel Smith of Sunderland, a fact that would cost him dearly after the Regulation.

During the uprising, Reuben Dickinson played his usual role in recruiting men. At least sixty men who served under him during the war joined the Regulation. So, too, did his son, two sons-in-law, and two young men who were courting his daughters. That, among other things, earned him a place on the attorney general's "Black List." Earmarked for harsh punishment, Dickinson fled to Vermont when the Regulation collapsed.[14] His creditors moved in for the kill and forced him to liquidate his Amherst holdings. He settled in Thetford, Vermont, where he farmed on "free" disputed land until his death.

Not all the Amherst rebels had followed Reuben Dickinson into battle during the Revolution. Nor were all of them former patriots. Two prominent Tories—John Field and John Nash—joined the rebellion. Field, who was a liquor dealer as well as a farmer, had once been a leader of the town. Like Moses Dickinson, he had been both a selectman and town moderator. During the Revolution, he had first been a Tory, but then recanted. Nash, who was also a liquor dealer, had been one of the town's more aggressive Tories and had been jailed by the Dickinsons and their patriot comrades during the war. True to form, he became one of the town's more aggressive Regulators—and, like Reuben Dickinson, earned a place on the attorney general's "Black List."

In trying to discredit the Regulation, the state often pretended that men like Nash and Field were typical rebels, that the Shaysites were mostly former Tories, men who at heart were still loyal to King George III. That was far from being the case. In fact, the state was more dependent on former Tories than were the rebels. In Amherst, of the thirteen men who actively sided with the state and took up arms to defend the courts, six were Tories. Among the six were three members of the Boltwood family. The Boltwoods were famous locally as rabid, unbending, unrepentant supporters of the British crown.

Also siding with the state was one of the town's most honored patriots, Ebenezer Mattoon, Jr. He was in an uncomfortable situation, to put it mildly. He was a government appointee and profited from his many government connections. Yet he had not only sided with the Dickinsons during the Revolution, he had fought under Reuben Dickinson and alongside Daniel Shays. To make matters worse, he was married to a Dickinson, and his sister Elizabeth and her husband Oliver Clapp were adamant supporters of the rebellion. Indeed, the Clapps operated the tavern at which the insurgents met. Elizabeth brewed the beer the rebels drank, while Oliver helped them formulate plans against the state.

Mattoon was also a leader of the "aggrieved brethren" who had opposed the Reverend David Parsons and founded the Second Church. His fellow church members included some of the richest families in town and also some of the poorest. Yet, the church was not divided, rich versus poor, creditor versus debtor. Members of the Second Church overwhelmingly supported the Regulation. Thirty-one took up arms against the state. The rest supported their friends in arms. Mattoon, the lone government employee, was the only member who sided with the state.

Mattoon felt so uncomfortable in this situation, or so threatened, that he temporarily moved his family out of town. Later, when peace returned, Mattoon went out of his way to get back in the good graces of his onetime friends, writing letters in their behalf, and in one instance even flat out lying to save a man in neighboring Pelham from the gallows.[15]

IN THE NEARBY town of Pelham, the key family was the Grays.[16] Of the 110 Pelham men who marched behind Daniel Shays, 20 in one way or another were members of the Gray family. Among their number was Daniel Gray, the richest man in town, who also was a deacon of the church and frequently was elected selectman and town moderator. Also participating was the leader of the clan, Deacon Ebenezer Gray, who served as town treasurer for over twenty-five years. These men carried much weight in town, far more than Daniel Shays, who although highly respected was a relative newcomer to Pelham with few family connections.

In terms of wealth, the Pelhamites were generally poorer than their Amherst neighbors. The soil was rockier, the winters one to two weeks longer, and the main outlet to long-distance trade—the Connecticut River—was farther away. In Pelham, no one family was as wealthy, collectively, as the Dickinsons of Amherst. Nonetheless, like in Amherst, the most rebellious family in Pelham—the Grays—was also the most prosperous. In terms of taxable wealth, the top three men in town were Grays. All but one took up arms against the state. The single exception was on his deathbed. His son joined the Regulation. Of the next seven men on the tax list, none were Grays. Three, including Dr. Hines, were rebels.

As in Amherst, the rebels in Pelham tended to be more affluent than their neighbors:[17]

	Grays	Other Rebel Families
Top 20%	5	19
2d 20%	1	7
3d 20%	1	12
4th 20%	0	9
Bottom 20%	2	4

The Grays and other Pelham rebels also had been fierce patriots during the Revolution. Support for the king was, in fact, almost nonexistent in Pelham. The townsfolk were primarily Scots-Irish, a term not used at the time but developed later to distinguish these people and others of similar ancestry from the Catholic Irish who migrated to America in the nineteenth century. Although they differed strikingly from the Catholic Irish, most

Conkey's Tavern. Reprinted from Carpenter & Morehouse, *History of the Town of Amherst* (Amherst, Mass., 1896), 135. Built in 1758, this tavern had long been a favorite watering hole for the men of Pelham. Here was where much of the politicking in town took place, and where many of the town's political decisions were made. And here was where the town's insurgents met and organized to do battle against the state. The owner of the tavern was a Regulator, as were many of his relatives.

being Lowland Scots in ethnic origin and fiercely Protestant, they shared one quality with their former countrymen: their hatred for the British ran deep. They learned this hatred literally "at their mother's knee." It was a key element in their folk history.

Their forebears, as they understood their heritage, had been hard-working Lowland Scots who had been moved to northern Ireland by the British government. There, they were to serve as the king's loyal garrison in the midst of his "papist" enemies. In exchange, the king and Parliament had promised to let them live and prosper as God-fearing Presbyterians. With much hard work, their ancestors had kept their end of this sacred bargain, turned Irish wasteland into productive farms, and added immensely to their British landlords' wealth. The landlords, in turn, had unmercifully exploited them, eventually cutting off their wool trade and jacking up their rents, first by two times and then by three times, while the British government had repeatedly violated its promises and tried to force them to conform to the "ungodly" practices of the Church of England.[18]

Then, in the summer of 1718, the first of their American ancestors migrated to the New World. While most Scots-Irish disembarked in Philadelphia, their ancestors landed in Boston. Immediately, they encountered hostility, even though they shared with Puritan Boston a common Calvinist heritage, as well as a mutual disdain for the Church of England. Puritan Boston looked down upon them and feared that they would devour the food supply. The provincial legislature in 1720 ordered them to get out of Boston within seven months. The hope was that they would move to the Massachusetts frontier and form a barrier against Indian raids. Some settled in Worcester County, built a Presbyterian church, only to have their "Puritan neighbors gather in a mob and totally destroy their work by chopping, sawing and burning in a cruel orgy of vandalism." Intolerance continued in the following years, and in the 1730s many of their forebears moved further west and settled distinctly Scots-Irish towns. One was Pelham, another Colrain.[19]

Like Scots-Irish settlers throughout the backcountry, the people of Pelham had a reputation for being different. They were noticeably taller than most New Englanders. They spoke with an Irish brogue. They grew potatoes. They raised and spun flax. Many claimed that they introduced both the potato and flax to Massachusetts. Many also claimed that they were incredibly tight fisted. Indeed, rumor had it that they walked barefoot to church, waiting until the last minute to put on their shoes, thus saving them from wear and tear. Borrowing and lending were also said to be very common among them; buying and selling rare.

Above all, they were known for being extremely clannish and for standing up for their own. They came out of a culture in which the "family" encompassed all kin within four generations, and in which all family members were expected to band together whenever danger threatened. In that culture, family members seldom lived isolated from each other. They tended to live near kinfolk, migrate with kinfolk, marry kinfolk, socialize with kinfolk, and exchange land with kinfolk.[20] These interlocking family networks could be formidable. They proved it time and again throughout the backcountry, reacting forcibly against outside threats and especially against British sympathizers.

The Pelhamites, in particular, had such a history. In 1762, Solomon Boltwood of Amherst, a sheriff's deputy and staunch supporter of the king, made his way up Pelham hill to serve a warrant. Five men and four women attacked him "with axes, clubs, sticks, hot water and hot soap in a riotous and tumultuous manner" and sent him scurrying back down the hill. Eleven years later, the Boston Committee of Correspondence sought support in western Massachusetts against British economic restrictions. Only seven towns responded. Pelham was one of the seven. It promised to resist British authority and support American liberty.[21]

Two years later, on the eve of the Revolutionary War, a mob of Pelhamites went many miles out of their way to terrorize British sympathizers. They made their way down Pelham hill, through Amherst and Hadley, across the Connecticut River to Hatfield, and seized two prominent Tories, the "River God" Israel Williams and his son. They then took their prisoners back across the river, to Hadley, where they confined them to a house, clogged the chimney and smoked them overnight, thus forcing them to sign a proclamation denouncing Britain's Intolerable Acts.[22] This hostility carried over into the war. Many Pelhamites enlisted, including four-fifths of the future Shaysites who had reached fighting age. Six served under Reuben Dickinson.

In the battle over the state constitution, the town championed local egalitarianism. It found fault with the rejected constitution of 1778 because it seemed "in some particulars too favourable to some Classes of Men while it excludes others." If anything, the town was even more critical of the 1780 constitution, the one that actually became the law of the land. Among other things, the town took issue with the governor's power to appoint all judicial officials on the grounds that "that is a priviledge that ought to be Lodged in the hands of the People, belonging to the Towns and Counties, where such persons dwell." Similarly, the town took issue with the governor's and governor's council's power to appoint militia officers on the grounds that all men sixteen years and older who "shall be Drafted, ought to have a Voice in the Choice of their own officers."[23]

Pelham, as a voice for local egalitarianism, was hard not only on distant authority figures. It was also notoriously hard on local authority figures. The town had dismissed its first pastor after nine years, driven its second pastor to an early grave, and gotten rid of its third pastor after a protracted salary dispute during the Revolutionary War. Thanks to this history, there was no ministerial authority in Pelham at the time of Shays's Rebellion. Indeed, the church was in a shambles.

Like their Puritan neighbors, the Scots-Irish expected their pastors to be educated. The town's first minister, the Reverend Robert Abercrombie, had met the town's exacting standards. He had been trained at Edinburgh University, the seat of all knowledge in Presbyterian circles. That, however, did not keep him from having a long-running quarrel with some townsfolk or being dismissed by the presbytery of Boston in 1755. After his dismissal, he remained in Pelham, and three of his sons subsequently took up arms against the state.

Since Abercrombie's dismissal, the town had had trouble finding and settling a minister. More often than not, the pulpit had been occupied by suppliers, men who were hired to deliver a handful of sermons and sent on their way. Then during the last long vacancy, in 1784, Deacon Ebenezer Gray made a grave mistake. He hired as the town's supplier a con man, Stephen Burroughs. Although only nineteen, Burroughs was an old hand at fooling people, having already successfully palmed himself off as a doctor as well as a preacher. Using his mother's maiden name, he introduced himself to Deacon Gray as the Reverend Davis and produced a letter attesting to his qualifications. Deacon Gray hired him, and Burroughs preached for thirty shillings a week from a handful of old sermons that had been written by his father, a legitimate New Hampshire minister. Months passed before he was exposed as an impostor.

Drummed out of Pelham, Burroughs got involved in alchemy and counterfeiting schemes, and in late 1785 he was convicted of passing fake money in Springfield and sentenced to three years in jail. From jail he further added to the misery of his Scots-Irish parishioners by concocting what came to be known as the "Hay Mow Sermon," a pamphlet ridiculing the Grays and other Pelhamites for their distinctive Irish brogue and traditions, their gullibility, and their role in Shays's Rebellion. He did them even more damage in his *Memoirs*, which first appeared in 1798 and was reprinted at least twenty times.[24]

IN WEST SPRINGFIELD, three families were central. Of the 141 men who bore arms against the state, 26 were connected by blood or marriage with the Day family, 24 with the Leonards, and 15 with the Elys.[25]

The most prominent of these men was Colonel Benjamin Ely, a wealthy landowner and easily the most popular man in town. Elected selectman seven times, town moderator six times, state representative five times, he was indicted for treason and barred from holding office in 1787. The next year the townsfolk elected him to represent them in the state legislature and at the state convention called to ratify the United States Constitution. In keeping with his constituents' wishes, he voted against ratifying the Constitution.

Also indicted for treason was Reuben Leonard, Jr. Thirteen years younger than Ely, he was just reaching his prime in town affairs at the time of Shays's Rebellion. The son of a deacon and prominent selectman, he was elected selectman in 1788 and held that office until 1797.

West Springfield, by and large, was a much wealthier community than either Amherst or Pelham. The land was better, and the town bordered the Connecticut River, the main transit for trade. As in Amherst and Pelham, the rebels were not just poor farmers. The better off, in fact, were slightly more supportive of the rebellion than were their poorer neighbors. Of the fifteen Elys who participated in the insurrection, for example, four were among the top 5 percent of town taxpayers, and another two were among the top 20 percent. Overall, the rebels came from these brackets:[26]

Top 20%	31
2d 20%	22
3d 20%	18
4th 20%	17
Bottom 20%	31

The West Springfield church was stable, "solid as a rock," according to parishioners. Yet, only a few years before, the church had come close to having the same problem as the Pelham church. The pastor of the First Church was Joseph Lathrop. Ordained in 1756, he ran the church with a firm hand for most of the sixty-five years of his ministry. But every now and then he became seriously ill, and on this occasion the town had to find a temporary replacement. John Watkins, an Englishman, appeared and tried to get hired as a supply minister. He, like Stephen Burroughs, was a fraud. Fortunately for the town's reputation, he was quickly discovered and booted out. By the time of the Regulation, Lathrop had recovered and again exercised authority over much of the community.[27]

Lathrop, in several respects, typified the clerical response in the Connecticut Valley to Shays's Rebellion. He condemned the insurrection without actually supporting the government. On December 14, 1786, he preached that "drawing the sword" against the government was wrong. Yet, at same time, he criticized the government, arguing that it should protect its "prudent and industrious members" and not put them in a position "to struggle in vain under an insupportable load." Rumor also had it that on the eve of the Springfield arsenal attack, Lathrop tried to convince Luke Day to back off. He allegedly told Day that his army was "deficient of good, true,

The Reverend Joseph Lathrop. Reprinted from *Account of the Centennial Celebration of the Town of West Springfield . . . 1874* (West Springfield, Mass., 1874), frontispiece. Ordained in 1756, the Reverend Lathrop was the pastor of West Springfield's First Church for the next sixty-five years, and from all accounts he governed his congregation with a firm hand. Yet, against his wishes, many members of his church joined the Regulation.

and trusty officers," that he was "engaged in a bad cause" and his men knew it, and that he ought to "disband them, and let them return peaceably to their homes; for, as sure as you advance upon the public stores, 'tis as certain that you will meet with sure defeat."[28]

Whatever Lathrop said, it only had limited effect on Day, Benjamin Ely, Reuben Leonard, Jr., and some of the other prominent members of Lathrop's congregation. Yet, at the same time, it undoubtedly dampened the turnout. Certainly, had Lathrop sided with the Regulation, rather than having had opposed "drawing the sword," the turnout from West Springfield would probably have been far more than 141 men.

IN WHATELY, TWO families were central. Of the seventy-six men who rebelled against the state, fifty-five were connected with the Graves and Smith families. In most cases, the connection was through women members of the two families. While only nine men named Graves and five named Smith bore arms, marching with them were eighteen men who had married their sisters or aunts and thirteen men who were the sons of such marriages.[29]

Typical was the extended family of Oliver Graves. Sixty-one years old at the time of the Regulation, Oliver was one of the few town elders who participated in the rebellion. He had been a selectman during the Revolution and had been elected to the first provincial congress. He was also a longtime deacon of the church and was always referred to as Deacon Graves. He had ten children, and one of his younger sons, Selah, joined him in taking up arms against the state. So did his brother's son Israel. He was also joined by three young men who were not blood relatives: Solomon Atkins, Jr., Josiah Davis, and Jonathan Edson. One had married his daughter Rebecca, another his daughter Ruth, and the third was engaged to his daughter Electa. The potential bridegroom, Atkins, was a twenty-five-year-old tanner who was already well on his way to becoming one of the town's wealthier citizens. He married into the family in March 1787, just weeks after the insurrection collapsed. He later became the town treasurer.

Both young Atkins and Deacon Graves were men of substance in 1786. Graves, as befit his social prominence, ranked in the top 20 percent of town taxpayers. And Atkins, despite his youth, was already in the top 20 percent. Marching with him were twenty-three men who were his age or younger. Most had been too young to have fought in the Revolution. Some were teenagers. Not one was from a down-and-out family. All came from the town's more prosperous families:[30]

	Youth Families	Other Rebel Families
Top 20%	14	17
2d 20%	8	9
3d 20%	0	9
4th 20%	0	6
Bottom 20%	0	5

Of the fifty-two men who were old enough to have fought in the Revolution, forty-two were veterans.

The town's minister, Rufus Wells, was an old hand in town politics. At the time of the Regulation, he had been in the pulpit for fifteen years, and he would remain in the pulpit for another forty-eight years. Obviously a survivor, he was also influential. If he consistently opposed the insurrection, as many later claimed, he clearly did not make full use of his persuasive powers. Not only did Deacon Graves support the rebellion, so did five of Wells's kinsmen.

For Wells and other town leaders, the situation changed dramatically soon after the rout of the Shaysites at Petersham. In an effort to capture rebel leaders, one detachment of state troops was sent after Captain Jason Parmenter of Bernardston, who had fled to Vermont but then returned home to get some household goods. The detachment ran into trouble. In a shoot-out with Parmenter's men, a young Whately man was killed. Buried in the neighboring town of Hatfield, he was hailed as a hero. The Reverend

The Reverend Rufus Wells. Reprinted from James M. Craft, *History of the Town of Whately, Mass., 1669–1899* (Conway, Mass., 1899), 151. The Reverend Wells was much like the Reverend Lathrop of West Springfield. A powerful figure in town, he had been in the pulpit for fifteen years when the rebellion broke out and would remain there for the next forty-eight years. Whether he matched Lathrop in his condemnation of the rebellion, however, is doubtful. Not only did the deacon of his church join the Regulation, but so too did five of his kinsmen.

Rufus Wells and the other town leaders decided that his memory had to be honored. On his tombstone was carved: "To the Memory of Mr. Jacob Walker, who, respected by the brave, beloved by his country's friends, dear to his relatives,—while manfully defending the laws and liberties of the Commonwealth, nobly fell by the impious hand of treason, on the 17th day of Feb'y, 1787, in the thirty-second year of his age."[31]

Later, in May and June, several Whately leaders became suppliers of the triumphant state army. Among other things, they sold Lincoln's men several hundred pounds of beef, pork, bread, and peas—and nearly a hundred gallons of rum. They made a nice profit. One of the biggest suppliers, especially of rum, was Gad Smith.[32] The owner of a large country store, hotel, slaughtering house, and coopering works, Smith was one of the town's wealthiest men. He ranked in the top 5 percent of town taxpayers. Married to a blood relative of the minister, Smith was anything but a staunch supporter of the government. Just a few weeks earlier, he had been a rebel, as had been his future son-in-law and twenty-two members of his extended family.

IN COLRAIN NO single family matched the Smiths, the Graveses, or the Dickinsons in providing rebel soldiers. Instead, a half-dozen families contributed far more than their share. And these families undoubtedly had

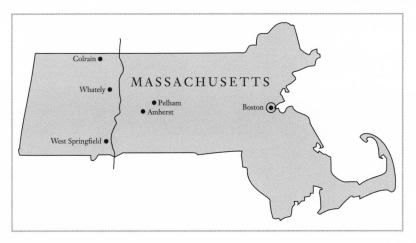

Colrain and other banner towns.

clout. Of the 156 men from Colrain who took up arms against the state, 32 either served as selectmen at one time or another or were the sons of selectmen.[33]

The oldest former selectman was Hezekiah Smith. Just turning sixty-one at the time he took up arms against the state, he had first been elected selectman in the 1760s, some ten years before the Revolution. Later a state representative, he also had been a major during the Revolutionary War. Nearest to him in age were John Clark and John Anderson. They too had been selectmen before the Revolution. Altogether, fifteen Colrain rebels were over forty-five years old. At the other end were forty-two youngsters who were still in their teens or early twenties. The vast majority—roughly two-thirds of the total—were between twenty-five and forty-five years of age. Of those old enough to have fought in the Revolution, over two-thirds had done so.

Like Pelham, Colrain was a Scots-Irish town. Named after a town in northern Ireland, it was founded in 1743, at roughly the same time as Pelham. Colrain was situated near the Deerfield River, the very route that the Mohawks had used on several occasions to attack Deerfield and settlements to the south. Its founders had obtained the land at rock-bottom prices from three Boston speculators. The speculators had paid just pennies an acre for the land and were anxious to quickly double their money. From the beginning, the town had close ties to Pelham, even though the two towns were more than thirty miles apart, and getting from one to the other was a long day's journey even in good weather. In the early days the two towns had even shared the same minister, the Reverend Robert Abercrombie, and for years young men in one town had gone to the other in search of potential brides.

Like Pelham, Colrain was also a hotbed of local egalitarianism. Its response to the 1780 constitution was unique. While it never objected to property as a basis for senate districts, and while it insisted that the office of governor be restricted to Protestants, it was the only town in the state to call for the abolition of all property qualifications for office holding and all property qualifications for voting. The right to vote for any office, it declared by a thirty-eight to four vote, should be extended to every male age twenty-one and over who was, in the eyes of the selectmen, "a friend to the Independance of Said State and of Sober life and Conversation." Similarly, by a twenty-seven to zero vote, the town objected to property qualifications for holding office on the grounds that "money was no Qualification in this Matter."[34]

Economically, Colrain was also much like Pelham. The land was somewhat flatter, and the soil was slightly less rocky, but both were hardscrabble communities. And, as in Pelham, those at the top of the economic ladder were more likely to support the Regulation than those at the bottom:[35]

Top 20%	19
2d 20%	17
3d 20%	22
4th 20%	8
Bottom 20%	10

At the time of Shays's Rebellion, however, Colrain differed from Pelham in two respects. First, it had a long-settled minister. The town had hired Samuel Taggert in 1777. For nearly ten years, he had successfully coped with the difficult personalities in town, and he would continue to do so for the next thirty years. He would remain in the pulpit, preaching the old-fashioned Calvinism that the Scots-Irish liked, until 1818.

Second, although the town provided more rebel soldiers than any other town, a handful of men in town openly opposed the Regulation. Of these men, the most notable were Colonel Hugh McClellan, a Revolutionary War hero, and Major William Stevens, a former artillery officer. Stevens had just opened a store in town, an event so recent that his name did not appear on the 1783 tax assessment. McClellan owned enough property to just barely qualify as one of the top 20 percent of town taxpayers. He, like Ebenezer Mattoon of Amherst, was clearly in an awkward situation. He was beholden to the state for his positions as justice of the peace and colonel of the local militia, but nearly all the men who fought under him during the Revolution became Regulators. At first, like the other leading men in Colrain, McClellan opposed the sitting of the courts and signed petitions to that effect. Then, as violence increased, he defected to the "ranks of law and order." Indeed, he served under General Shepard in defense of the Springfield arsenal. Stevens, the former artillery major, directed the firing of the cannon at the Battle of Springfield.

Once the Regulation was over, McClellan and Stevens were singled out for reprisals. Their fellow townsmen vowed to hang them if James White and Matthew Clark, two town leaders under indictment, were hanged by the state. Neither rebel was hanged. Stevens, the newcomer, soon left town for central New York. Justice of the Peace McClellan, like Ebenezer Mattoon of Amherst, administered the oath of allegiance to many of his fellow townsmen. He also literally went the extra mile to get back into their good graces. In February 1787, he journeyed some ninety miles by horse through heavy snow and freezing temperatures, to the state house in Boston to plead the case of a neighbor, Samuel Boyd, who had served under him as a sergeant during the Revolution.[36]

THE TALE OF Colonel McClellan and Sergeant Boyd was part of a much larger story. The state generally had the backing of high-ranking officers like Colonel McClellan, but not Revolutionary veterans of lesser rank. The latter, like Sergeant Boyd, often joined the Regulation.

That was not the view, to be sure, of the top officers in the old Revolutionary army. In the fall of 1786, for example, the cavalry commander "Lighthorse" Henry Lee sent a report to Washington. "It must give you pleasure to hear," wrote Lee, that the "officers and soldiers are on the side of the government unanimously." Six months later, Washington received a similar account from his former artillery commander Henry Knox. Only a "few wretched officers," said Knox, sided with Shays. Otherwise, all the officers of the late army, even though they had never been adequately paid, staunchly supported the state.[37] Such claims were made time and again, especially by General Knox, Washington's chief correspondent.

Knox's view was clearly the view from above. He had once been a Boston bookbinder and shopkeeper, but he had left that life well behind him. His devoted wife had inherited a huge chunk of southeastern Maine, one-fifth

Henry Knox. Engraving by John F. E. Prud'homme after a portrait by Gilbert Stuart. Courtesy American Antiquarian Society. This portrait captures the image that Knox always tried to convey: George Washington's dependable artillery commander whose cannons drove the British out of Boston and helped win the Revolution. The three-hundred-pound general portrayed the Shaysites in the darkest terms and had an enormous influence on Washington.

of the original Waldo patent, and largely because of her wealth he had become one of the richest men in New England.[38] He corresponded frequently with other rich men, and his portrayal of the rebellion gained a wide following, especially among his wealthy friends. It was later repeated in scores of town histories and a handful of general histories. It thus came to have credibility.

Knox's portrayal had little to do with reality, however. It was just wishful thinking, the view of a major general who coveted order and dreamed of a society in which ordinary men followed the dictates of their betters. Had Knox bothered to do a simple head count, he would have found that of the some four hundred veteran officers of the Massachusetts Line, probably the majority were neutral during Shays's Rebellion, many were supportive of the insurgents, and at least thirty were active leaders of the uprising.

The rebellious leaders, moreover, were not the "wretched officers" that Knox depicted to Washington. Many, in fact, had distinguished war records, and some had attained the status of war heroes. Daniel Shays, whom the Marquis de Lafayette had honored with a gold-handled sword, was just the best known. Also honored and probably held in even higher esteem was Captain Adam Wheeler of Hubbardston. A veteran of both the French and Indian War and the Revolution, he had been singled out by his commanding officer, Colonel William Heath, for conspicuous bravery in the Concord skirmish, an event that had already gained legendary status throughout New England.[39]

Scores of men had served under Wheeler, first in Doolittle's Massachusetts Regiment, then the Fourth Continental Infantry, and then the Sixth Massachusetts. In calling out the men in his hometown to join the insurrection, Wheeler left no doubt that he saw himself and the Regulator movement in the Revolutionary tradition:

We have lately emerged from a bloody war, in which liberty was the glorious prize aimed at, and as liberty is the prize that I so early stepped forth in the defence of the country to gain, and so cheerfully fought for, so liberty is the prize I still have in view, and in this glorious cause I am determined to stand with firmness and resolution.[40]

WHILE IT IS uncertain how many veterans responded to Wheeler's refrain, it is clear that far more sided with the rebels than with the state. In the rebel towns, as one would expect, this was especially true. In towns such as Amherst, Pelham, West Springfield, Whately, and Colrain, the old soldiers of the Revolution were ten times as likely to bear arms in behalf of the Regulation than in behalf of the state. Virtually alone were men like Ebenezer Mattoon and Hugh McClellan.

More telling is what happened in the non-Regulator towns. Here, one might expect hundreds of veterans to turn out in behalf of the state, to respond to the call to arms, just as they had to the Lexington alarm. Such did not happen. Consider, for example, the case of Northampton. A shire town, its residents had been wakened time and again by angry farmers from the outlying area marching on the court, banging drums, and periodically breaking men out of jail. The town was conspicuous in its support of the government. In September 1786, Solomon Allen and fifty-three North-ampton volunteers marched twenty miles south to help General William Shepard defend the Supreme Judicial Court meeting in Springfield. Months later, in January 1787, Captain Hezekiah Russell, in response to Shepard's call to arms, rounded up seventy-one Northampton men and led them to Springfield to defend the arsenal. Altogether, 108 Northampton militiamen took up arms in behalf of the state at one time or the other, and 18 of these men did so twice.

Neither unit, however, was comprised of the "old soldiers" that General Shepard counted on. The two captains, Allen and Russell, had been briefly in the Revolutionary War, and so had their senior officers. Between them, they had less than three months' service. Most of the men under their command had been mere boys at the time of the Revolution. What about the veterans, yesterday's heroes? There were 363 veterans in Northampton, and some 300 in the surrounding towns. Only 23 responded to the call to arms.[41]

The situation was no better in General Shepard's hometown of West-field. Of 295 veterans living in Shepard's hometown, only 14 responded to his call for help.[42] That was especially telling. The general was not just another resident. He was the town's most honored citizen and easily its biggest war hero. Like Luke Day of neighboring West Springfield, he had spent a full eight years in the Revolutionary army. He had led many West-field men into battle. He had a huge presence in town and church affairs. He was an enthusiastic supporter of the state government and one of the most vehement critics of Day and the other rebels. He lobbied for harsh punishments and hangings. And he was the most prominent voice for law and order.

Yet, when it came to getting his former Revolutionary comrades to join him in supporting the state, Shepard had little luck. With some coaxing, he got sixty-five of his fellow townsmen to follow him into battle. That at least was more military support than the rebels enjoyed in Westfield. The insurgents had the armed support of only forty-two Westfield residents. But half of those men were veterans, and hence the rebels had more of the town's veterans in their ranks—seven more, to be exact—than did the general.[43]

The vast majority of the town's veterans, however, did nothing. They sat on the sidelines and ignored the call to arms. To Shepard's embarrassment, most of these men had served under him during the war. That fact would be conveniently ignored after the Regulation. Indeed, many years later, the town historian would even claim that the town's foremost hero had the backing of the town's military men. He would also imply that only a handful of former soldiers joined the rebellion and that patriots throughout western Massachusetts supported the state.[44] It was in keeping with Knox's view of the insurrection. It was also make-believe.

THIS LEADS, IN turn, to a bigger question. Why did so many men throughout western Massachusetts remain "neutral" during the uprising? And why, more particularly, did veterans in Amherst, Pelham, and Greenwich march to the drumbeat of the Regulator movement, while veterans in nearby Hadley and South Hadley stayed at home?

These are tough questions to answer. Probably the best explanation comes from one of General Lincoln's aides. Unlike the Westfield historian, the aide had few illusions. He saw hostility all around him. It varied from place to place, but rarely had he and his comrades been welcomed with open arms. Support for the state in western Massachusetts was obviously sparse. The state could count on high-ranking Revolutionary officers. It could count on some support from shire towns like Northampton. It had some support from "people of property." But nearly everyone else was "restless and disaffected."

Why, then, did they not join the rebellion? The aide attributed it to two factors. One was the rebel leaders. They lacked the prestige, the command presence, to rally men outside their home communities. The other factor was the clergy. It was their conservatism, and the respect that the people had for them, that kept thousands from joining the insurgents. In a sense, then, the state and its leaders had been fortunate. If the rebels had a "respectable leader at their head," noted the aide, "and the clergy engaged on the same side, the Commonwealth would exhibit a scene that would alarm the continent."[45]

The aide undoubtedly had a strong case, especially with regard to the clergy. Dozens of pastors denounced the Regulation from their pulpits. It violated God's holy writ, declared the Reverend Samuel Hopkins of Hadley. It was wicked, the work of the devil, said the Reverend Benjamin Judd of Ware.[46]

Not all of these pastors spoke with one voice, however. In condemning the rebellion, some also censured the state and its leaders. Instead of treating the Regulators' indictment of the governing elite as groundless, they incorporated some of the charges against Bowdoin and his allies into their sermons and reminded their congregations of the Apostle Paul's admonition that good fathers did not provoke their children to anger. Others wholeheartedly supported the governor and his men and held the state up as equitable and just. Denouncing the Regulation was clearly one thing, supporting the state another.

Some ministers never crossed the line. Those who did sometimes lost the backing of their congregations. The Reverend Thomas Allen, for instance, had been a major power in Pittsfield since shortly after graduating from Harvard in the 1760s. He had carried the torch for the Revolution, traveling the Berkshires, trumpeting the patriot cause in one small church after another. He had led the fight for constitutional government. The town was proud of him. Then came the Regulation, and he threw his support behind the state. In the eyes of his parishioners he went too far. To protect himself and his family, he decided that he had to have a gun at his side, even when he went to bed.[47]

Allen survived the uprising and held onto his pulpit. Less fortunate was the Reverend Eleazar Storrs of Sandisfield. A Yale graduate, Storrs had never been as political as Allen, but for years he had been a major force in his community and highly respected. With the coming of the Regulation, Storrs denounced the insurgents and vigorously supported the state. It cost him dearly. Members of his congregation concluded that he was out of touch, that he lacked sympathy for their needs. They never forgave him and eventually sacked him.[48]

Also fired for his zeal was the Reverend Benjamin Judd of Ware. Hired just a year before the rebellion, he used his pulpit as a forum to denounce the Regulators, declaring that he would as "soon pray for the Devils in hell" as for the insurgents. He also insisted that even "if the Devil was Governor or Ruler the People ought to Obey Him." So impassioned were his remarks that two leading members, Deacon Maverick Smith and Abijah Davis, stormed out of church "in contempt of the pastor, or what he had delivered." Then, along with another deacon and two other members, they stopped attending church. The pastor filed charges against them, and they in turn filed charges against him. A local ecclesiastical council then stepped in to restore order. They censured Deacon Smith and several other dissidents, denounced the Regulation as "a crime of the most aggravated nature," and declared the Reverend Benjamin Judd to be "an honest faithful minister in Christ." That did him little good. Two months later, by a sixty-three to thirteen vote, the town dismissed him.[49]

WHAT COLONEL MCCLELLAN experienced in Colrain was thus commonplace. Despite being the acknowledged commander of the local militia and having a strong record in getting men to follow him during the Revolution, the colonel was out of step with his neighbors. He was bucking the will of his community. It was a lost cause. Even his old sergeant took up arms against him.

Throughout the backcountry, the predilection of family, kin, and community generally prevailed. That was especially true in Scots-Irish towns like Colrain and Pelham. They had a long tradition of sticking together. They also had a long tradition of resisting outside authority. For them, assembling a company of warriors was relatively easy. But it also seems to have been relatively easy for tight-knit communities that came out of the New England Puritan tradition. What is striking about most of the rebels is that they came out of unified cultures. Class divisions are almost impossible to find. Towns that supported the Regulation were not divided, rich versus poor, creditor versus debtor. As a rule, people either moved as one or did not participate.

John Brooke, in his study of Worcester County, makes much of religious strife and the lack of ministerial authority. Yet just as many Shaysite towns had long-settled ministers as had vacant pulpits. For every Pelham, there was a West Springfield and a Colrain. In Middlesex County, three of the four major Shaysite towns had ministers who had been settled for ten years or more; in Worcester County, five of nine towns; in Hampshire County, eight of fifteen towns. The only county in which vacancies were rampant was Berkshire County, but that was true of virtually every town in Berkshire County, not just the Shaysite communities. With the Revolution came a shortage in new ministers, as Harvard and other suppliers failed to graduate enough to meet the demand. Especially hard hit were the hill towns of far western Massachusetts.[50]

Religious turmoil, moreover, was not confined to the Shaysite towns. Fights over the minister's salary were endemic throughout rural New England. So too were theological, liturgical, and political altercations. Among the communities that bore the scars of such controversies were four Shaysite strongholds—Amherst, Groton, Princeton, and Shutesbury— where the Revolution had pitted irate parishioners against Tory pastors. Groton in 1776 found a suitable replacement in Daniel Chapin, who would serve for the next fifty years. Amherst in 1783 created a second church. Princeton, after a vacant pulpit for ten years, finally filled it in 1786. Shutesbury's troubles dragged on until 1806.

Yet even in towns that were riven over religious matters, there was unity in subcultures. In Amherst, for example, members of the Second Church were virtually "at war" with the Tory pastor of the First Church and his supporters. This war, moreover, was not just a passing fancy. It would last some twenty more years. Yet, apart from the government appointee Ebenezer Mattoon, members of the Second Church overwhelmingly sided with the Regulation.

Without such community loyalties, Shays's Rebellion would never have become a reality. The "poor and desperate" did not come out of every nook and cranny in western Massachusetts to do battle against the state and its "grasping" elite. Nor did the vast majority of debtors who found themselves in court or in debtors' prison. More "hard-pressed debtors" lived in Hadley than in Amherst or Pelham. And more lived in Granville than in West Springfield or Colrain. Yet these men never took up arms against the state. Only in tight-knit communities where men and women acted as one were rebel leaders like Reuben Dickinson, James White, and Luke Day able to raise hundreds of men to join the Regulation and hopefully restore "communal order."

REVERBERATIONS

court closings and skirmishes. It failed as a revolution. Yet, long after the rebels fled the battlefield, the insurrection reverberated through American society.

Much of the backlash was due to the Boston elite. Had they treated Daniel Shays as simply a small-town rebel leader, the aftermath might have been different. But they portrayed him instead as a major villain, a threat to the entire nation, an archetype for anarchy. He thus became memorable, hailed and damned long after they were forgotten, the subject of wild tales and much curiosity.

Typical was the experience of the Salem clergyman William Bentley. In August 1793, just six years after the rebellion's collapse, he traveled west to Springfield. His host took him to the federal arsenal and showed him where General Shepard had stationed his regiment and the ground over which Shays had "so precipitately retreated." He was also told that Shays had recently been seen in the area, begging from house to house in Deerfield, a small town thirty miles north of Springfield, and had "gained eleven dollars from such as had favored his party." The "true courage of this unhappy man," concluded Bentley, was still widely respected.[1]

Pelham eventually put up a marker memorializing the rebels and their cause. Sheffield did the same for the "last battle" of the rebellion. Westfield built a statue honoring General Shepard. Amherst named a street after

Daniel Shays. Years later, the federal government named a highway after the defeated leader.

MORE IMPORTANT THAN these public memorials, however, was the Regulation's long-term impact on its participants, the Commonwealth of Massachusetts, and the nation as a whole.

For some, the immediate outcome was dire. The nominal leader, Daniel Shays, fled the state, lost his farm, and despite rumors to the contrary never again took up residence in Massachusetts. John Bly and Charles Rose went to the gallows. Sixteen others spent months anticipating a hangman's noose before gaining their freedom. Judge William Whiting lost his judgeship, paid £100 in fines, and faced seven months in jail. State Representative Moses Harvey lost his seat in the legislature, paid £50 in fines, and had to stand an hour at the Northampton gallows with a rope around his neck. Hundreds of others had to cope with indictments filed by the state, or damage suits filed by neighbors, and some four thousand temporarily lost their right to vote, sit on juries, hold office, and work as teachers and tavernkeepers.

On the winning side, General Lincoln gained acclaim as a conquering hero. No longer was his surrender of an entire army at Charleston, South Carolina, the focal point of his military career. Instead, polite society made much of his all-night march from Hadley to Petersham and his rout of Shays's forces. The story of that winter night was told time and again, long after Lincoln resigned his special commission as major general of Governor Bowdoin's army, long after Lincoln's death in 1810.

But approval of the general also had its limits. He ran for lieutenant governor in 1787, shortly after his military triumph. He did well in the eastern counties, poorly in the west, and statewide finished second in the popular voting. He ran twice again, winning in 1788, losing the following year. He eventually accepted a patronage job from the national government under George Washington as head of the Boston Customs Office. It was lucrative, but hardly a position of the highest distinction.

Less successful politically was Lincoln's former commander, Governor Bowdoin. The governor gained enormous respect among his fellow speculators. They toasted him and his victory. But he was no match for John Hancock. In the spring 1787 election he captured only one vote for every three for Hancock. Two years later, the ratio was even worse, one for four.

DESPITE BOWDOIN'S SORRY political career, state officials continued to portray his foremost adversaries, the Regulators, as hopeless failures.

They were wrong. Overall, the Regulation made a difference. If one of the insurgents' chief goals was to bring the speculators to heel, and to stop the state from shifting money from the backcountry to Boston, the Regulators emerged far better off than they were before. Indeed, they emerged victorious.

From 1780 to 1786, speculators in state securities had been in the saddle. In the early 1780s the state legislature had consolidated the state debt at an extremely high value, at least twice what any other American government was willing to pay the holders of its notes. The legislature had also decided to pay interest in specie and retire the entire state debt, principal as well as interest, by the late 1780s. To service the interest charges, the legislature had established a state impost and excise system. Then in 1786, it had assigned revenues from direct taxes, chiefly land and poll taxes, to service the debt.

With Shays's Rebellion, this system came to an end. The new 1787 legislature passed a moratorium on debts and cut direct taxes "to a bone." The burden of taxation, formerly placed on polls and estates, shifted to indirect taxes. From 1781 to 1786, direct taxes had averaged nearly £300,000 a year. In 1787 no direct taxes were levied; in 1788, the total was £78,387; in 1789, £37,508; in 1790, £29,564.[2] Direct taxes thus fell to about 10 percent of what they had been.

Under the new system, indirect taxes no longer went to speculators either. Previously, excise and import duties had been earmarked to pay interest on state notes. Now, these revenues were shifted to pay general state expenses. The state made an earnest attempt to sell its public lands and thus reduce taxes, but little effort was made to find new revenues to service securities. The loss of revenue from impost and excise taxes hurt speculators severely. Specie interest payments ceased. Interest on the state debt fell into arrears. The value of securities on the Boston market fell by 30 percent.[3]

Meanwhile, with the state no longer levying heavy direct taxes to pay off speculators and other noteholders, backcountry towns focused on paying off their debts and collecting back taxes. The average backcountry family thus still had a tax bill, but nothing like the earlier ones. In 1786, the average family in the western half of the state had to pay nearly £3 in poll taxes for every male sixteen years or older. In the next five years combined, the total was less than half that amount. The annual rate in towns such as Amherst, Pelham, and Colrain dropped from twenty-five shillings to less than two shillings.[4]

ALMOST AS WELL off were the scores of Regulators who, facing indictments in Massachusetts, fled to the independent republic of Vermont. Although they had to start over again, carve out new lives for themselves, they no longer had to cope with a state government that was the servant of the Boston gentry. They also knew that the Green Mountain republic would be a safe haven. Its leaders, Ethan Allen and Governor Thomas Chittenden, had refused to cooperate with Massachusetts officials during the rebellion.

Labeling the Massachusetts elite "a pack of Damned Rascals," Allen had scoffed at the Bowdoin administration's cry for help. Twice, General Lincoln turned to Governor Chittenden for aid in capturing runaway rebels. The governor, on each occasion, said that he would see what he could do, and then did nothing. From his perspective, it was not Vermont's duty "to be aiding in hauling them away to the halter." Of a different persuasion were some Vermont assemblymen who feared that any connection with the rebels might jeopardize Vermont's security. In February 1787, they called on Chittenden to denounce the "horrid & wicked rebellion." He refused to do so. Then, with the support of a bare majority of the legislature, they passed a resolution requiring him to act. In response, Chittenden issued a proclamation, warning Vermonters that they should not "harbour, entertain or conceal" Daniel Shays and three other top insurgent leaders. At the time, Shays and several other rebels were staying at the farm next to the governor's.[5]

Vermont's inaction worried not only the Massachusetts gentry. It also worried the great land barons of New York. In their eyes, the Green Mountain republic had long been a bad example. It had no taxes, it attracted army deserters and other riffraff, and it refused to honor the property rights of land speculators from neighboring states. Its population was growing by leaps and bounds. There was even talk that Vermont, with its growing population, might annex the insurgent region. There was also talk that it might rejoin the British Empire.

Alexander Hamilton, a powerful force in the New York assembly, offered the New York elite a solution. As far as he was concerned, Vermont was already an independent republic and they had to accept that fact. Overthrowing the Green Mountain Boys, argued Hamilton, was out of the question. An invading army would have to reckon not only with mountains, thick forests, and deep gorges but with a "whole tribe of Yankees." And even if a New York victory were certain, they would then have to subjugate some of the most cantankerous people on earth—a task that only their worst enemies would wish upon them. Once New Yorkers accepted the fact that con-

Thomas Chittenden. Reprinted from E. P. Walton, ed., *Records of the Council of Safety and Governor and Council of the State of Vermont* (Montpelier, 1873–80), vol. 1, frontispiece. Although Chittenden never received as many accolades as the flashier Ethan Allen, he was one of the heroes of independent Vermont. Like Allen, he had little use for the men who governed Massachusetts, and as governor he thwarted their efforts to capture Daniel Shays and other rebel leaders.

quering Vermont, reversing the Vermont revolution, was a lost cause, they could deal with the real problem that now faced them.

That, contended Hamilton, stemmed from the fact that Vermont was a totally independent republic not "confederated" with the United States. Hence its leaders were free to pursue their outlaw ways, connive with the British one day, the Shaysites the next. Vermont's leaders, moreover, clearly knew what they were doing. To enhance their own power, they had sought connections with the British in Canada and "wisely" encouraged settlement by "an exemption from taxes, and availing themselves of the discontents of a neighboring state." Were they a threat to New York as well as Massachusetts? Undoubtedly, they were. They continually tempted the inhabitants of neighboring states to join them. Their intentions were to make "proselytes to their government," and their methods were "too well calculated to accomplish their designs."

Terms with the Vermonters, concluded Hamilton, thus had to be reached before they became more "formidable" and encroached even more on New York. What they wanted was clear. Above all else, they yearned for guaranteed borders, security, statehood. By standing in their way, New Yorkers were just asking for trouble, virtually encouraging civil unrest and British intrigue. It was time to face reality, to reverse course, and to make peace with Allen, Chittenden, and the Green Mountain Boys.

So, in March 1787, Hamilton introduced a bill in the New York assembly directing the state's congressional delegation to support statehood for Vermont. That raised a hue and cry among New York's biggest land claimants. They thundered about the sacred rights of property, a concept close to Hamilton's heart. The New York assembly balked at accepting Hamilton's proposal. An attorney for the claimants was allowed to present their case to the assembly. Debate was heated. In the end, however, Hamilton got his way.[6]

Ethan Allen responded by disavowing the Shaysites, turning down Luke Day's and Eli Parsons's offer of leadership, ordering the two men out of Vermont, and publicizing his actions. Yet, quietly, the leaders of Vermont still gave Shaysites refuge, only turning over to Massachusetts two horse thieves in the fall of 1787.[7]

In 1789, Hamilton worked out a further settlement with Vermont's leaders. In exchange for New Yorkers giving up their Vermont land claims, Vermont would pay them $30,000 in cash. Governor George Clinton of New York opposed this arrangement, but the legislature accepted it and ultimately agreed to sweeten the deal by giving the land claimants an eighty-mile-square tract in western New York as further compensation. With that, many prominent New Yorkers dropped their opposition to Vermont's admission to the United States, and a year later Vermont entered the Union.[8]

Independent Vermont proved to be a haven for many former Shaysites. Reuben Dickinson, facing indictment in Massachusetts and forced to sell his Amherst holdings, first fled to Brattleborough and then settled in the town of Thetford farther north along the Connecticut River. The winters were longer. Viable markets were many miles away. The river-bottom land, however, was "free" as no one as yet had "good" title to it. There, the former Amherst selectman lived his twilight years, a "free" man in a town that was even more self-sufficient than Amherst had been before the Revolution.[9]

Politically, Vermont towns like Thetford were ideal for fierce localists like Dickinson. There were no cities in Vermont, much less any hub city like Boston that had economic and political power over the rest of the state. The mountainous terrain and harsh winters, moreover, worked against central control. By and large, each mountain valley was cut off from its neighbors for much of the year. In the dead of winter and long into spring, no governor was able, even if he had been so inclined, to tell the people of Thetford what to do. Thetford was largely on its own. So too was every

Alexander Hamilton. Engraving by John F. E. Prud'homme after a miniature by Archibald Robertson. Courtesy American Antiquarian Society. A powerful force in New York politics at the time of the Regulation, Hamilton already had the reputation as a doer, a man who weighed the options, made the tough decisions, and forged ahead. He prided himself on being a man of action and moved and dressed with military crispness. This portrait, in the eyes of many, captured his personality.

other Vermont village. The only governing bodies that truly mattered, therefore, were the local town meetings. To a man like Dickinson, that was the way it should be.

Similarly, Simeon Hazleton carved out a new life for himself in Sandgate, Vermont. Like Dickinson, Hazleton had been a Minuteman in 1775 and later a captain in the Massachusetts Line. A onetime slaveowner, he had been one of Hardwick's most prominent citizens at the time of the Regulation. Even the state authorities deemed Hazleton a "gentleman." As a leader of the Hardwick Regulators under Adam Wheeler, he had been indicted for treason by the Worcester Grand Jury. With the sheriff bearing a warrant for his arrest, Hazleton fled to Vermont. Following in the footsteps of an earlier generation of Hardwick men who had sought refuge in Bennington, he joined scores of other Shaysites in taking cover in the town of Sandgate just north of Bennington. There, he quickly reestablished himself as a community leader and was chosen time and again to represent the town in the Vermont assembly.[10]

Hazleton's story, to be sure, was unusual. Most of the men who joined him in fleeing to Sandgate never enjoyed his political success. They never had the benefit of his social status in Massachusetts. They never obtained it in Vermont. But, like Hazleton, they acquired land and saw themselves as "free" men, living in a polity in which local self-governance was the rule and in an independent republic that was free of debt and not answerable to Governor Bowdoin, William Phillips, and other Massachusetts speculators.

NO LONGER ABLE to get money from the fleeing rebels, or from the state, Phillips and other Massachusetts speculators looked elsewhere for largesse. Nice profits still could be made by those who timed the market right. The value of notes still rose and fell in response to rumors, news, and acts of Congress. Brokers still advertised in Boston newspapers their willingness to buy notes. Purchasing for the long term might no longer make good sense, but Phillips and other wealthy Bostonians still acquired large amounts for the sake of short-term marginal gains.[11]

Some speculators, in fact, managed to get themselves into situations whereby they benefited when the value of notes fell. Most of these men were land speculators who had contracted to buy huge tracts of frontier lands and pay for the land over several years in government notes. For them, a depressed securities market was a bonanza. It enabled them to fulfill their land contracts with cheap money. If they timed the market right and bought the securities they needed at rock-bottom prices, they could acquire broad acres for far less than the land was worth.

Again, however, timing was crucial. Nathaniel Gorham and Oliver Phelps, two enthusiastic land speculators, learned this the hard way. Under a scheme that they had worked out in the mid-1780s, they contracted to buy the lands owned by Massachusetts in western New York. The terms called for three annual payments in consolidated notes totaling £300,000. Had they been able to complete the deal in 1786, they would have benefited from a falling securities market. Notes that were selling for five shillings on the pound in 1786 fell to three shillings, sixpence the following year. But the deal was not consummated until early 1788, and that proved to be disastrous, as securities subsequently quadrupled in price.[12]

Most Massachusetts noteholders, however, were not in this position. They benefited when notes rose in value and in 1787 faced a bleak future if the value of notes continued to fall. After Shays's Rebellion and the events in Rhode Island, many of these noteholders feared the worst. They imagined the state debt being scaled down and paid off in paper money. Their only hope, so many argued, was the federal government. But the present federal government, under the Articles of Confederation, lacked the power to tax and the means to pay off noteholders. Under these circumstances, the speculators' only real hope lay in revising the Articles of Confederation and establishing a reformed federal government that would assume and pay the state debt. Many Massachusetts noteholders thus joined the agitation for a more powerful national government.

THE MOVEMENT FOR a stronger national government was well on its way when the Regulation began. Since 1781, when the Articles of Confederation went into effect, the Congress had been able to win the war and negotiate a favorable peace. It also had one huge asset in that it controlled western lands ceded by the British in the peace treaty. But the Congress had not been able to enforce the terms of the peace treaty or pay the nation's debts. It had no executive to do its bidding and no courts to enforce its laws and treaties. It could not tax. Many had thus concluded that the Articles needed to be changed, that Congress had to be granted additional powers.

But this was no easy matter. Changing the Articles of Confederation required the consent of the legislatures of all thirteen states, and suggested changes had repeatedly been turned down by the Rhode Island assembly or some other state legislature. Moreover, some of the nation's power brokers wanted more than a few minor alterations. Leading this group was Alexander Hamilton of New York. Since 1782, in the New York assembly as well as in correspondence, court cases, and essays, Hamilton had labored relentlessly to convince others that wholesale revision of the Articles was necessary. He wanted to reduce—or, better yet, eliminate—the power of states. He also wanted to diminish the influence of farmers and artisans and enhance the power of landlords and merchants. He sought a powerful national government run by men "whose principles are not of the *leveling kind.*"[13]

Well before Shays's Rebellion, this way of thinking had become the talk of Boston. With little prompting from the likes of Hamilton, early Massachusetts nationalists—especially Henry Knox, Stephen Higginson, James Bowdoin, and the officers of the Cincinnati—had concluded that the federal government under the Articles needed to undergo drastic alterations. The Confederation government, in their judgment, was the laughingstock of the Atlantic world. It was incapable of taking care of the men who had fought the Revolution. It was incapable of negotiating favorable commercial treaties with foreign nations. It lacked the money and power to pay off the United States debt at face value.

Many Massachusetts nationalists, however, had second thoughts on how to proceed. Should the Articles of Confederation be revised piecemeal? Step by step? Or wholesale? The latter, they feared, could produce a major power shift to the wrong sort of men. Clearly, the great slave masters of the South, the owners of vast estates and scores of slaves in tidewater Virginia and South Carolina, wanted a larger voice in the federal government. So did Robert Morris, the powerful Philadelphia financier, and his nationalist cronies. Could fundamental changes in the Articles be made without giving such men a decisive voice in the national government? The question haunted Massachusetts nationalists.

Massachusetts nationalists also had to cope with naysayers in their own social circle. In the spring of 1785, for example, Governor Bowdoin proposed a convention of all the states to reconsider the general powers of the Continental Congress. He had been encouraged to do so by William Phillips and some sixty Boston merchants, as well as a committee of Boston tradesmen and manufacturers.[14] The state legislature endorsed the proposal and ordered the state's three congressional delegates to present it to Congress. The three delegates, however, ignored the instructions. They deemed the proposal "dangerous." They feared that it might bring changes for the worse. "Too much precipitation may injure us," declared Rufus King, a young Harvard graduate and well-connected lawyer. Yet nothing came of their disobedience. Instead of censuring King and his cohorts for failing to follow instructions, the Massachusetts legislature in November withdrew the proposal.[15]

Hopes for change were again dashed in 1786. In January, Virginia issued an invitation for an interstate commercial convention at Annapolis in September. The purpose was to find some solution to the commercial problems that plagued the gentry. Eight states accepted. Massachusetts was one of the eight, but again there were second thoughts among the Massachusetts elite. King again raised objections. So did Theodore Sedgwick of Stockbridge. What were the Virginians up to? Were southern slaveholders really concerned about the problems facing Massachusetts merchants? Or were they just trying to get a whip hand over the northern states? In this atmosphere, the Massachusetts legislature dithered in selecting delegates for the convention, many likely delegates hemmed and hawed about going to Annapolis, and by the time Massachusetts got a delegation to Annapolis the convention was over.[16]

The convention, to the dismay of the nationalists, was also a bust. Only five states sent delegates in time for the meeting, and with so few states in attendance the convention decided it was futile to proceed. The conven-

Rufus King. Engraving by T. Kelly after a Gilbert Stuart portrait. Courtesy American Antiquarian Society. As a delegate to the Continental Congress, King initially thwarted Governor Bowdoin and others who wanted to drastically revise the Articles of Confederation. Although he shared their desire for a stronger central government, he thought that tinkering with the Articles might have dangerous repercussions. With the Regulation, he changed his tune and joined their campaign for a wholesale overhaul of the federal government.

tion, however, endorsed an address drafted by Alexander Hamilton that called on the thirteen states to send delegates to a new convention, to be held the following May in Philadelphia, to discuss not only commercial problems but all matters necessary "to render the constitution of the Federal Government adequate to the exigencies of the Union." Would this convention be any more successful than Bowdoin's aborted proposal? Than the Annapolis embarrassment?

Within months, Shays's Rebellion gave the nationalists the edge they needed. It provided the spark on which to advance the nationalist cause and play on the fears of others.[17] Stephen Higginson, once both a nationalist and a skeptic, was almost joyful for the opportunity. Now in his midforties, the Salem merchant had for years hoped for a fundamental revision of the Articles of Confederation. But the previous year, he had concluded that nothing good was likely to come from the revisionist crusade. Now, he had hope and was determined to give "the Tide a right direction." Without any military experience, he joined the cavalry unit that set off from Cambridge to capture Shattuck, Parker, and Page. He also helped raise money for Lincoln's army. And he especially urged friends to get involved in the campaign for a stronger national government. "The present moment," he counseled

Knox, "is very favorable . . . for increasing the dignity and energy of Government. What has been done, must be used as a stock upon which the best Fruits are to be ingrafted."[18]

Even more eager to take advantage of the situation was General John Brooks. A leading member of the Cincinnati, the general had impressive political connections and had risen quickly in Massachusetts society. Only twenty-three years old when the Revolutionary War began, he had been appointed commander of the Seventh Massachusetts before he reached his twenty-seventh birthday and had held that position for the remainder of the war. He and his men had been in the first line of battle at Yorktown. Luke Day, among others, had served under him. Now in his midthirties, Brooks was a strong backer of the Bowdoin administration and Lincoln's expedition. As long as the insurrection was eventually crushed, Brooks was happy to see it continue. He saw nothing but good coming from it. He even hoped that the rebels would become more audacious. "Should the insurgents begin to plunder," wrote Brooks, "I think it will have a good effect." It would provide good propaganda for the cause of a stronger national government.[19]

So quick were Higginson, Brooks, and Knox's friends in the Cincinnati to take advantage of Shays's Rebellion that they convinced Mercy Warren, the wife of another Massachusetts general, that they were anything but innocent bystanders. In the eyes of Warren, who was one of the Revolutionary generation's leading commentators, they were undoubtedly agents provocateurs. They had "artificially wrought up" the rebels to obtain "a more strong and splendid government."[20] Also suspicious was George Richards Minot, the clerk of the state legislature. From his perspective, the rout at the Springfield arsenal "was almost too decisive a victory for the friends of government to gain, as it was likely to shut the door against opposition."[21]

Indeed, in some instances, fearful men had already lost touch with reality. Especially noteworthy was the ardent land speculator Nathaniel Gorham, president of the Confederation Congress. By November 1786, he had become convinced that the entire country was falling apart, that all his hopes and land schemes were in danger.

He became desperate. In his fear of "democratic excesses" and "mob rule," he called for a new king, someone to replace the ousted George III, a genuine European blueblood to rule over a limited American monarchy. He tried to sound out Prince Henry of Prussia. Would the prince accept an American throne? The prince rejected the proposal as foolhardy.[22]

Nathaniel Gorham. Etching by Max Rosenthal after a Charles Willson Peale portrait. Courtesy American Antiquarian Society. The calm and contented gentleman of this portrait was anything but calm and contented during the Regulation. Instead, he thought his whole world was being turned upside down and that men of his stripe desperately needed a king to restore order. A major land speculator, Gorham was also the president of the Continental Congress.

Also susceptible to pressure was George Washington. As late as August 1, 1786, just days before the closing of the Northampton court, the stately general rejected an invitation to become involved in public affairs. He was emphatic about it.[23] He had no use for the Articles of Confederation, but he was optimistic about economic recovery and determined to stay out of national politics. He had served the country long and well. He was now retired and set on remaining so. But, like many of his economic class, Washington feared abolition of debt. And, more than others, he trembled at the thought of the Revolution, the centerpiece of his distinguished career, giving way to anarchy.

The news coming out of Massachusetts in late 1786 frightened Washington. And scores of nationalists, led by General Knox, played on the fears of their former commander in chief. From New Haven, former aide David Humphreys told Washington that the malcontents were animated by "a licentious spirit prevailing among the people: a levelling principle; a desire of change; & a wish to annihilate all debts public & private."[24]

More pointed was Knox. "It is indeed a fact," explained Washington's former artillery commander, "that high taxes are the ostensible cause of the commotions, but that they are the real cause is as far remote from truth as light from darkness. The people who are the insurgents have never paid any, or but very little taxes—But they see the weakness of government; They feel at once their own poverty, compared with the opulent, and their own force, and they are determined to make up the latter, in order to remedy the former." What, then, is their goal? "Their creed is, 'That the property of the United States has been protected from confiscation of Britain by the joint exertions of all, and therefore ought to be the common property of all, and he that attempts opposition to this creed is an enemy to equity and justice, and ought to be swept from off the face of the earth.'"[25]

Such talk squared with Washington's biases. Like Governor Bowdoin, the wealthy general was a major land speculator, the absentee owner of nearly sixty thousand acres in the backcountry. For forty years, he had invested in every land scheme that had come his way. In acquiring these properties, he had frequently dealt with men and women who had moved away from the seaboard and carved out farms in the wilderness. His estimation of their worth had not risen since the 1740s. They were "as ignorant a set of people as the Indians."[26]

Like Governor Bowdoin, moreover, Washington had a tendency to lump all backcountry folk together and see them as potential enemies. From his perspective, they had no respect for absentee owners like him who had spent years mapping, surveying, and purchasing backcountry tracts. Instead, they habitually trampled on his rights and tried to cheat him out of his land and timber. They ignored the clear markings on his properties. They also ignored his overseers who warned them off the land before they tried to settle. They just moved onto the land and caused him endless trouble.

Washington thus fully sympathized with the problems that Governor Bowdoin had in keeping squatters off his Maine lands. Backcountry folk, in Washington's judgment, were anything but virtuous yeomen. They were a wretched lot, not to be trusted, and certainly not to be the bone and sinew of a great nation.

Washington also listened to those who envisioned British agents lurking in the shadows. Rumors of British involvement in the Massachusetts uprising made their way along the Atlantic seaboard from Boston's counting houses to New York, Philadelphia, and points south, especially among the rich and well-born. Edward Carrington reported on talk around Congress: "It is said that a British influence is operating in this mischievous affair." Echoed James Madison: There was "good ground to believe" that the Shaysites were "secretly stimulated by British influence." Concluded the more cautious Washington: "There are surely men of consequences and abilities behind the curtain who move the puppets. . . . They may be instigated by British counsel."[27]

By November 18, less than two weeks after receiving Knox's distressing letter, Washington began to prepare himself to return to public life. He decided that the crisis demanded his personal attention, that the entire country was in danger of falling apart, that the uprising in Massachusetts was a dire threat to the nation that he had done so much to create. Had the British not predicted that the American government, left in the hands of Americans, would soon dissolve? "How melancholy," wrote Washington, "is the reflection, that in so short a space, we should have made such strides towards fulfilling the prediction of our transatlantic foe!"[28] Further reports from Knox and others in December and January only reinforced that view. Washington thus redoubled his efforts to obtain a stronger national government—one that would provide national aid in suppressing local disturbances.

Did Washington actually believe that Shays's Rebellion represented a genuine threat to the nation? Undoubtedly, he did. Even after the insurgents were routed at the Springfield arsenal, he still expected the political fabric of the nation to be "much tumbled and tossed, and possibly wrecked altogether."[29] He thought it "not probable that the mischiefs will terminate." Maybe when "this spirit first dawned, probably it might easily have been checked; but it is scarcely within reach of the human ken, at this moment, to say when, where, or how it will end. There are combustibles in every State which a spark might set fire to."[30]

Shortly after receiving Knox's alarming letter, Washington received a message from James Madison. The leading officials of Virginia, Madison indicated, had taken the liberty of putting the general's name at the head of the list of delegates to represent the state at the upcoming Philadelphia convention. Would Washington lead the delegation? The final decision was of course up to him, but his presence would give the entire enterprise "very solemn dress, and all the weight which could be derived from a single State."[31]

To accept, Washington had to go back on his word. He had publicly taken an "oath of retirement." He had been adamant about it. Did he dare risk his reputation on a convention that might produce only heartache and folly? Washington wrestled with the matter for months, but once the other states had chosen "respectable" delegates, all of his correspondents insisted that he must attend. And like them, he too saw Shays's Rebellion as inextricably tied to the inadequacies of the Articles of Confederation. The weaknesses of the present government, in his judgment, thus had to be corrected. As he explained to the Marquis de Lafayette: "I could not resist the call to a convention of the States which is to determine whether we are to have a Government of respectability under which life, liberty, and property will be secured to us, or are to submit to one which may be the result of chance or the moment, springing perhaps from anarchy and Confusion, and dictated perhaps by some aspiring demagogue."[32]

What if the news from Massachusetts had been different? What if it had not frightened Washington out of retirement? What if he had rejected James Madison's challenge to sacrifice his tranquillity and head the Virginia delegation at the upcoming Philadelphia convention? Rock Brynner, in a fine dissertation on Shays's Rebellion and the Constitution, makes the case that Washington's presence at the Constitutional Convention was pivotal.

True, Washington did not say much at the convention. But, as the towering figure of his age, larger than life, a virtual monument long before his likeness was carved into stone, "his participation in the formation of the new constitution provided the most effective propaganda the nationalists could engage to accomplish their objective." With Washington heading the Virginia delegation, with Washington accepting the post as presiding officer of the convention, the fifty-five men who met in Philadelphia that summer had to be taken seriously. So did fervent nationalists in Boston and elsewhere. He was their "trump card."[33]

SHAYS'S REBELLION NOT only energized Washington. It created waves of alarm across the thirteen states. News reports like those Washington read in the *Pennsylvania Packet* had a similar effect upon many of his fellow Virginians—including Governor Edmund Randolph, Congressmen Henry Lee and Edward Carrington, protégé James Madison, and planter Archibald Stuart—who in turn amplified their alarm in letters to Washington. It also brought many hesitant Massachusetts men like lawyers Rufus King and Theodore Sedgwick in full support of changing the nation's political fabric.

The nationalists, by the spring of 1787, were thus riding high and able to dictate much of what happened at the Philadelphia convention. The meeting was very much to their liking. Most of the delegates were merchants, lawyers, large landholders, and major slaveowners. The final document would say "We the People," but ordinary "people" had no say in its creation. Indeed, only a few delegates had ever rubbed shoulders with the lowly. Among the few was Alexander Hamilton, who had begun life as the illegitimate son of a woman of dubious virtue on the tiny Caribbean island of Nevis. He had come a long way since his childhood, gaining fame as

George Washington Presiding over Constitutional Convention. Library of Congress. Just the presence of Washington at the Constitutional Convention was crucial. Had he not come out of retirement and attended the convention, the meeting undoubtedly would have had less clout. The other delegates, to be sure, were men of great prestige, but none as yet had been deemed demigods. Washington, in contrast, was already a towering figure, larger than life, the nation's most influential citizen. With Washington as presiding officer, everyone in the country had to take notice.

Washington's brilliant aide-de-camp, wealth as the son-in-law of a great New York landlord, and power as an extremely capable New York lawyer and politician. More typical was James Madison, who was raised in comfort on a large Virginia plantation and had little experience with life's darker side. He had already written a private essay, "The Vices of the Political System of the United States," which set forth most of the changes he wanted.

Madison, Hamilton, and the other delegates were all patriots. They were also republicans, committed to the idea that a government must rest on the consent of the people. But for the most part they were not democrats. They thought the country, if anything, suffered from too much democracy. They had no faith in ordinary farmers and artisans running society or governing wisely or well. Extending the franchise to such men might be appro-

James Madison. Reprinted from John Fiske, *The Critical Period of American History, 1783–1789* (Boston, 1888), 245. Raised in comfort on a Virginia plantation, Madison was typical of most of the delegates to the Constitutional Convention in that he had experienced few of the hard knocks of life. He differed from the others, however, in the time and effort he was willing to devote to hammering out a new national covenant. Having already written an essay setting forth most of the changes that he wanted, he worked diligently to see that they were incorporated and thus came to be seen as "the father of the Constitution."

priate—or at least debatable. Allowing them to hold major public office, however, was generally dismissed as absurd. The general conviction was that ordinary people, especially in Rhode Island and Massachusetts, were out of control and that there were "combustibles," as Washington termed them, in every state. "The insurrections in Massachusetts," said Madison, "admonished all the States of the danger to which they were exposed."[34]

The specter of Shays's Rebellion not only hung over the convention, it also crystallized antidemocratic sentiment. "The evils we experience flow from the excess of democracy," declared Elbridge Gerry, in explaining the troubles in Massachusetts.[35] Gerry, a Marblehead merchant and protégé of Sam Adams, was not alone in this sentiment. Similarly, Oliver Ellsworth of Connecticut drew on Shays's Rebellion in arguing against letting the people elect delegates to the House of Representatives. The task should be in the hands of state legislatures, contended Ellsworth. The people lacked the necessary wisdom. As evidence of the people's folly, he noted that "Massachusetts cannot keep the peace one hundred miles from her capitol and is now forming an army for its support."[36]

The need in Massachusetts and elsewhere for a trustworthy army also arose time and again. Charles Coatesworth Pinckney of South Carolina raised the specter of Shays's Rebellion in disparaging the effectiveness of the militia. It clearly had performed poorly in Massachusetts. He had "scanty faith" in the militia in any state. "There must (also) be a real military force. . . . The United States has been making an experiment without it, and we see the consequence in their rapid approaches to anarchy." He thus called for a standing army. He also wanted the national government to have the power to use its army to suppress insurrections in any state without "the application of its legislature."[37] John Langdon of New Hampshire agreed with Pinckney: "The apprehension of the national force, will have a salutary effect in preventing insurrection."[38]

Others clearly thought the South Carolinian's proposals went too far. The states would not tolerate such high-handedness. The militia had too much support. Having a standing army in time of peace, moreover, violated one of the cardinal precepts of the Revolution. George Mason of Virginia spoke against it. He proposed, instead, giving the central government the power necessary to regulate the state militia. He wanted more uniformity. He worried about the lack of discipline.[39] His fellow Virginian James Madison also wanted the central government to regulate the militia. Pointing out that a strong militia was needed to suppress rebellions in the states, Madison insisted that the states would always fall short of the mark. They just would not do the job. They had neglected their militia in the past, and the neglect would only get worse. "The Discipline of the Militia" was thus a "*National* concern, and ought to be provided for in the *National* Constitution."[40]

Every detail was debated again and again. Yet, while never agreeing on the particulars, all the delegates agreed something had to be done. Hence powers were included in the final document to shackle the likes of Daniel Shays and to cope with unreliable state militias. The Constitution gave the federal government the power to "suppress Insurrections," protect the states from "domestic Violence," and suspend the right of habeas corpus in "cases of Rebellion or Invasion." It also provided for a national army under the command of the president and gave Congress the authority to nationalize the state militias. In 1794 George Washington, as president and commander in chief, would use these powers fully. To suppress the Whiskey Rebellion in western Pennsylvania, he mobilized thirteen thousand men—an army of grenadiers, dragoons, foot soldiers, and artillery almost as large as any he took to the field during the Revolutionary War.

THE CONSTITUTION ALSO suited the pocketbook needs of Boston and other seaboard merchants. It expanded their potential market to the nation

Washington as commander in chief during the Whiskey Rebellion, 1794. Woodcut by Frederick Kemmelmeyer. Courtesy American Antiquarian Society. In a sense, this woodcut was out of focus. The centerpiece was clearly Washington and his horse. More telling, however, were the soldiers in the background. Just seven years earlier, under the Articles of Confederation, not even Washington would have been able to raise thirteen thousand men to put down a domestic rebellion. Now, under the Constitution, he did.

as a whole and was built on the principle that their need for long-distance trade and uniform law was more important than the specific customs of small communities. To Congress went the power to regulate interstate and foreign commerce, to coin and regulate money, register patents and copyrights, establish weights and measures, fashion bankruptcy laws, and create a postal service. States had to give "Full Faith and Credit" to other states' legal decisions. Never again could states "emit Bills of Credit, make anything but Gold or Silver Coin a Tender in Payment of Debts," or pass any law "impairing the Obligation of Contracts."

To get such measures, the constitutional delegates from Massachusetts and other northern states had to do what Sedgwick and others had once feared. They had to grant southern slave masters, particularly the Virginians, a much larger voice in national politics. Madison and other southern leaders insisted that slaves as well as free persons be counted in determining the size of the state delegations to the House of Representatives and the electoral college. That would greatly enhance southern power, as slaves made up 40 percent of all Virginians and 55 percent of all South Carolinians. And, as slaves would have no say in choosing the representatives that their numbers earned, it would also mean that the southern white man's vote would be worth more than the northern white man's vote.

Gouverneur Morris, speaking for Pennsylvania, attacked "slave representation" from every possible angle. The very idea was an abomination, said Morris, offensive in every possible way. Of the Massachusetts delegates, only Elbridge Gerry put up much of a fight. "Blacks are property," argued Gerry, "and are used to the southward as horses and cattle to the northward." Why should they be counted, any more than northern "horses or oxen"?[41]

In the end, northern delegates ignored Morris's arguments and accepted the so-called "three-fifths compromise," whereby five slaves counted as three free persons for both political representation and direct taxes. During debate, Morris predicted that nothing would come of the direct tax provision, that it was just a fig leaf to cover the fact that "extra" power in the House of Representatives and the electoral college had been given to southern aristocrats who hold their "fellow creatures . . . to the most cruel bondages." Time would prove that Morris was basically right. Direct taxes were levied only four times in the next seventy-two years, while the larger voice that southern slave masters obtained in the House and the electoral college had enormous impact, affecting not only scores of congressional decisions but virtually every aspect of the nation's political fabric.

To get the desired commercial clauses, Massachusetts and other northern delegates also had to agree to what came to be known as the "dirty compromise." Others, especially some of the southern delegates, opposed allowing a simple majority of the Congress to regulate trade. They wanted to make certain that only the least controversial trade regulations got through Congress. In a debate over this issue, Charles Pinckney of South Carolina moved that a two-thirds majority be required for all commercial regulations. That would have made it difficult, if not impossible, to get the trade regulations that New England merchants desperately wanted.

Pinckney and his Deep South colleagues, however, were willing to deal. Unlike the tidewater Virginians, they did not have an oversupply of slaves. They wanted more slaves at the cheapest possible prices. They thus wanted the importation of slaves from Africa to remain legal and vehemently opposed Virginia's proposal to outlaw the African slave trade. They also wanted a clause in the Constitution ensuring that fugitive slaves would be returned to their masters.

In the end, a deal between the New England delegates and the South Carolinians was obviously struck. The "dirty" particulars are hard to track down, and thus exactly what happened is still a matter of debate. Nonetheless, the outcome is clear. On the one hand, South Carolina joined the northern states to defeat the motion requiring a two-thirds vote when it came to the regulation of commerce. Only a simple majority was required. In exchange, New Englanders supported one exception to this clause. For the next twenty years, Congress was forbidden from abolishing the African slave trade or imposing a tax of over $10 on an imported slave. In addition, the fugitive slave clause was allowed to pass without debate or a recorded vote.[42]

*C*LIMAX

EVEN BEFORE THE CONSTITUTION WAS SIGNED, THE campaign for ratification began. The supporters of the Constitution, who now called themselves Federalists, launched a fierce battle, first in Congress, then in the states. It was a dirty fight.

Throughout, Federalists kept their critics on the defensive, continuously identifying themselves with George Washington and their opponents with Daniel Shays. The *Pennsylvania Gazette* began hammering on these twin themes, day after day, even before it published the Constitution. "Every state has its SHAYS," wrote one correspondent, "who, either with their pens—or tongues—or offices—are endeavoring to effect what *Shays* attempted in vain with his sword." Indeed, behind every objection to the Constitution lay "the spirit of Shays." Moreover, should "the federal government be rejected (AWFUL WORDS)," none other than Daniel Shays would seize control of Massachusetts.[1] With great fanfare, the *Gazette* then printed the first copies of the Constitution. A few days later, it published a declaration from another correspondent proclaiming that all Federalists "should be distinguished hereafter by the name of WASHINGTONIANS, and the ANTIFEDERALISTS, by the name SHAYITES, in every part of the United States."[2]

To a large extent, that came to pass. From Maine to Georgia, supporters of the Constitution damned their opponents as "Shaysites."

THE REALITY, OF course, was quite different. Not all those who opposed the work of the Philadelphia convention were sympathetic to the Regulation. Like the Constitution's sponsors, its critics were a diverse lot. Some out of conviction preferred the Articles of Confederation. More influential, according to most accounts, were state officeholders and their dependents who enjoyed great status under the old system and feared being diminished under its replacement to mere bit players. Still others, perhaps the largest group, supported a handful of revisions to the Articles of Confederation, but dreaded living under a consolidated government like the one that had been created in Philadelphia. To them, strong government and national consolidation were horrid ideas. Even worse was what these ideas would eventually foster: "a *permanent* ARISTOCRACY."[3]

The first battleground was in Congress. The Federalists moved fast and let nothing get in their way. A leading Virginian, Richard Henry Lee, tried to attach amendments to the Constitution before it was shipped to the states for ratification. Most of his amendments would later be proposed at the Massachusetts ratifying convention, and later still would become the basis for the Bill of Rights. But in Congress, they got nowhere. They were even expunged from the official record, and over Lee's objections the unamended Constitution went to the states for approval. To outsiders, moreover, it looked as if the unamended Constitution had Lee's approval. Each state delegation had but one vote and collectively the Virginia delegation had supported the document. The "appearance of unanimity," declared Washington, was of "great importance," as not everyone had the opportunity "to peep behind the curtain" and "the multitude often judge by externals."[4]

Lee did not accept defeat quietly. Not only did the Virginia aristocrat become a leading opponent of the Constitution, he was widely credited— and perhaps mistakenly credited—for a pamphlet that soon appeared under the pseudonym "Federal Farmer." Espousing a sharply different rendition of recent events, the pamphleteer claimed that the real evil in American society lay not with Daniel Shays and his followers. In fact, there were "two very unprincipled parties in the United States. . . . One party is composed of little insurgents, men in debt, who want no law, and who want a share of the property of others; these are called levellers, Shaysites, &c. The other party is composed of a few, but more dangerous men, with their servile dependents; these avariciously grasp at all power and property."[5]

To Lee's chagrin, the Federalists quickly organized broad support in the six states most likely to ratify the Constitution: Delaware, Maryland, New

Jersey, Connecticut, South Carolina, and Georgia. To build further momentum, in September 1787, they sought to get the Pennsylvania legislature to call an election before the state's Antifederalists had time to organize. To prevent a quorum, sixteen Antifederalist legislators fled the assembly. The sergeant at arms, with the help of a mob, forcefully rounded up two of the runaways. A quorum was declared, and the ratification convention was called for early November.

At the convention, the Federalist floor leader James Wilson made much of the "combustibles" that so worried Washington the previous winter. It was "not generally known," contended the well-known legislator, "on what a perilous tenure we held our freedom and independence at that period. The flames of internal insurrection were ready to burst out in every quarter . . . and from one end to the other of the continent, we walked on ashes, concealing fire beneath our feet."[6] Wilson and his Federalist colleagues prevailed, forty-six to twenty-three.

A few weeks later, attention focused on Massachusetts. Here, everyone agreed, was the decisive contest. The state was the second most populous in the Union. It was thus crucial, declared Henry Knox, that the state set a "bright example" for the other critical states, Virginia and New York, to follow.[7] Madison was pessimistic. The news from Massachusetts, he told Washington, was "very ominous." Not only did the supporters of the Constitution have to cope with "the antifederal party." They also had to contend with the "insurgents" and "the province of Mayne." He feared that "the voice of that State would be in the negative." If that happened, all their hard work was doomed. Virginia would follow suit. The Constitution never would be ratified.[8]

THE SOURCES OF Madison's pessimism were many. One was Elbridge Gerry, a fellow delegate to the Constitutional Convention. Like Madison, Gerry was secure in his wealth. The son of a rich Marblehead merchant, he had inherited the family business, added to it, and amassed thousands of acres in western lands. He was also proof that not all note speculators thought alike. He zealously defended the rights of speculators at the Constitutional Convention, declared national noteholders the heroes of the Revolution, and called for a specific constitutional provision to repay them. Yet, despite holding thousands in securities, Gerry had broken with Madison and refused to sign the Constitution.

Throughout the convention, Gerry had favored what he called a federal government. In it, the states—mainly through their legislatures—would

Elbridge Gerry. Reprinted from James T. Austin, *The Life of Elbridge Gerry* (Boston, 1828), frontispiece. As a rule, note speculators and wealthy merchants sang the praises of the men who wrote the Constitution. Gerry was the exception that proved the rule. Not only did he oppose their handiwork, he wrote the most widely reprinted pamphlet that called for its rejection by the state ratifying conventions.

play a pivotal role. He objected to national control over the state militia, national officials entering the territories without territorial consent, and direct popular election of the House of Representatives. He urged that state legislatures be granted the authority to choose members of the House, instruct them on how to vote, and replace them at any time. He also wanted the states, through their governors, to choose the nation's top executives. In addition to a federal structure, Gerry championed a bill of rights to curtail the powers of the new national government.

In November 1787, Gerry had published his reasons for not signing the Constitution. The message was succinct and hard-hitting. The Constitution had too many nationalist features, too many consolidationist features, not enough protections for the states and the people. The people lacked adequate means to control their representatives, and their right of election was insecure. The Congress had too many ambiguous and dangerous powers. The powers of the president were wrongly blended with those of the Congress, and the president had undue influence over the legislative process. The new judicial system was certain to be "oppressive." Allowing the president with "the advice of two thirds of a *quorum* of the Senate" to make important national treaties was absurd. It placed too much power in the hands of a few. On top of all that, the whole system was "without the security of a bill of rights."[9]

Gerry's article had clout. First appearing in the *Massachusetts Centinel*, it was reprinted some forty times.[10] But in the eyes of Rufus King, a fellow delegate to the Constitutional Convention, Gerry was not the problem. Not only did Gerry share the Federalist belief that the nation's political problems stemmed from "the excess of democracy," he was a long-term member of the governing elite, and the main opposition in Massachusetts hardly came from men of his stripe. In fact, Gerry was an anomaly, one of the few members of the Massachusetts gentry who opposed the Constitution.[11]

Also anomalous, in King's judgment, was Gerry's mentor Sam Adams. Most of the Boston hard-liners who had called for the blood of Daniel Shays and his followers now enthusiastically supported the Constitution. Adams was the notable exception. The task of ratifying it caused him to "stumble at the threshold." The old Revolutionary did not put up much of a fight, however. During the ratification debate his son died, and that took much of the fight out of him. Also his political base, largely Boston tradesmen, wanted the Constitution. Over four hundred of them, at the probable instigation of Federalist leaders, met at the Green Dragon Inn on Union Street and unanimously endorsed ratification. Paul Revere then delivered the Green Dragon resolution to Adams. The next day, Adams threw his support behind the Constitution. All he asked was that its proponents agree to submit a list of suggested amendments along with the ratification.[12]

What about the specific objections that Gerry and others raised about the Constitution? These objections, said King, could be overcome. But the "apprehension that the liberties of the people are in danger, and a distrust of men of property or education have a more powerful effect upon the minds of our opponents than any specific objections against the Constitution." Overcoming "that baneful passion," King explained to Madison, was next to impossible. There was nothing specific to rebut. "Their Objections are not directed against any part of the constitution, but their Opposition seems to arise from an Opinion, that is immoveable, that some injury is plotted against them, that the System is the production of the Rich, and ambitious; that *they* discern its operation, and that the consequence will be, the establishment of two Orders in the Society, one comprehending the Opulent and Great, the other the poor and illiterate. The extraordinary Union in favor of the Constitution in this State of the Wealthy and sensible part of it is in confirmation of these opinions and every exertion hitherto made to eradicate it, has been in vain."[13]

THE PROBLEM THAT King and Madison faced in Massachusetts stemmed largely from the rout of Daniel Shays and his followers. Ordinary citizens had no idea what had been said or done at the Constitutional Convention, or any sure way to judge the merits of Gerry's argument. But distrust of the governing elite was widespread. An army of mercenaries hired by Boston's wealthiest citizens had paraded through the countryside. Thousands of men had been forced to take an oath of allegiance to the state and its rulers. Seething with resentment, many now questioned the motives of the New England delegates to the Philadelphia convention. Indeed, many assumed that the proposed Constitution was just another aristocratic weapon to crush the "little people."

This widespread fear of the governing elite, coupled with the fear of Shays and his forces, had also energized Massachusetts politics. Bowdoin and his supporters had been thrown out of office, and they were now the main proponents of the new Constitution. In 1786, when Bowdoin was in charge, many of the towns had initially been lax about sending representatives to Boston. The house numbered only 190 men. The following spring, the number climbed to 266. In January 1788, when the ratifying convention convened, the number climbed again, by nearly another hundred, to 364. Never before had so many backcountry towns been represented. Nearly two-thirds of these newly represented towns opposed the Constitution. Thanks to the new interest in state politics, reckoned the Maine Antifederalist Samuel Nasson, his side had a forty-eight-vote majority when the delegates began deliberation.[14]

SOME OF NASSON's allies on that cold January day represented the insurgency. How many is open to debate. Henry Knox, who as always tended to exaggerate, blamed "the late insurgents and all those who abetted their designs" for "four-fifths of the opposition." He insisted that "the principle of insurgency expanded" lay behind all hostility to the Constitution. In agreement was Knox's friend, Henry Jackson: "The whole opposition, in this commonwealth, is that cursed spirit of insurgency that prevailed last winter." More circumspect was General Lincoln: "We find ourselves exceedingly embarrassed by the temper which raged the last winter in some of the counties. Many of the insurgents are in the Convention; even some of Shays's officers. A great proportion of these men are high in the opposition."[15]

Lincoln's observation was at least partly true. Despite measures to strip the rebels of their right to hold office, to represent their towns, or even to vote, the old backcountry tradition of not paying heed to the wishes of Boston had prevailed. At least twenty-nine communities chose well-known insurgents to represent them at the ratifying convention. Noteworthy was the town of Rehoboth, the only Shaysite community of any significance in Bristol County. The previous spring, the town had helped elect Phanuel Bishop, a wealthy innkeeper and staunch supporter of the rebellion, to the state senate. The senate had refused to seat him. Anything but repentant, the town sent him to the ratifying convention, again to do battle against the seaboard elite.[16]

Equally recalcitrant was the tiny town of Charlton. Their choice, the Reverend Caleb Curtis, had once been the perfect example of the kind of minister that Sam Adams and other revolutionary leaders needed. Not only had Curtis exhorted his flock to take up arms against King George III, he also had resigned his ministry to serve in the Massachusetts legislature. Ten years later, in December 1786, he was still exhorting his flock, this time against Adams and the new state government. "Do not mind your Governor," he had counseled local militiamen, "nor your General Warner, nor your Colonel Towne, nor your Ammidowns, but in the name of God turn out and stop the sitting of the court, and I will support you with my life and Fortune." For such remarks, he had been arrested, jailed, indicted for seditious practices by the Worcester County Grand Jury, tried before Justice of the Peace Joseph Wheeler, and fined £200. His fellow townsmen, however, admired his grit and chose him to represent their sentiments at the ratifying convention.[17]

Similarly, the town of Groton in Middlesex County sent Benjamin Morse, a fifty-seven-year-old wheelwright and former compatriot of Job Shattuck, to the convention.[18] From West Springfield was dispatched Benjamin Ely, who was still the town's most popular leader, despite having earned a prominent spot on the attorney general's "Black List."[19] Also blacklisted by the state, and in some cases indicted and jailed, were:

Asa Fisk, the delegate from South Brimfield
Timothy Blair, the delegate from Blandford
Isaac Pepper, the delegate from Ware
Silas Fowler, the delegate from Southwick
Elihu Colton, the delegate from Longmeadow
Benjamin Josselyn, the delegate from New Braintree
Samuel Willard, the delegate from Uxbridge
Josiah Whitney, the delegate from Harvard[20]

In addition to these men were several delegates who had managed to escape the court system, yet had been singled out by the authorities for their rebellious activities. Notable was Agrippa Wells, the representative of Bernardston. A war hero and militia captain, he had violated the Militia Act. Instead of following orders and leading his men against the rebels, he had formed a company of rebels and led them against the state.[21] Also noteworthy were two justices of the peace, John Hurlburt of Alford and Ephraim Fitch of Egremont. The former had been so open in his support of the rebellion that the state had stripped him of his commission.[22] The latter puzzled the authorities. His activities had been equally notorious and had come to the attention of the chief justice of the state supreme court and the justices of Berkshire court. They agreed that he "should have been indicted for treason," but somehow he had managed to escape prosecution.[23]

Not all Shaysite communities were so blatant in their choice of delegates. Had the town of Colrain wanted to make a statement, it easily could have done so. On hand were several highly respected town leaders who had been blacklisted by the attorney general, indicted by a grand jury, or even jailed. Instead, the townsfolk chose Samuel Eddy to be their delegate. Eddy had signed the oath of allegiance. So had his son and his cousin. But none of the Eddys had drawn special attention to themselves.[24]

Amherst was even more discreet. In choosing Daniel Cooley, the town selected a man who at first glance had no ties at all with the rebellion. A Yale graduate and member of the First Church, Cooley appeared to be neutral. He never took the oath, and he never came to the attention of the state. But he had six relatives in the valley who had sided with the rebellion. And the town gave him no leeway. The town told him how to vote.[25]

The practice Amherst followed in instructing Cooley was common throughout the backcountry. It was an old tradition, one that had flourished in medieval England. It had faded away in England when members of the House of Commons came to be seen as representing the interests of the entire country, all of Britain, and later the entire British Empire. It had yet to fade away in rural Massachusetts. The practice of "voting instructions" to their representatives had begun in the first years of settlement. It still had wide support. The towns still felt themselves to be largely autonomous with few interests in common with those of the central government in Boston. They also saw themselves as the benefactors rather than the beneficiaries of the central government. Having this mind-set, they made sure that their representatives spoke for them.

As the representative of Amherst, Daniel Cooley claimed that he was not just following instructions. He was also voting his "conscience." His instructions were to oppose the Constitution. He did so.[26] So too did the delegates from the other Shaysite towns. Of the fifty-two towns in which the insurgency had the most support, not a single one sent a delegate to the ratifying convention who supported the Constitution.[27] In another tally, the historian David Szatmary calculates that of the ninety-seven towns with "Shaysite sympathies," only seven backed the Constitution.[28]

RUFUS KING AND the other sponsors of the Constitution thus faced an uphill battle at the Massachusetts ratifying convention. Not only did they have to confront old enemies, they lacked popular support. They spoke for a document that began with "We the People," but it was not the "people" who had demanded a new national government. Instead, the Constitution was the handiwork of a small segment of governing elite, and everyone knew it. To prevail, noted George Richards Minot, the clerk of the state legislature, King and his allies had "to *pack* a Convention whose sense would be different from that of the people."[29]

To do so, King and the other champions of the Constitution capitalized on their assets. They had the necessary talent, including three men who had sat at the Philadelphia convention and helped formulate the Constitution: Nathaniel Gorham, Caleb Strong, and King. Also on their side were former Governor Bowdoin, Generals William Heath and Benjamin Lincoln, the Stockbridge lawyer Theodore Sedgwick, and Theophilus Parsons, the author of the Essex Result. They also had the support of fourteen of the seventeen clergymen who attended the convention. This, Lincoln explained to Washington, was "very fortunate for us" for the clergy "have in this State a very great influence over the people, and they will contribute much to the general peace and happiness."[30] Finally, they could take comfort in the fact that forty-six towns were not represented. Had every town in Massachusetts sent delegates, the struggle would have been even more uphill.

To buy time and to keep the opposition from trashing the entire document, King and his allies maneuvered to have the Constitution debated line by line. Each step of the way, they had to ward off hostile comments from rural delegates with old grievances to settle, as well community leaders who shared Elbridge Gerry's ingrained fear of centralized power. The direct tax clause of the Constitution, for example, generated much debate. Many contended that direct taxes were likely, just as they had been in Massachusetts, and that the Constitution gave slaveowners a huge tax break. Why, critics asked, had the Massachusetts delegates to the Constitutional Convention agreed to count only three out of five slaves for direct taxes? Under this provision, a hardworking Yankee farmer would pay as much in taxes for "three infant children" as a wealthy Virginia planter would pay for "five sturdy, full grown negroes." To counter this argument, King and other supporters of the Constitution claimed that direct taxes would be levied only in times of crisis. Time would prove that they were right.

Overall, the Constitution's advocates had little trouble handling such issues. Their real problem was overcoming the widespread fear of the governing elite. Every critic, it seemed, envisioned the "little people" being stomped on by "the well-born," "the great men," and "the aristocracy." Phanuel Bishop, the Rehoboth rebel, told the delegates that with the further concentration of power into the hands of the seaboard elite, "the liberties of the yeomanry are at an end." More pointed still was Amos Singletary, a sixty-seven-year-old, home-taught delegate from the small town of Sutton in Worcester County. Said Singletary: "These lawyers, and men of learning, and moneyed men, that talk so finely, and gloss over matters so smoothly, to make us, poor illiterate people, swallow down the pill, expect to get into Congress themselves; they expect to be the managers of this Constitution, and get all the power and all the money into their own hands, and then they will swallow up all us little folks, like the great leviathan, Mr. President; yes, just as the whale swallowed up Jonah. This is what I am afraid of."[31]

To overcome this fear, the champions of the Constitution had to make deals. Much chicanery was involved. In the end, the house clerk, George Richards Minot, an ardent Federalist and a seasoned observer of deal-making, was appalled. "Never was there a political system introduced by less worthy means," wrote Minot.[32] But what were these unworthy means? What did Minot's Federalist colleagues do that so troubled him? That is still uncertain.

On the one hand, Minot's colleagues clearly agreed to support amendments to the Constitution. From the beginning, their opponents had lambasted them for trying to defend a document with no bill of rights, arguing that the new national government was certain to be as repressive as the Massachusetts government, and yet would be bound by no restrictions whatsoever. The opposition had also scored points against the Constitution in demanding a larger House of Representatives, jury trials in civil cases, restrictions on national courts, more power for the states, and no direct taxes except when impost and excise duties failed to meet expenses.

By January, they had convinced one of the Federalist floor leaders, Nathaniel Gorham, that it would be impossible "to gain the question with-

Old State House, Boston. Reprinted from Justin Winsor, *The Memorial History of Boston* (Boston, 1881), 4:12. Here was where 364 delegates met in January 1788 to consider the fate of the Constitution. Initially, the document seemed to have little chance of being ratified. James Madison, among others, thought it was doomed. Then, as debate dragged out, some delegates went home, and the supporters of the Constitution went to work putting together a majority. After much wheeling and dealing, as well as promising to support a bill of rights, they prevailed, 187 to 168.

out some amendments."[33] By late January, others agreed with Gorham, and the archconservative Theophilus Parsons was given the task of fashioning amendments that would take some of the sting out the opposition's objections and win over ten to fifteen votes.[34]

The Federalists also got John Hancock to throw his considerable political weight behind the Constitution. Hancock had been lukewarm about the Constitution—if not downright hostile—and so had many of his followers. A delegate to the convention, he had been elected chair, but had never bothered to attend. Then, on January 31, he took the chair and as presiding officer proposed a series of amendments drafted by his longtime political enemy Theophilus Parsons. Sam Adams, another longtime enemy, seconded them. A week later, with nine "recommended" amendments, the Constitution passed, 187 to 168.[35]

Hancock's role was undoubtedly crucial. Without him, noted the Boston merchant Caleb Gibbs, "it was more than probable that *important* question would have been lost."[36] But why did Hancock reverse himself and suddenly throw his weight behind the Constitution? Rufus King claimed that the Federalists got his help by promising him "the universal support of Bowdoin's friends" in state politics. But that was not much of an enticement. Hancock already dominated state politics. He did not need the help of Bowdoin's friends. King also claimed that the Federalists promised to make Hancock president if Washington turned down the office.[37] That may have been more enticing, but only if Hancock thought that Washington would turn down the presidency and that Massachusetts Federalists had the necessary clout to deliver on their promise.

There was a third explanation, one that historians have generally ignored, but one that circulated widely at the time. That was the charge, made in a Boston newspaper and on the convention floor, that the Constitution's supporters got the votes they needed by bribing a handful of their opponents with "Large sums of money . . . brought from a neighboring state." The charge was never proven or disproven. Years later, Henry Dawson, the editor of *Historical Magazine*, insisted that he had been told by the son of a prominent New York Federalist that "enough members of the Massachusetts Convention were bought with money *from New York* to secure ratification of the new system by Massachusetts." Dawson did not dispute the assertion; he had heard as much before and assumed that it was true.[38]

Whatever happened, the Massachusetts ratifying convention endorsed the Constitution, along with nine amendments, by nineteen votes. Of the 364 delegates who had been sent to Boston, 355 were present when the final vote was taken. The delegates from the four coastal counties supported the Constitution overwhelmingly, 102 to 19. Those from the three Maine counties supported it narrowly, 25 to 21. Those from the five western counties opposed it, 60 to 128. Daniel Cooley of Amherst did what he was told. So did Benjamin Ely of West Springfield, Samuel Eddy of Colrain, and all the delegates from the other hard-core Shaysite communities. All voted no.[39]

RATIFICATION OF THE Constitution was a blessing for most speculators. Months before, when news that the Philadelphia convention had finished writing the Constitution reached Boston, securities shot up 25 percent in value. With ratification, they shot up again, another 30 percent.[40]

Again, not every speculator benefited. Ironically, that was especially true

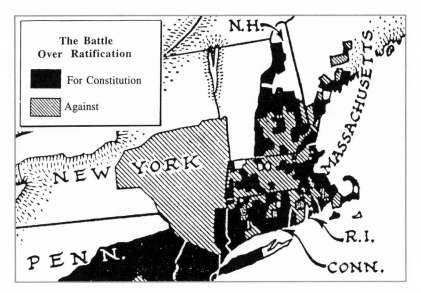

The battle over ratification of the Constitution.

of Nathaniel Gorham, the seasoned legislator who had called for a new king
during the Regulation. Gorham had championed the Constitution at the
Philadelphia convention and had fought hard for it at the Massachusetts
ratifying convention. Yet, once the value of securities began to soar, he was
in trouble. So too was his partner, Oliver Phelps. Their scheme to buy the
lands owned by Massachusetts in western New York became far more costly than anticipated. No longer could they get three hundred thousand
pounds in consolidated notes for just a few thousand pounds. Notes that
had been selling for three shillings, sixpence on the pound were no longer
to be found. Could they get the state legislature to change the terms of the
contract? They had the necessary political connections. They succeeded.
Yet, they were still in trouble. As one state after another ratified the Constitution, the notes kept rising in value.[41]

Again, however, most Massachusetts noteholders were not in this position. They benefited when notes rose in value, and with ratification their
financial futures looked promising. Indeed, for most of them, 1788 was a
good year. They no longer worried so much about the impact of Shays's
Rebellion and the events in Rhode Island. Nor did they fret as much about
the state debt being scaled down and paid off in paper money. For years,
their only real hope had lain in revising the Articles of Confederation and

Washington en route to his Inauguration. Library of Congress. After receiving unanimous electoral support for president, Washington slowly made his way to New York, the nation's temporary capital. Along the way, he was greeted by throngs of men, women, and children. Hailed especially as the protector of American women—first the women of 1776, now the women of 1789—Washington loved every minute of it.

establishing a reformed federal government that would assume and pay the state debt. Now, they had the new government that they wanted.

The new government fulfilled their hopes. In April 1789, after receiving unanimous electoral support for president, George Washington journeyed to New York, the temporary federal capital. Almost every town along the way organized an official welcome and celebration, and New York City went wild, with arches over the streets, booming guns in the harbor, and girls strewing flowers in his path as he made his way to his living quarters. The president's love of pomp, his many servants, his coach blazoned with his coat of arms, his aristocratic habits troubled men and women who lived in the backcountry. But to his Federalist followers, his lifestyle conveyed a sense of stateliness and well-being.

Although the Constitution made no mention of a cabinet, no one seriously expected that Washington would be without advisors. Congress authorized the creation of four departments—War, Treasury, State, and Attorney General. Washington chose his old comrade Knox to head the War Department. For Treasury, he chose his former aide-de-camp Alexander Hamilton. The choice of Knox played to the biases of the New England gentry. The choice of Hamilton proved to be far more significant.

In 1789 the House of Representatives called on the thirty-four-year-old treasury secretary to devise a means of retiring the Revolutionary War debts and establishing public credit. Hamilton eagerly accepted the assignment. Scarred by the stigmas of illegitimacy and childhood poverty, he was a driven man, always restless, always craving more respectability. He was determined to be a major figure in the new government. He also had few doubts about what needed to be done. He firmly believed that selfishness governed all human behavior. Yet, at the same time, he also believed that the poor were "turbulent and changing," seldom apt to "judge or determine right," while the rich and well-born were more steadfast, more persistent in pursuing their goals, and thus more dangerous to any government that got in their way. To succeed, then, the new government had to have the support of the rich and well-born.[42]

Hamilton thus set out to link the interests of the rich and well-born with those of the new government. The old government had suffered from huge financial problems. It had lacked the revenue to be effective. It had lacked good credit. The national debt was hopelessly complex, consisting of a bewildering assortment of bills of credit, loan office certificates, and notes issued by hospital departments, commissaries, quartermasters, and the like, as well as arrears of interest on all of these obligations. Somehow the new government had to overcome these liabilities and be put on a firm financial footing. Without revenue, it too would be ineffective. Without a solid reputation for repaying the nation's debts, it too would lack the ability to borrow money.

In January 1790, Hamilton presented his plan to Congress. He recommended funding the $56 million federal debt at par, converting the hodgepodge of outstanding federal notes into interest-bearing bonds with a definite time to run before maturity, and enabling creditors to exchange depreciating federal notes at face value for the new bonds. He also recommended that the federal government assume responsibility for the $21.5 million in war debts still owed by the individual states, treat these notes the same as federal securities, but postpone interest payments until January 1792.

Hamilton's plan touched off a furious debate in Congress. Many congressmen clearly did not understand the details of funding and assumption. Many complained bitterly that he had made the twin proposals hopelessly complex just to confuse Congress. Leading them was the very able James Madison, whom Hamilton had expected to be on his side. At times Madison sounded just like the dissidents in Massachusetts. Had the original owners of federal notes not sold them for a song to speculators? Why should the latter be paid full price? Would it not be a violation of public faith to do so? He then proposed a compromise: "Let them have the highest price which has prevailed in the market; and let the residue belong to the original sufferers."[43]

The debate then quickly became even more heated. Hamilton and his congressional allies argued that Madison's proposal would not only be a patent violation of national honor but it would plunge the Treasury Department into an administrative quagmire. How was the Treasury, with only a handful of employees, to make the fine discriminations urged by Madison? Was Congress prepared to waste money on needless administration? Madison's supporters, in turn, claimed that Hamilton's plan was designed to aid rapacious speculators at the expense of poor soldiers and southern backwoodsmen. The Massachusetts congressional delegation had heard the debate before, many times.

Had Hamilton recommended only the payment of the federal debt at par, this question of fairness might have had little impact. Half of the legislators were noteholders, and only a handful were truly concerned with the lot of poor soldiers and southern backwoodsmen. But in coupling funding of the national debt with assumption of the state debts, Hamilton considerably raised the stakes. His goal was obvious. He intended to strengthen the national government at the expense of the states by diminishing the ties of state creditors to the states and binding them to the central government. If their future wealth and well-being was linked to the success of the federal government, rather than to the states, their hearts and minds would follow. "Men," Hamilton firmly believed, "will naturally go to those who pay them best."[44]

The members of Congress, for the most part, fully understood Hamilton's purpose. How they reacted, however, depended only partly on whether they shared his goal. Also central was the size of the debt of their respective states and how much of it had been paid off. Heavy was the debt burden in South Carolina, light in neighboring North Carolina and Georgia. Thus, to no one's surprise, the delegates from South Carolina harped on the merits of Hamilton's proposal, while those from Georgia and North Carolina made much of "stockjobbers" and "corruption." Virginia still had a large debt but had paid off much of it and figured to be a net loser with Hamilton's plan. The Virginia delegation, again to no one's surprise, took the lead in opposing assumption.

Had Hamilton's proposal been debated solely on its merits, it probably would have gone down to defeat. But to salvage his program, Hamilton forfeited New York's claim as the nation's capital. Southern congressmen, especially the Virginians, were anxious to have the nation's capital located in the South. They hoped that such a location would make Congress more susceptible to southern influence. They also wanted the account books juggled in Virginia's favor. In one of the most famous deals in American history, Hamilton let them have their way. In exchange for Jefferson and Madison's rounding up the necessary southern votes to get assumption through Congress, he agreed to recalculate Virginia's debt and round up northern votes to locate the federal city at Georgetown on the Potomac. On July 10, 1790, he delivered on his end of the bargain. Two weeks later, funding and assumption squeaked through the House by six votes.

FROM THE PERSPECTIVE of the Massachusetts delegation, salvaging Hamilton's program was well worth the cost. On most issues that faced the new government, the eight Massachusetts men in the House had been at odds. Should there be a single secretary of the treasury or a board to handle fiscal issues? Should federal judges receive higher or lower salaries than state judges? Should congressional districts be small or large? Should all the amendments suggested by state ratifying conventions come before the House for approval?

All these issues had badly split the Massachusetts delegation. At one extreme were the representatives of Boston and Essex County, Fisher Ames and Benjamin Goodhue, who supported the Washington administration at every opportunity and considered themselves the heart and soul of the Federalist Party. At the other was Elbridge Gerry, the Marblehead merchant who had opposed the Constitution.[45] Yet, on assumption, they were united. Indeed, getting Hamilton's program through the House had been their first priority.

The pressure from back home had been intense. During the winter of 1789–90, the likelihood that the commonwealth was going to renege on its debts had once again become the talk of Boston. What then would powerful creditors like William Phillips and Jonathan Mason do? Would they shift over to the opposition if the state debt were not assumed by the federal government? Would they prove that Hamilton was right, that rich men acted in accord with their pocketbooks? Many Massachusetts Federalists thought as much.

Their Antifederalist rivals, meanwhile, also lobbied vigorously for assumption as long as it did not lead to direct taxes. What else should the federal government spend the newly enacted customs duties on? High salaries? No, it would be much better to ease the burden on Massachusetts and its citizens. Even newspapers from western Massachusetts joined the crusade, again with the proviso that direct taxes must be avoided at all costs.

Needled by consistent pressure from back home, Massachusetts congressmen put aside their differences and worked together to get Hamilton's program through the House and the Senate. Gerry spearheaded the debate against Madison's proposal to discriminate against speculators. He also led the fight against cutting the proposed interest rates. He then joined forces with Goodhue in arguing that the defeat of assumption would lead to heavy direct taxes, new rebellions, and the rapid development of "factions" built around state and national creditors. Theodore Sedgwick, who now represented western Massachusetts in Congress, maintained that Shays's Rebellion had been caused by the imposition of direct taxes, and that assumption would end the need for such taxes and thus turn these once-hostile Massachusetts farmers into ardent supporters of the new national government. Without assumption, Sedgwick indicated, he would not support funding of the national debt.[46]

The deal finally worked out by Hamilton to let the South have the nation's capital thus barely caused a ripple of concern among the Massachusetts delegation. It was not "of two paper dollars consequence whether Congress sat at New York, Philadelphia, or on the Potomac," declared George Thacher of Maine.[47] Like Ames and Gerry, Goodhue and Sedgwick, the Maine congressman had spent months trying to get assumption through Congress. On other issues, he had prided himself on being "independent-minded," sometimes siding with Gerry, more often with Ames and Goodhue. On this issue, he had heard plenty from his constituents. They had been loud and clear. Especially vocal had been Thomas Wait, the owner of Maine's only newspaper: *"What in God's name have you been doing, Gentlemen?"*[48]

FROM ANY PERSPECTIVE, Hamilton's assumption and funding program was a boon for Massachusetts. Under his program, the United States agreed to assume the debts of the individual states to the amount of $21.5 million. Governor Hancock reported at the time that the consolidated debt of Massachusetts was £1,583,086, equal to $5,276,955 in the new national currency, or roughly one-fourth of the total debt to be assumed.[49] Only South Carolina benefited more.

In Boston, speculators were ecstatic. Rumors of assumption had already sparked a sudden rise in the price of Massachusetts securities. Brokers had been scouring the countryside for over a year for additional notes. Leonard Bleecker, an agent in faraway South Carolina, had been ordered to buy securities there—$200,000 if the price was right, $400,000 if credit could be obtained.[50] Once assumption became the law of the land, securities continued to skyrocket in value.

The terms of the assumption bill fostered high hopes. For the amount any state owed a creditor, the creditor received from the federal government three loan certificates: one for four-ninths of the total due, another for one-third, the last for the remaining two-ninths. The first paid 6 percent interest commencing on January 1, 1792; the second, 3 percent also commencing on January 1, 1792; the third, 6 percent commencing on January 1, 1801. Some speculators grumbled that the interest could have been higher, or that it could have been paid sooner. Some noted that national notes, which began bearing interest immediately, were more valuable. But all agreed that the new notes were far more valuable than the old state notes.

The market soon erased all doubt. The state's consolidated notes, which had traded at about 20 percent of par value in July 1789, rose to almost 72 percent by June 1792, while national notes rose from 24 percent to 112 percent.[51] In just three years, the notes in William Phillips's and Jonathan Mason's possession nearly quadrupled in value. The banker Phillips had about $94,000 worth; his partner Mason about $89,000. They were overshadowed only by merchant Samuel Breck's $104,000 and broker Nathaniel Prime's $196,000.[52]

Eventually, $5,055,451 of the Massachusetts debt ended up in Hamilton's program. Of this amount, $347,097 was owed to institutions. The remaining $4,708,354 was owed to 1,480 individual creditors. Nearly half of these creditors were ordinary folk with certificates worth less than $500. Of the monetary total, just over 3 percent was for them. The bulk of the monetary total, about 80 percent, was to go to speculators who lived in or near Boston. Nearly 35 percent was for seventy-two men and women who held certificates valued at between $10,000 and $25,000, and over 37 percent for thirty-five big operators who held certificates valued at over $25,000. At the very top were a handful of men like Phillips and Mason.[53]

These powerful men profited handsomely from Hamilton's financial program. They toasted the treasury secretary. And, as he hoped, they became closely tied with the new national government that he worked diligently to strengthen. To celebrate their good fortune, they called for the erection of a public monument in Boston. It was "to commemorate that train of events which led to the American Revolution and finally secured liberty and independence to the United States." On it were to be listed the key events. The list began with "Stamp Act passed 1765." It ended with "Public debt funded Aug. 4, 1790."[54]

IN WESTERN MASSACHUSETTS, few farmers shared in this largesse, but they too shared in the state's financial good fortune. The state's immense debt had finally been lifted from their shoulders, and the new federal debt would barely affect their everyday lives.

For one thing, Hamilton's plan was far less burdensome than the old state debt redemption program that had so upset their lives. The state leaders had regarded the state debt as something that had to be paid off in the near future. They had intended to be rid of it by the end of the 1780s. Much of the country's leadership thought like they did. Hamilton did not. He saw government borrowing as a benefit. Whereas taxation decreased money available for private capital expansion, borrowing did just the opposite. For every dollar the government borrowed, the national economy expanded by two. The government received one dollar to expand the economy, and in return the lender had a transferable certificate that increased the amount of private capital.

Hamilton thus had no intention, much less desire, to actually pay off the new $75.6 million national debt. He was only interested in keeping up interest payments, ensuring the good credit of the United States, and tying the rich and well-born to the national government. He purposely created a permanent debt to tie merchant capitalists, men like William Phillips and Jonathan Mason, to the new federal regime. When bonds became due, he had no intention of finding new tax money to pay them off. His intention was to issue new bonds to take their place. His plan was to recycle the debt, not pay it off or eliminate it entirely, as the leaders of Massachusetts had vainly tried to do.

Hamilton's plan was thus far less painful. To eliminate the Massachusetts debt, the state leaders had worked out a scheme that would cost the state taxpayers over $1 million annually in direct taxes. Farmers with grown sons were especially hard hit. Somehow they had to come up with hard coin for land and poll taxes. Hamilton in 1792 required only $4.6 million from the entire nation to pay the interest on the $75.6 million national debt, and another $1 million to cover the operating expenses of the federal government. None of this money, moreover, was to come from poll taxes or land taxes. No farmer had to scrounge about to find hard coin. Instead, the money was to come mainly from custom duties and excise duties.

For farmers in western Pennsylvania, the excise tax on whiskey was so irksome they rebelled. For Massachusetts farmers, however, the new taxes were relatively painless. Many of them, especially those in hardscrabble towns like Pelham and Colrain, were subsistence farmers. Rarely did they buy goods from the outside world. With the reduction of the state debt, moreover, their state and local taxes continued to decline. The tax on polls, which had totaled nearly three pounds per poll in 1786, dropped to one shilling, nine pence in 1791 and 1792. It dropped another pence in 1795 and remained at this figure until 1802.[55] The heavy tax burden that prompted many to rebel in 1786 thus no longer existed.

BY THIS TIME, defenders of the state and its policies had relegated the rebellion to history books. The first was published in 1788, just a year after Lincoln's victory. Written by George Richards Minot, a thirty-year-old Boston lawyer and clerk of the lower house of the Massachusetts legislature, it set the tone for much that was to follow.

Minot was anything but an unbiased observer. His job as house clerk, which he had had since 1782, required him to cater to the whims of the governing elite. He was very good at it, and every year the members had reelected him by unanimous vote. Minot was also a full-fledged member of Boston gentry. As the youngest son of a prosperous merchant, Boston landowner, and speculator in Maine land, he had enjoyed elite status since his birth. He had followed in his father's footsteps in going to Harvard, but had not become a merchant. Instead, he had studied law under Judge William Tudor. Then, thanks to Tudor and other well-placed Bostonians, he had become the clerk of the house and subsequently the secretary of the Massachusetts convention that ratified the United States Constitution.[56]

As a Boston blueblood, lawyer, and government official, Minot saw the Regulation as a threat to his way of life. Yet he was not just anxious to protect men and women like himself. He was also concerned about the reputation of the state. How would the people and rulers of Massachusetts be judged by their fellow Americans? By Europeans? By history? Would the outside world conclude that the yeomen of Massachusetts were unfit for self-government? Would the republican government of Massachusetts be deemed a failure? That worried him.

He also worried about the various hostile forces in Massachusetts, which in his eyes were many, combining against the governing elite. What might be done to prevent that? At one point, he secretly called for the "decapitation" of Daniel Shays. That, he noted in his diary, "would have dissolved a common tie" and rendered the opinions of the government's numerous opponents "harmless speculations."[57]

Minot had few illusions about the governing elite. He knew that the Hancock men and the Bowdoin men were usually at loggerheads, and that to praise one group would only irritate the other. He also knew that some of his Federalist friends were unscrupulous. He was appalled by the methods that Theodore Sedgwick used to get elected to the Massachusetts ratifying convention. He was even more distressed by the way the Constitution had been ratified in Massachusetts. He preferred to see such chicanery as "*Bad* measures in a *good* cause." In any case, he was not about to let such thoughts get outside the confines of his diary. He decided to present both the Hancock men and the Bowdoin men in a positive light, not as acting selfishly in behalf of themselves or their own factions, but as struggling side by side in behalf of the common good, constitutional government, and the administration of justice.[58]

Minot thus left many of his true thoughts out of his history. No reader would ever discern that he once wished for Shays's beheading. Minot did not even portray Shays as a monster. Nor did he castigate the rebels in every other sentence. Instead, the rank and file were presented as simply deluded farmers down on their luck. At times, moreover, he made it clear that a large segment of the population sympathized with them. They were anything but evil men unfit for republican government. They had simply been misled, but only temporarily. In the end, they had acknowledged their mistakes and accepted the rule of law.

More telling, however, was Minot's treatment of state authorities. He hid virtually all their warts. No reader would ever realize that at least one chief justice, along with hundreds of Revolutionary veterans, had blamed the commonwealth's troubles on an attempt by the Boston aristocracy to "plunder" the state's taxpayers for personal gain. Missing also was much of the harsh treatment recommended by the hard-liners and the unpopularity of the Bowdoin administration in much of the state. The refusal of the militia to rally behind the governor was downplayed, as were the problems General Lincoln had in recruiting veterans and the animosities that made it difficult, if not impossible, for the Hancock men and the Bowdoin men to work together. Indeed, whenever Minot took up matters that had divided

THE

HISTORY

OF THE

INSURRECTIONS,

IN

MASSACHUSETTS,

In the YEAR MDCCLXXXVI,

AND THE

REBELLION

CONSEQUENT THEREON.

BY GEORGE RICHARDS MINOT, A. M.

PRINTED AT *WORCESTER,* MASSACHUSETTS,
BY ISAIAH THOMAS. MDCCLXXXVIII.

Title page of Minot's *History* (Worcester, Mass., 1788). In telling the story of the Regulation, this book was notable in what it omitted. Nonetheless, it became the standard
account of Shays's Rebellion. The book sold well in Boston. It was also a hit with George
Washington, who regarded it as a judicious account of the insurrection. But in western
Massachusetts, the heartland of the Regulation, sales were poor.

the governing elite, he was careful not to name names and to present both sides as pursuing the common goal of restoring law and order.

"Thus," concluded Minot, "was a dangerous internal war finally suppressed, by the spirited use of constitutional power, without the shedding of blood by the hand of the civil magistrate; a circumstance, which it is the duty of every citizen to ascribe to its real cause, the lenity of government, and not to their weakness; a circumstance too, that must attach every man to the constitution, which, from a happy principle of mediocrity, governs its subjects without oppression, and reclaims them without severity."[59]

SO THE STORY came to be told. It was repeated widely, not only in the parlors of Boston but on plantations in Virginia and the Carolinas.

Minot sent complimentary copies of his book to George Washington, John Adams, and other national figures. Washington liked the book. He congratulated Minot on the "intrinsic merit of the work" as well as "its perspicuity & impartiality." On the same day, he told Benjamin Lincoln that the book seemed to be "executed with ingenuity, as well as to be calculated to place facts in a true point of light, obviate the prejudices of those who were unacquainted with the circumstances & answer good purposes in respect to our government in general."[60]

In Boston and areas that had remained loyal to the state during the Regulation, the book sold well. Sales were also satisfactory in Maine. But in Hampshire County, to Minot's dismay, sales were poor. Even men who had subscribed to the book before it was published refused to pay for it. Despite Minot's concluding argument that the state was once again one big happy family, the notion that the state house was the servant of the Boston establishment still persisted in western Massachusetts.

IN A SENSE, nothing has changed since those days. The Boston gentry succeeded in getting the Regulation called Shays's Rebellion, thus marginalizing the rebels and their cause, and evading such ticklish questions as "What needed regulating?"

Meanwhile, the notion that the state government was just a hireling of the Boston elite never abated in western Massachusetts. It still persists today. In the 1930s and early 1940s, the focus was on the Quabbin, a project that led to the flooding of much of east Pelham where Daniel and Abigail Shays had once farmed, along with three other towns in the Swift River Valley, to create a reservoir for metropolitan Boston. Today, the focus is on the "Big Dig," a project that has siphoned off billions of tax dollars to build

Alleged site of Shays's farm. From the author's collection. Most of the area in which Daniel and Abigail Shays once farmed now lies under water, thanks to the construction of the Quabbin Reservoir, a massive project that flooded four towns. On reservoir property, however, there are still a few remnants from the past. One is this wooded parcel, on which an old cellar hole is still visible. Some locals insist that it was part of Shays's farm.

a tunnel underneath Boston. Scarcely a year passes without some political leader in western Massachusetts harking back to the days of Daniel Shays.

Few traces from those days still remain, however. After fleeing Massachusetts, Shays eventually settled in western New York. He died there in 1825, at age seventy-eight, having outlived Bowdoin by thirty-two years, Lincoln by fifteen years. The farm that he and Abigail left behind was obliterated 110 years later by the construction of the Quabbin Reservoir. So too was the road that Dr. Nehemiah Hines took to the meeting of the Pelham selectmen, as well as the whole town of Greenwich from which his kinsman Captain Joseph Hines led troops against the Northampton court. All that remains are a few cellar holes. Some locals insist that one in particular was once part of Shays's homestead. Others have doubts.

Yet, despite the obliteration of Shays's home base, Daniel Shays has become a folk hero, and the rebellion that bears his name has inspired novels, plays, ballads, films, folk-singing groups, and even Web sites. Tributes have come from men and women of all political persuasions. One came from the novelist Gore Vidal, another from President Ronald Reagan, who in 1987 set aside an entire week to honor the defeated leader and his men. Perhaps most telling, however, was a decision made in 1994 by the original public Internet provider for western Massachusetts. The Web site needed an address. It had to reflect both the "unfair conditions imposed upon the struggling local economy" and "an attempt to improve the welfare of all working people." It also had to be memorable. The provider decided only one name would do: "ShaysNet.com."[61]

Yet, despite the diverse appeal of Shays's Rebellion, much of the "true story" has been long forgotten. The uprising occurred more than two hundred years ago. The fierce localism and family ties that sparked it no longer exist. The greed that also sparked it was obscured by George Richards Minot and scores of other government officials. Governor Bowdoin and his supporters eventually succeeded in shifting the odium from themselves and discrediting all their opponents as lowlifes trying to avoid payment of their debts. Other distortions subsequently crept in, some from the right, some from the left, providing President Reagan with one story to tell, Gore Vidal and the Internet provider with another.

Nearly all these accounts include drams of truth along with hefty doses of myth and propaganda. What is missing, oddly enough, are the main actors, the thousands of backcountry families who made the Regulation possible, the men and women who had to cope with a revolution that had failed them, one which in their judgment had merely shifted power from one set of "plunderers" to another, and the thousands of ordinary men who decided to either take up arms against the state or remain neutral. Only by coming to grips with them, understanding their hopes and grievances, does an uprising that appealed to some of the first families of western Massachusetts as well as the down-and-out emerge from the shadowy world of half-truths and begin to make sense.

NOTES

Abbreviations

AAS   American Antiquarian Society, Worcester, Mass.
MA   Massachusetts Archives, Boston.
MHS   Massachusetts Historical Society, Boston.
WMQ   *William & Mary Quarterly*, 3d series.

Prologue

1. See, for example, Richard B. Morris, "Insurrection in Massachusetts," in Daniel Aaron, ed., *America in Crisis: Fourteen Crucial Episodes in American History* (New York, 1952), 21–49; Robert J. Taylor, *Western Massachusetts in the Revolution* (Providence, 1954), chaps. 6 and 7; Marion L. Sharkey, *A Little Rebellion* (New York, 1955); Robert A. Feer, "Shays's Rebellion" (Ph.D. diss., Harvard, 1958); David P. Szatmary, *Shays' Rebellion: The Making of an Agrarian Insurrection* (Amherst, Mass., 1980).

2. Humphreys to Washington, November 1 and 9, 1786, in W. W. Abbot et al., eds., *The Papers of George Washington: Confederation Series*, 6 vols. (Charlottesville, Va., 1995), 4:324–25, 350–51.

3. Knox to Washington, October 23, 1786, in Abbot et al., *Papers of George Washington: Confederation Series*, 4:300.

4. Madison to Washington, November 8, 1786, in William T. Hutchinson et al., *The Papers of James Madison*, 17 vols. (Chicago, 1962–91), 9:166.

5. Washington to Henry Knox, December 26, 1786, February 3, 1787, in Abbot et al., *Papers of George Washington: Confederation Series*, 4:481–82; 5:9.

6. Washington to Lafayette, June 6, 1787, in Abbot et al., *Papers of George Washington: Confederation Series*, 5:222.

Chapter 1. Defiance

1. C. O. Parmenter, *History of Pelham* (Amherst, Mass., 1898), 503–5. In the case of Dr. Hines and other obscure individuals mentioned in this book, I used the "family reconstitution" technique to gather biographical data. I did this for 1,062 rebels and 564 government supporters. I relied heavily on town histories, the New-England Genealogical Society's vital records of the towns of Massachusetts to 1850, town tax assessments, local church and court records, and genealogical accounts of individual families. I found the manuscript United States census returns, which some historians have used for such research, to be of less value. The census takers invariably missed dozens of residents in each community, and if one were to take the returns seriously one might mistakenly conclude that the missing individuals had moved, died, or never lived in the community. For Dr. Hines and other Pelham residents, the collection of documents assembled by Robert Lord Keyes of the Pelham Historical Society is especially valuable.

2. Francis B. Heitman, *Historical Register of Officers of the Continental Army* (Washington, D.C., 1914), 291, 492; Mary Ann Nicholson, ed., *The Family of Daniel Shays* (Boston, 1987), 12.

3. Computed from "Table on Ranked Evaluations, 1784," in Daniel W. Shelton, "'Elementary Feelings': Pelham, Massachusetts, in Rebellion" (honors thesis, Amherst College, 1981), and Pelham Tax Evaluations, November 2, 1784, Special Collections, DuBois Library, University of Massachusetts, Amherst.

4. *Massachusetts Gazette* (Springfield), August 14, September 22, 1786.

5. Selectmen of Pelham to Selectmen of Amherst, July 18, 1786, Jones Library, Special Collections, Amherst, Mass.

6. *Massachusetts Gazette* (Springfield), August 14, September 22, 1786; Sylvester Judd diary, August 21, 1786, Forbes Library, Northampton, Mass.

7. *Hampshire Herald*, September 5, 1786.

8. John Bruce testimony, Supreme Judicial Court (Hampshire County), April term, 1787, in Minutes of Criminal Trials, 1780–89, Robert Treat Paine Papers, MHS.

9. *Hampshire Herald*, September 5, 1786; *Massachusetts Gazette*, 8, September 26, 1786; MA 189:5; 318:4, 6.

10. All accounts of this incident came from government sources, mainly reports to Governor Bowdoin: MA 190:230–35; 318:7, 9, 24; *Worcester Magazine*, first week in September 1786; *Massachusetts Centinel*, September 9, 1786. For a heroic and much exaggerated description of Artemas Ward's behavior, see Charles Martyn, *The Life of Artemas Ward* (New York, 1921), 282–87.

11. Jonathan Warner to Governor Bowdoin, n.d.; William Greenleaf to Governor Bowdoin, n.d.; Artemas Ward to Governor Bowdoin, September 5, 1786—all in MA 190:229–30, 235, 234.

12. *Independent Ledger*, 11 September 1786; *Boston Gazette*, September 18, 1786; William V. Wells, *The Life and Public Service of Samuel Adams*, 3 vols. (Boston, 1865), 3:225.

13. Accounts from government sources, mainly reports to Governor Bowdoin: MA 190:253–60a, 318:13–16.

14. David Cobb to Governor Bowdoin, September 13, 1786, MA 190:262; Bowdoin to Cobb, September 14, 1786, MA 318:18; *Worcester Magazine*, third week in September 1786.

15. John Paterson to Caleb Hyde, September 10, 1786, Caleb Hyde to Governor Bowdoin, September 13, 1786, MA 190:241, 263–64; J. E. A. Smith, *The History of Pittsfield, Mass., 1734–1800* (Boston, 1869), 402; Thomas Egleston, *The Life of John Paterson: Major General in the Revolutionary Army* (New York, 1894), 171–72.

16. General William Shepard to Governor Bowdoin, September 25 and 29, 1786; account of Judge Nathan P. Sargent and Judge David Sewall, October 2, 1786, MA 190:266, 289–94; *Hampshire Gazette*, October 4, 1786; *Worcester Magazine*, second week of October 1786; David P. Szatmary, "Shays' Rebellion in Springfield," in Martin Kaufman, ed., *Shays' Rebellion: Selected Essays* (Westfield, Mass., 1987), 10–11.

17. The governor's men had a different slant on this story. In their accounts, the governor's behavior was always honorable; the rebels' dishonorable. See Jeremy Belknap, *History of New Hampshire*, 3 vols. (Boston, 1791), 2:470–75; and "Letters of William Plumer, 1786–1787," Colonial Society of Massachusetts, *Publications*, 11 (1910): 390–96. For conflicting details, compare Jere R. Daniell, *Experiment in Republicanism: New Hampshire Politics and the American Revolution, 1741–1794* (Cambridge, Mass., 1970), 199; David P. Szatmary, *Shays' Rebellion* (Amherst, Mass., 1980), 78–79; and Alan Taylor, "Regulators and White Indians: The Agrarian Resistance in Post-Revolutionary New England," in Robert A. Gross, ed., *In Debt to Shays: The Bicentennial of an Agrarian Rebellion* (Charlottesville, Va., 1993), 147–50.

18. Benjamin Homer Hall, *History of Eastern Vermont* (New York, 1858), 548–51; A. M. Caverly, *History of the Town of Pittsford, Vermont* (Rutland, Vt., 1872), 248–61; Robert E. Shalhope, *Bennington and the Green Mountain Boys: The Emergence of Liberal Democracy in Vermont, 1760–1850* (Baltimore, 1996), 189–90; Michael A. Bellesiles, *Revolutionary Outlaws: Ethan Allen and the Struggle for Independence on the Vermont Frontier* (Charlottesville, Va., 1993), 247–48.

19. Bills of indictment, Robert Treat Paine Papers, MHS; Sidney Kaplan, "Veteran Officers and Politics in Massachusetts, 1783–1787," *WMQ* 9 (January 1952): 51; "Names of the Persons Before Supreme Judicial Court, Northampton, April 1787," Suffolk County Court, File 159008; Smith, *The History of Pittsfield*, 406–7.

20. Dr. William Whiting, "Some Brief Remarks on the Present State of Publick Affairs," in Stephen Riley, "Doctor William Whiting and Shays' Rebellion," *Proceedings of the American Antiquarian Society* 66 (January 1956): 132.

21. Dr. William Whiting, "Some Remarks on the Conduct of the Inhabitants of the Commonwealth of Massachusetts . . . December 1786," in Riley, "Doctor Whiting and Shays' Rebellion," 124, 131–32, 151–53.

22. Notes from the trial of Dr. William Whiting, Robert Treat Paine Papers, MHS; Whiting, "Some Brief Remarks," 127; Theodore Sedgwick to Bowdoin, October 5, 1786, MA 190:277; William Whiting to Robert Treat Paine, March 19, 1787, Paine Papers, MHS; Stephen Higginson to Nathan Dane, March 3, June 16, 1787, Dane Papers, Beverly Historical Society.

23. *Journals of the Continental Congress, 1774–1789* (Washington, D.C., 1934), 31:891–96; Rufus King to Elbridge Gerry, October 19, 1786, in Charles R. King, ed.,

The Life and Correspondence of Rufus King, 6 vols. (New York, 1894), 1:191–92; Henry Knox to Bowdoin, October 22, 1786, in Knox Papers, MHS; Governor Bowdoin message to the General Court, October 27, 1786, *Acts and Resolves of the General Court, 1786 and 1787*, 948–49; Robert A. Feer, "Shays's Rebellion" (Ph.D. diss., Harvard, 1958), 269–70, 284–85.

24. Charles Pettit to Benjamin Franklin, October 18, 1786, Edward Carrington to Edmund Randolph, December 8, 1786, both in Edmund C. Burnett, ed., *Letters of Members of the Continental Congress*, 8 vols. (Washington, D.C., 1936), 8:487, 517; William North to Henry Knox, October 29, 1786, Knox Papers, MHS; Elbridge Gerry to Rufus King, October 29, 1786, in King, *Life and Correspondence*, 1:197. For the correct date of the Gerry letter, see Feer, "Shays's Rebellion," 271 n. 2.

25. John M. Palmer, *General von Steuben* (New Haven, Conn., 1937), 339–40.

26. "Instructions to senior officer of the troops to be raised in Massachusetts by virtue of the act of Congress of the 20th of October 1786," MA 190:25; Henry Jackson to Henry Knox, November 12, 1786 to March 31, 1787, Knox Papers, MHS; Joseph Parker Warren, "The Confederation and Shays Rebellion," *American Historical Review* 11 (October 1905): 42–67.

27. Wells, *Adams*, 3:246; *Massachusetts Centinel*, September 13, 1786; William Pencak, "Samuel Adams and Shays's Rebellion," *New England Quarterly* (March 1989): 64; John C. Miller, *Sam Adams: Pioneer in Propaganda* (Boston, 1936), 374.

28. Feer, "Shays's Rebellion," 255–58; Szatmary, "Shays' Rebellion in Springfield," 12–13; Szatmary, *Shays' Rebellion*, 84; Franklin Russell Mullaly, "The Massachusetts Insurrection of 1786–1787" (M.A. thesis, Smith College, 1947), 61.

29. Szatmary, "Shays' Rebellion in Springfield," 12–13; Szatmary, *Shays' Rebellion*, 84; Mullaly, "Massachusetts Insurrection," 61; Miller, *Sam Adams*, 374.

30. *Worcester Magazine*, last week in November 1786, first week in December 1786; MA 189:33, 35; Feer, "Shays's Rebellion," 318.

31. MA 189:46, 50, 51, 52; *Worcester Magazine*, first week in December 1786; Feer, "Shays's Rebellion," 323–25.

32. Mullaly, "Massachusetts Insurrection," 53. For Northampton volunteers, see Captain Solomon Allen's payroll, September 1786, MA 192:474; Captain Russell's payroll, January 1787, MA 192:503. For list of veterans, see James Russell Trumble, *History of Northampton*, 2 vols. (Northampton, 1898–1902), appendix, 616–33; and "Hampshire County Soldiers and Sailors in the War of the Revolution," Forbes Library, Northampton, Mass. (1939), which is an index to *Massachusetts Soldiers and Sailors of the Revolutionary War*, 17 vols. (Boston, 1896–1908).

33. Thomas Keefe Callahan, "The Voice of the People of This County: The Birth of Popular Politics and Support for the Shaysite Insurrection in Groton, Massachusetts" (M.A. thesis, Harvard, 1992), 28–29.

34. *Commonwealth v. Shattuck et al.*, Middlesex, April term, 1782, Supreme Judicial Court File Book, 148930, MA; Callahan, "Voice of the People," 38; *Commonwealth v. Shattuck et al.*, Middlesex, April term, 1784, Supreme Judicial Court File Book, 85–86, MA; Van Beck Hall, *Politics Without Parties: Massachusetts, 1780–1791* (Pittsburgh, 1972), 187; MA 190:253–60a, 318:13–16.

35. MA 189:36, 38, 41a, 44, 45, 49, 402; *Worcester Magazine*, first week in Decem-

ber 1786, second week in December 1786, second week in January 1787; Shrewsbury Town Petition, January 15, 1787, Shays Rebellion Collection, AAS; Callahan, "Voice of the People," 54; Szatmary, *Shays' Rebellion*, 83, 93.

36. *Worcester Magazine*, January–February 1787; Petitions, Shays Rebellion Collection, AAS; Feer, "Shays's Rebellion," 342–43 n. 1.

37. "List of Persons who the [Worcester] Grand Jurors found Bills against for Treason," April term, 1787, Ward Family Papers, Box 16, AAS; Indictments for Treason, Sedition, Worcester, 1787, Suffolk County Court, File 155325; John Gill testimony and Captain Webb testimony in Isaac Chenery case, Arrests and Trials of Worcester (County) Insurgents, 1787, Shays Rebellion Collection, Folder 5, AAS; John Noble, "A Few Notes on the Shays Rebellion," *Proceedings of the American Antiquarian Society* 15 (October 1902): 212–13.

38. Szatmary, "Shays' Rebellion in Springfield," 13; Samuel Lyman to Samuel Breck, December 27, 1786, *The Bowdoin and Temple Papers, Collections of the Massachusetts Historical Society* (Boston, 1907), 66:122–24; Feer, "Shays's Rebellion," 331–32.

39. By this time, there had been a steady barrage of reports about the failure of both the militia and the people in western Massachusetts to support the state government. At first, state leaders had trouble accepting the fact that they were so thoroughly disliked. Gradually, most got the message. Cf. Proclamation, September 2, 1786; Message of Governor Bowdoin to the Massachusetts House and Senate, September 28, 1786; Message of Governor Bowdoin to the Massachusetts House and Senate, February 3, 1787; House and Senate Resolution, February 4, 1787—all in MA 189:1–2; 190:267–76, 325–32; 189:108–9; and Theophilus Parsons to Nathaniel Tracy, n.d., in Theophilus Parsons, *Memoir of Theophilus Parsons* (Boston, 1859), 128–31.

Chapter 2. Crackdown

1. Merrill Jensen, *The New Nation* (New York, 1950), 56; Douglas Southall Freeman, *George Washington: A Biography*, 6 vols. (New York, 1948–54), 5:385–86; Clifford K. Shipton, "Benjamin Lincoln: Old Reliable," in George Allan Billias, ed., *George Washington's Generals* (New York, 1964), 202–3.

2. James Bowdoin to Rufus Putnam, January 17, 1787, Wetmore Family Papers, Yale Library; Stephen Higginson to Henry Knox, January 20, 1787, Knox Papers, MHS; Benjamin Lincoln to George Washington, December 4, 1786 through March 4, 1787, W. W. Abbot et al., eds., *The Papers of George Washington: Confederation Series*, 6 vols. (Charlottesville, Va., 1995), 4:422; List of Subscribers, MA 189:66, 217–18; Receipts on Loan to Suppress the Rebellion, 1787, MA; "To the Forty Thousand Pound Loan established by the Act of the General Court, passed the 6th February 1787," Treasurer's Office, Journal B, 1786–87, pp. 477–78, MA.

3. Robert A. Gross, "The Confidence Man and the Preacher: The Cultural Politics of Shays's Rebellion," in Robert A. Gross, ed., *In Debt to Shays: The Bicentennial of an Agrarian Rebellion* (Charlottesville, Va., 1993), 301–4, 315–19.

4. David P. Szatmary, *Shays' Rebellion* (Amherst, Mass., 1980), 85, 89; Prince Hall to Bowdoin, November 26, 1786, in William Grimshaw, *Official History of Freemasonry*

Among the Colored People of North America (New York, 1903), 81; John Quincy Adams diary, January 18, 1787, Adams Papers (microfilm), MHS.

5. Carpenter & Morehouse, *The History of the Town of Amherst, Massachusetts* (Amherst, Mass., 1896), 125–27; Szatmary, *Shays' Rebellion*, 88, 104. For government payrolls, see MA, vols. 191–92, passim.

6. Robert Holt testimony, Shays Rebellion Box, Robert Treat Paine Papers, MHS.

7. Elnathan Haskell to Colonel Pratt, January 31, February 1, 1787, Knox Papers, MHS; Robert A. Feer, "Shays's Rebellion" (Ph.D. diss., Harvard, 1958), 376.

8. John Bruce testimony, Supreme Judicial Court (Hampshire County), April term, 1787, in Minutes of Criminal Trials, 1780–89, Robert Treat Paine Papers, MHS; Black List County of Hampshire, Robert Treat Paine Papers, MHS; William Shepard to James Bowdoin, December 4, 1786, MA 318:202; William Shepard to the Militia, December 5, 1786, in Orsamus Turner, *History of the Pioneer Settlement of Phelps and Gorham's Purchase* (Rochester, N.Y., 1851), 483; William Williams, in Paul Ford, ed., *Essays on the Constitution of the United States* (New York, 1892), 157; Edward Carrington to Governor Edmund Randolph, December 8, 1786, in Edmund C. Burnett, ed., *Letters of Members of the Continental Congress*, 8 vols. (Washington, D.C., 1936), 8:516; James Madison to George Mutter, January 7, 1787, in William T. Hutchinson et al., eds., *The Papers of James Madison*, 17 vols. (Chicago, 1962–91), 9:321; George Washington to David Humphreys, December 26, 1786, in W. W. Abbot et al., eds., *The Papers of George Washington: Confederation Series* (Charlottesville,Va., 1995), 4:478.

9. Cf., for example, *Massachusetts Centinel*, January 17, 20, 1787; Rufus Putnam to Governor Bowdoin, January 8, 1787, *Collections of the Maine Historical Society* (Portland, 1847), 2:250–54; James Winthrop to Bowdoin, December 13, 1786, MA 318:47; Levi Shepard to Bowdoin, December 28, 1786, *The Bowdoin and Temple Papers, Collections of the Massachusetts Historical Society* (Boston, 1907), 66:125; Lewis Glazier, *History of Gardner* (Worcester, Mass., 1860), 80.

10. John Bryant to Samuel Hodgson, May 14, 1785, Springfield City Library; *Journals of the Continental Congress, 1774–1789* (Washington, D.C., 1934), 31:675–76; Joseph Parker Warren, "The Confederation and Shays Rebellion," *American Historical Review* 11 (October 1905): 44; David P. Szatmary, "Shays' Rebellion in Springfield," in Martin Kaufman, ed., *Shays' Rebellion: Selected Essays* (Westfield, Mass., 1987), 13.

11. William Shepard to Henry Knox, December 20, 1786, Knox Papers, MHS; *Springfield Republican*, December 21, 1894, as quoted in Szatmary, "Shays' Rebellion in Springfield," 13.

12. Daniel Stebbins diary, 1:48–49, Forbes Library, Northampton, Mass.

13. Luke Day, "To the Commanding Officer of Springfield," *Worcester Magazine*, February 1787.

14. Stebbins diary, 1:47–49.

15. Henry Parsons, *The Parsons Family: Descendants of Cornet Joseph Parsons, Springfield, 1636–Northampton, 1655*, 2 vols. (New York, 1912), 1:134; Elnathan Haskell to Colonel Pratt, January 30, 1787, Knox Papers, MHS.

16. Daniel Shays interview, *Massachusetts Centinel*, January 17, 20, 1787.

17. Granby town meeting, January 31, 1787, in Knox Papers, MHS; General Lincoln to Colonel Price, February 2, 1787, Porter-Phelps-Huntington Papers, Amherst College.

18. F. W. Minot diary, February 3, 1787, in Theodore Sedgwick Papers, MHS.

19. Thomas Egleston, *The Life of John Paterson: Major General in the Revolutionary Army* (New York, 1894), 185–88; John H. Lockwood, *Westfield and Its Historic Influences*, 2 vols. (Springfield, Mass., 1922), 1:120–21; John H. Lockwood, *Western Massachusetts: A History, 1636–1925*, 2 vols. (New York, 1926), 1:174–75.

20. Lincoln to Bowdoin, February 4, 1787, in Frederick J. Allis, Jr., and Wayne A. Frederick, eds., *The Benjamin Lincoln Papers* (Cambridge, Mass., 1977), microfilm; David B. Mattern, *Benjamin Lincoln and the American Revolution* (Columbia, S.C., 1995), 171.

21. Diary of an Officer in Lincoln's Army, January 28–February 12, 1787, in Theodore Sedgwick Papers, MHS; Feer, "Shays's Rebellion," 379.

22. Quoted in Franklin Russell Mullaly, "The Massachusetts Insurrection of 1786–1787" (M.A. thesis, Smith College, 1947), 75.

23. Dr. Jeremy Belknap to Ebenezer Hazard, February 2, 1787, in Jeremy Belknap, *Belknap Papers*, 3 vols. (Boston, 1877–91), 1:455–56.

24. *Acts and Laws of the Commonwealth of Massachusetts, 1780–1797*, 11 vols. (Boston, 1890–97), 4:423–30, 165–68; Van Beck Hall, *Politics Without Parties: Massachusetts, 1780–1791* (Pittsburgh, 1972), 229; "To the Forty Thousand Pound Loan established by the Act of the General Court, passed the 6th February 1787," Treasurer's Office, Journal B, 1786–87, pp. 477–78, MA.

25. William Shepard to James Bowdoin, February 18, 20, 1787, *Bowdoin and Temple Papers*, 66:142–43, 147; James Sullivan to Rufus King, February 24, 1787 in Charles R. King, ed., *The Life and Correspondence of Rufus King*, 6 vols. (New York, 1894), 1:214; Lincoln to James Bowdoin, February 14, 20, 22, 1787, *Bowdoin and Temple Papers*, 66:136–37, 145, 156–58; Lincoln to Henry Knox, February 17, March 14, 1787, Knox Papers, MHS; Richard D. Brown, "Shays's Rebellion and the Ratification of the Federal Constitution in Massachusetts," in Richard Beeman, Stephen Botein, and Edward C. Carter II, eds., *Beyond Confederation: Origins of the Constitution and American National Identity* (Chapel Hill, N.C., 1987), 116.

26. Stephen Higginson to Henry Knox, February 13, 1787, "Letters of Stephen Higginson," in *Annual Report of the American Historical Association* (Washington, D.C., 1896), 1:751.

27. Richard D. Brown, "Shays Rebellion and Its Aftermath: A View from Springfield, Massachusetts, 1787," *WMQ* 40 (October 1983): 609–15; Brown, "Shays's Rebellion and the Ratification of the Federal Constitution in Massachusetts," 118–19.

28. *New Hampshire Mercury*, February 28, 1787. See also Electa F. Jones, *Stockbridge, Past and Present* (Springfield, 1854), 188; J. E. A. Smith, *The History of Pittsfield, Mass., 1734–1800* (Boston, 1869), 404–5; "Guns along the Housatonic: The Story of Shays Rebellion," *Berkshire Magazine* (Summer 1974): 33; Szatmary, *Shays' Rebellion*, 107.

29. "Statement of Ira Allen," *Records of the Governor and Council of the State of Ver-*

mont (Montpelier, 1875), 3:380; Royall Tyler, Report to General Lincoln, March 1787, Tyler Papers, Vermont Historical Society; Michael A. Bellesiles, *Revolutionary Outlaws: Ethan Allen and the Struggle for Independence on the Vermont Frontier* (Charlottesville, Va., 1993), 253.

30. Lord Dorchester to Lord Sidney, February 28, 1787, Sidney to Dorchester, April 5, 1787, Colonial Office 42, vol. 50, Public Archives of Canada, Ottawa; *Hampshire Gazette*, June 6, 1787; Szatmary, *Shays' Rebellion*, 108–9, 118.

31. Lincoln to James Bowdoin, February 14, 20, 22, 1787, *Bowdoin and Temple Papers*, 66:136–37, 145, 156–58; Lincoln to Henry Knox, February 17, March 14, 1787, Knox Papers, MHS; Feer, "Shays's Rebellion," 395–98.

32. Mullaly, "Massachusetts Insurrection," 78; George Richards Minot, *The History of the Insurrections in Massachusetts* (Worcester, Mass., 1788), 148–49.

33. Jones, *Stockbridge, Past and Present*, 190; Feer, "Shays's Rebellion," 390; Lockwood, *Western Massachusetts*, 1:185.

34. Jones, *Stockbridge, Past and Present*, 191–96.

35. Original papers relating to Shays's Rebellion, Berkshire Atheneum, Pittsfield, Mass.; *Worcester Magazine* (1787) 2:648; *Independent Chronicle*, March 8, 1787; Richard E. Welch, Jr., *Theodore Sedgwick, Federalist* (Middletown, Conn., 1965), 51–53; Sarah C. Sedgwick and Christina S. Marquand, *Stockbridge, 1739–1939* (Great Barrington, Mass., 1939), 16–64; Feer, "Shays's Rebellion," 402–5.

36. Journal of Thomas Thompson, April 2, 1787, Stevens Collection, University of Vermont, Burlington; Szatmary, *Shays' Rebellion*, 112–13.

37. *New Hampshire Gazette*, June 2, 1787; *Hampshire Gazette*, June 27, 1787; Thomas Ives to Theodore Sedgwick, June 25, 1787, MA 190:21; Suffolk County Court, File 160536.

38. Joseph Henshaw to James Bowdoin, February 14, 1787, *Bowdoin and Temple Papers*, 66:135–36.

39. "Report of the Commissioners, April 27, 1787," MA 189:277–81; *Independent Chronicle*, May 3, 1887; Robert J. Taylor, *Western Massachusetts in the Revolution* (Providence, 1954), 164–65; Feer, "Shays's Rebellion," 414.

40. James Sullivan to Rufus King, February 25, 1787, King Papers, New York Historical Society; Thomas Amory, *Life of James Sullivan*, 2 vols. (Boston, 1859), 1:172–75; 2:145.

41. John Noble, "A Few Notes on the Shays Rebellion," *Proceedings of the American Antiquarian Society* 15 (October 1902): 213–22.

42. Noble, "A Few Notes on the Shays Rebellion," 202–4.

43. Stephen Riley, "Dr. William Whiting and Shays' Rebellion," *Proceedings of the American Antiquarian Society* 66 (1967): 119–66; Increase Sumner to Elizabeth Sumner, April 8, 1787, as quoted in *Berkshire Eagle*, September 30, 1946; warrant of arrest to Sheriff of Berkshire County, February 1, 1787, MA 189:100–101; "List of Some Names in the County of Berkshire for Gen. Lincoln's Suppression," MA 189:102; trial and conviction of William Whiting, February-April 1787, Supreme Judicial Court, File 160304.

44. Bills of indictment, Robert Treat Paine Papers, MHS; "Names of the Persons Before Supreme Judicial Court, Northampton, April 1787," Suffolk County Court,

File 159008; Sidney Kaplan, "Veteran Officers and Politics in Massachusetts, 1783–1787, *WMQ* 9 (January 1952): 51.

45. "Samuel Buffington's Narrative," February 21, 1787, *Bowdoin and Temple Papers*, 66:153–55; bills of indictment, Robert Treat Paine Papers, MHS; "A Return of Prisoners now confined in Gaol in Northampton . . . 9 April 1787," Robert Treat Paine Papers, MHS; Randall Conrad, "A Captain with the Insurgents: Jason Parmenter of Bernardston," in Kaufman, *Shays Rebellion*, 67–79.

46. William Cushing et al. to James Bowdoin, Northampton, April 8, 1787, MA 190:417–19; indictment, March 20, 1787, documents relating to Shays's Rebellion, Berkshire Atheneum, Pittsfield, Mass.; Suffolk County Court, File 160538; Increase Sumner to Elizabeth Sumner, April 8, 1787, as quoted in *Berkshire Eagle*, September 30, 1946; C. M. Hyde and Alexander Hyde, comps., *History of Lee, Massachusetts* (Springfield, Mass., 1878), 158–59; Lockwood, *Western Massachusetts*, 1:185.

47. Stebbins diary, 1:54; *Independent Chronicle*, July 5, 1787; Conrad, "A Captain with the Insurgents," 67–79.

48. *Hampshire Gazette*, May 23, 30, June 27, 1787.

49. Thomas Cushing to Harry Newman, April 9, 1787, Cushing Family Papers, MHS; Paul Brandes, *John Hancock's Life and Speeches* (Lanham, Md., 1996), 189; Nathan Dane to Rufus King, May 31, 1787, King Papers, New York Historical Society.

50. Amory, *Life of James Sullivan*, 1:203–7.

51. Indictment, March 20, 1787, documents relating to Shays's Rebellion, Berkshire Atheneum, Pittsfield, Mass.; Suffolk County Court, File 160538; "Guns along the Housatonic," 35; Marion L. Starkey, *A Little Rebellion* (New York, 1955), 248.

52. "Return of Prisoners under charge of . . . Gen. Lincoln . . . at Pittsfield, March 8 and 12, 1787," MA 319:348, 350; Suffolk County Court, File 160576; Governor's Council, Pardon Files, Series 328, MA; Governor's Council, Pardons Not Granted, 1785–1810, Series 771, MA.

53. "Extracts from the Last Words and Dying Speeches of John Bly and Charles Rose . . . ," *Worcester Magazine*, second week of January 1788, p. 186.

Chapter 3. Oath Takers and Leaders

1. "Report of the Commissioners, April 27, 1787," MA 190:277–81. The oaths are in MA 190:67–225. They have to be used with care, as some men took the oath more than once.

2. Sidney Kaplan, "A Negro Veteran in Shays' Rebellion," *Journal of Negro History* 33 (April 1948): 123–29; bills of indictment, Robert Treat Paine Papers, MHS; "Names of the Persons Before Supreme Judicial Court, Northampton, April 1787," Suffolk County Court, File 159008; Lois McClellan Patrie, *A History of Colrain, Massachusetts, with Genealogies of Early Families* (Troy, N.Y., 1974), 90; MA 190:119, 146.

3. *Hampshire Herald*, September 5, 1786; *Massachusetts Gazette*, 8, 26 September 1786; MA 189:5; 318:4, 6.

4. Biographical information for Day was gleaned from George Edward Day, *A*

Genealogical Register of the Descendants in the Male Line of Robert Day . . . , 2d ed. (Northampton, Mass., 1848), 17, 23, along with town histories, town records, and court records. Bernie Lally, the town historian of West Springfield, provided me with a wealth of information and documents about Day and his neighbors.

5. "West Springfield's Minuteman Company," in Esther M. Swift, *West Springfield, Massachusetts: A Town History* (Springfield, Mass., 1969), 321; *Massachusetts Soldiers and Sailors of the Revolutionary War* (Boston, 1898), 579–80; Francis B. Heitman, *Historical Register of Officers of the Continental Army* (Washington, D.C., 1914), 189; Fred Anderson Berg, *Encyclopedia of Continental Army Units* (Harrisburg, Pa., 1972), 68, 73, 149; Kenneth Roberts, ed., *March to Quebec: Journals of Members of Arnold's Expedition* (New York, 1938); John Richard Alden, ed., *The War of the Revolution* (New York, 1952), vol. 1, chap. 13; Willard M. Wallace, *Traitorous Hero: Life and Fortunes of Benedict Arnold* (Freeport, N.Y., 1954), 55–93.

6. Wallace Evan Davies, "The Society of the Cincinnati in New England, 1783–1800," *WMQ* 5 (January 1948): 3–25; Henry Knox to John Adams, August 21, 1776, Knox Papers, MHS; Louis Clinton Hatch, *The Administration of the American Revolutionary Army* (New York, 1904), 82–84; Sidney Kaplan, "Veteran Officers and Politics in Massachusetts, 1783–1787," *WMQ* 9 (January 1952): 34–40; Sidney Kaplan, "Pay, Pension, and Power: Economic Grievances of the Massachusetts Officers of the Revolution," *Boston Public Library Quarterly* 3 (January and April 1951): 15–34, 127–41; Charles Royster, *A Revolutionary People at War: The Continental Army and American Character, 1775–1783* (Chapel Hill, N.C., 1979), 353–54.

7. Henry Laurens to George Washington, May 5, 1778, as quoted in Hatch, *Administration of the American Revolutionary Army*, 82; Royster, *A Revolutionary People at War*, 354–57.

8. Sidney Kaplan, "Rank and Status among Massachusetts Continental Officers," *American Historical Review* 56 (January 1951): 318–26; Kaplan, "Pay, Pension, and Power," 15–34, 127–41; Jackson Turner Main, *The Social Structure of Revolutionary America* (Princeton, N.J., 1965), 213–15; Gerhard Kollmann, "Reflections on the Army of the American Revolution," in Erich Angermann et al., eds., *New Wine in Old Skins: A Comparative View of Socio-Political Structures and Values Affecting the American Revolution* (Stuttgart, 1976), 153–76.

9. Computed from data: West Springfield Tax List, 1775, Connecticut Valley Historical Museum, Springfield, Mass. Again, I am indebted to Bernie Lally, the town historian of West Springfield, who discovered this and other tax records while rummaging through an unindexed box of long-neglected documents.

10. Computed from data: West Springfield Assessment, June 26, 1786, Connecticut Valley Historical Museum, Springfield, Mass.

11. *Two-in-One Book: Hampshire County House of Correction, 1784–1830*, Forbes Library, Northampton, Mass.

12. Kerry Landen, "'Money Makes the Mare Go': Debtor-Creditor Relations and the Abolition of Imprisonment for Debt in Massachusetts" (seminar paper, University of Massachusetts, spring 1995), 3–4; Robert A. Feer, "Imprisonment for Debt in Massachusetts Before 1800," *Mississippi Valley Historical Review* 48 (September 1961): 255–60; Jonathan M. Chu, "Debt Litigation and Shays's Rebellion," in Robert

A. Gross, ed., *In Debt to Shays: The Bicentennial of an Agrarian Rebellion* (Charlottesville, Va., 1993), 84–86; William E. Nelson, *Americanization of the Common Law: The Impact of Legal Change on Massachusetts Society, 1760–1830* (Cambridge, Mass., 1975), 41–45, 148.

13. All information on the Northampton jail in this paragraph and the following comes from *Two-in-One Book: Hampshire County House of Correction.*

14. Feer, "Imprisonment for Debt," 259–60.

15. Computed from data: *Two-in-One Book: Hampshire House of Correction,* and oaths of allegiance, MA 190:67–225. Of the eighteen hundred Hampshire County rebels, another four were jailed in the years following the rebellion: Nathan Powers and Darius Rice of Greenwich, and John Billing and John Field of Amherst.

16. James M. Craft, *History of the Town of Whately, Mass., 1661–1899* (Conway, Mass., 1899), 233–34, 237; George Sheldon, *A History of Deerfield, Massachusetts,* 2 vols. (1895; reprint, Deerfield, Mass., 1972), 2:56–60; Heitman, *Historical Register of Officers of the Continental Army.*

17. Computed from data: *Two-in-One Book: Hampshire County House of Correction,* and oaths of allegiance, MA 190:67–225.

18. Mary Ann Nicholson, ed., *The Family of Daniel Shays* (Boston, 1987), passim.

19. Nicholson, *The Family of Daniel Shays,* 12; petition of Timothy Hinds, May 1787, MA 189:367; bills of indictment, Robert Treat Paine Papers, MHS; "Names of the Persons Before Supreme Judicial Court, Northampton, April 1787," Suffolk County Court, File 159008.

20. The numerical information in this and the following paragraphs was computed from data in the oaths of allegiance, MA 190:67–225.

21. Patrie, in her *History of Colrain,* lists only eighty-eight rebels, mainly those who took the oath before Justices of the Peace Hugh McClellan of Colrain and Hugh Maxwell of neighboring Heath. Missing from her list are sixty-eight Colrain men. Most of these men took the oath before other justices of the peace; a few were under indictment or in jail; a few were simply left off her list. For a complete list, see the oaths of allegiance in the MA 190:90–91, 118–19, 138, 146, 173; Black List County of Hampshire, Robert Treat Paine Papers, MHS; bills of indictment, Robert Treat Paine Papers, MHS; "A Return of Prisoners now confined in Gaol in Northampton . . . 9 April 1787," Robert Treat Paine Papers, MHS; "Names of the Persons Before Supreme Judicial Court, Northampton, April 1787," Suffolk County Court, File 159008; and "Number & Names of the People in Colrain that have Taken Arms Against Government in the year 1786 & 1787," Colrain Town Records, Pocumtuck Valley Memorial Association Library, Old Deerfield, Mass. The last document lists the participants by their military rank.

22. "Maj. Shepard's Estimate of the No. of Insurgents in Hampshire, Dec. 14, 1786," *The Bowdoin and Temple Papers, Collections of the Massachusetts Historical Society* (Boston, 1907), 66:116–17.

23. David P. Szatmary, *Shays' Rebellion* (Amherst, Mass., 1980), 113; Mason Green, *Springfield, 1636–1886* (Springfield, Mass., 1888), 330; *Hampshire Gazette,* April 11, 1787; Benjamin Lincoln to Colonel Murray, April 16, 1787, Robert Treat Paine Papers, MHS.

24. See especially Szatmary, *Shays' Rebellion*, chaps. 2 and 3. See also Robert J. Taylor, *Western Massachusetts in the Revolution* (Providence, 1954), chaps. 6 and 7; and Marion L. Starkey, *A Little Rebellion* (New York, 1955).

25. *New Haven Gazette*, December 14, 1786; E. P. Walton, ed., *Records of the Governor and Council of the State of Vermont*, 8 vols. (Montpelier, 1873–80), 3:360; Laurel Thatcher Ulrich, *A Midwife's Tale: The Life of Martha Ballard Based on Her Diary, 1785–1812* (New York, 1990), 86–87; Jere R. Daniell, *Experiment in Republicanism: New Hampshire Politics and the American Revolution, 1741–1794* (Cambridge, Mass., 1970), 183–205; Rachel N. Klein, *Unification of the Slave State: The Rise of the Planter Class in the South Carolina Backcountry, 1760–1808* (Chapel Hill, N.C., 1990), 126–34; Jean B. Lee, *The Price of Nationhood: The American Revolution in Charles County* (New York, 1994), 228–58; Main, *Social Structure of Revolutionary America*, 159–60; Terry Bouton, "A Road Closed: Rural Insurgency in Post-Independence Pennsylvania," *Journal of American History* 87 (December 2000): 858–62.

26. Taylor, *Western Massachusetts in the Revolution*, 78–87, 99–102; Theodore M. Hammett, "Revolutionary Ideology in Massachusetts: Thomas Allen's 'Vindication' of the Berkshire Constitutionalists," *WMQ* 33 (October 1976): 514–27.

27. Robert E. Moody, "Samuel Ely: Forerunner of Shays," *New England Quarterly* 5 (January 1932): 105–8; Franklin Bowditch Dexter, *Biographical Sketches of the Graduates of Yale College*, 5 vols. (New York, 1903), 3:67–69; Samuel Ely, "Two Sermons Preached at Somers, March 18, 1770, when the Church and People Were Under Peculiar Trials" (Hartford, 1771); Samuel Ely, *The Deformity of a Hideous Monster, Discovered in the Province of Maine* (Boston, 1797); diary of Jonathan Judd, February 14, April 12, May 6, 17, 1782, Forbes Library, Northampton, Mass.; Joseph Hawley to Caleb Strong, June 24, 1782, Hawley Papers, Box 1, New York Public Library; John Hancock, message, June 17, 1782, in E. M. Bacon, ed., *Supplement to Acts and Laws of Massachusetts* (Boston, 1896), 141; John H. Lockwood, *Western Massachusetts: A History, 1636–1925*, 2 vols. (New York, 1926), 1:115–18; Stephen A. Marini, "The Religious World of Daniel Shays," in Gross, *In Debt to Shays*, 267–69; Alan Taylor, *Liberty Men and Great Proprietors: The Revolutionary Settlement on the Maine Frontier, 1760–1820* (Chapel Hill, N.C., 1990), 105–8.

28. Van Beck Hall, *Politics Without Parties: Massachusetts, 1780–1791* (Pittsburgh, 1972), 195, 192. For a similar interpretation, see Forrest McDonald and Ellen Shapiro McDonald, *Requiem: Variations on Eighteenth Century Themes* (Lawrence, Kans., 1988), 65–66.

29. Calculated from two databases: participants in Shays's Rebellion and parties in debt suits. The latter database was constructed from the records of the Court of Common Pleas, Hampshire County, vol. 18, MA, microfilm no. 00886429.

30. Szatmary, *Shays' Rebellion*, 29, claims that 31.4 percent of Hampshire men sixteen years of age or older were involved in debt suits. That number, although very specific, is way too high. In most Hampshire towns, as in Colrain, a handful of men were sued repeatedly, and that drove up the number of lawsuits.

31. Colonel Christian Febiger to J. Sobotken, September 27, 1784, in "Extracts from a Merchant's Letters, 1784–1786," *Magazine of American History* 8 (1882): 352. See also Samuel Otis to Joseph Otis, February 6, 1785, Otis Papers, Columbia Uni-

versity; Martin Gay to Benjamin Holmes, October 7, 1785, Gray-Otis Collection, Columbia University; Stephen Higginson to John Adams, December 30, 1785, "Letters of Stephen Higginson," in *Annual Report of the American Historical Association* (Washington, D.C., 1896), 1:732; David P. Szatmary, "Shays' Rebellion in Springfield," in Martin Kaufman, ed., *Shays' Rebellion: Selected Essays* (Westfield, Mass., 1987), 3–4; Robert Haas, "The Forgotten Courtship of David and Marcy Spear," *Old-Time New England* 7 (January 1962): 67; William B. Weeden, *Economic and Social History of New England, 1620–1789*, 2 vols. (New York, 1963), 2:819; McDonald and McDonald, *Requiem*, 61–62.

Chapter 4. The Revolutionary Government and Its Beneficiaries

1. MA 189:429; C. O. Parmenter, *History of Pelham* (Amherst, Mass., 1898), 373; Carpenter & Morehouse, *The History of the Town of Amherst, Massachusetts* (Amherst, Mass., 1896), 126; *Hampshire Gazette*, October 4, 1786.

2. *Oxford English Dictionary*, 2d ed. (Oxford, 1989). See also George Rude, *The Crowd in History* (New York, 1964), 42.

3. John S. Bassett, "The Regulators of North Carolina, 1765–1771," in *American Historical Association Annual Report for the Year 1894* (Washington, D.C., 1895), 141–212; Marvin L. Michael Kay, "The North Carolina Regulation, 1766–1776: A Class Conflict," in Alfred F. Young, ed., *The American Revolution* (DeKalb, Ill., 1976), 71–124; James P. Whittenburg, "Planters, Merchants, and Lawyers: Social Change and the Origins of the North Carolina Regulation," *WMQ* 34 (1977): 215–38; Paul David Nelson, *William Tryon and the Course of Empire: A Life in British Imperial Service* (Chapel Hill, N.C., 1990), 70–89; Arthur Palmer Hudson, "Songs of the North Carolina Regulators," *WMQ* 4 (October 1947): 470–85. For this and other backcountry uprisings, see also Richard Maxwell Brown, "Back Country Rebellions and the Homestead Ethic in America, 1740–1799," in Richard Maxwell Brown and Don E. Fehrenbacher, eds., *Tradition, Conflict, and Modernization: Perspectives on the American Revolution* (New York, 1977), 83–85.

4. Richard Maxwell Brown, *The South Carolina Regulators* (Cambridge, Mass., 1963); Richard J. Hooker, ed., *The Carolina Backcountry on the Eve of the Revolution: The Journal and Other Writings of Charles Woodmason, Anglican Itinerant* (Chapel Hill, N.C., 1953); Rachel N. Klein, *Unification of the Slave State: The Rise of the Planter Class in the South Carolina Backcountry, 1760–1808* (Chapel Hill, N.C., 1990), 47–51.

5. *Boston Chronicle*, July 18–25, 1768; *Massachusetts Spy* (Boston), June 13, 1771.

6. Irving Mark, *Agrarian Conflicts in Colonial New York* (New York, 1940), chaps. 4–5; Patricia U. Bonomi, *A Factious People: Politics and Society in Colonial New York* (New York, 1971), chap. 6; Sung Bok Kim, *Landlord and Tenant in Colonial New York: Manorial Society, 1664–1775* (Chapel Hill, N.C., 1978), 281–415; Oscar Handlin, "The Eastern Frontier of New York," *New York History* 18 (1937): 50–75; Edward Countryman, "'Out of Bounds of the Law': Northern Land Rioters in the Eighteenth Century," in Young, *The American Revolution*, 37–69.

7. Michael A. Bellesiles, *Revolutionary Outlaws: Ethan Allen and the Struggle for*

Independence on the Vermont Frontier (Charlottesville, Va., 1993), chaps. 1–7; Robert E. Shalhope, *Bennington and the Green Mountain Boys: The Emergence of Liberal Democracy in Vermont, 1760–1850* (Baltimore, 1996), chaps. 1–5; Countryman, "'Out of Bounds of the Law,'" 37–69.

8. Edwin P. Hoyt, *The Damndest Yankees: Ethan Allen and His Clan* (Brattleboro, Vt., 1976), 32, 40, and passim.

9. Dr. William Whiting, "Some Brief Remarks on the Present State of Publick Affairs," in Stephen Riley, "Doctor William Whiting and Shays' Rebellion," *Proceedings of the American Antiquarian Society* 66 (January 1956): 131–32.

10. Because of its treatment of Tories and pacifists, historians are at odds over just how "democratic" the Pennsylvania constitution was. Cf. Elisha P. Douglass, *Rebels and Democrats: The Struggle for Equal Political Rights and Majority Rule During the American Revolution* (Chapel Hill, N.C., 1955), chap. 14; Eric Foner, *Tom Paine and Revolutionary America* (New York, 1976), chap. 4; Anne M. Ousterhout, "Controlling the Opposition in Pennsylvania During the American Revolution," *Pennsylvania Magazine of History and Biography* 105 (January 1981): 3–34; Owen S. Ireland, *Religion, Ethnicity, and Politics: Ratifying the Constitution in Pennsylvania* (University Park, Pa., 1995); and Francis Jennings, *The Creation of America: Through Revolution to Empire* (New York, 2000), chap. 28.

11. Bellesiles, *Revolutionary Outlaws*, 136–40; Jackson Turner Main, *The Sovereign States, 1775–1783* (New York, 1973), 176–77; Chilton Williamson, *Vermont in a Quandary* (Montpelier, 1949); Nathaniel Hendricks, "A New Look at the Ratification of the Vermont Constitution of 1777," *Vermont History* 34 (1966): 136–40; Gary A. Aichelle, "Making the Vermont Constitution: 1777–1824," *Vermont History* 56 (Summer 1988): 166–90; Robert J. Taylor, *Western Massachusetts in the Revolution* (Providence, 1954), 78–79.

12. Irwin H. Polishook, *Rhode Island and the Union, 1774–1795* (Evanston, Ill., 1969), 41–42; John P. Kaminski, "Democracy Run Rampant: Rhode Island in the Confederation," in James Kirby Martin, ed., *The Human Dimensions of Nation Making: Essays on Colonial and Revolutionary America* (Madison, Wis., 1976), 244.

13. John Adams, "Thoughts on Government" (1776), in Charles Francis Adams, ed., *Works of John Adams*, 10 vols. (Boston, 1850–56), 4:185–203.

14. Oscar Handlin and Mary Handlin, eds., *The Popular Sources of Political Authority: Documents on the Massachusetts Constitution of 1780* (Cambridge, Mass., 1966), 192–93; Main, *The Sovereign States, 1775–1783*, 179.

15. Michael Zuckerman, *Peaceable Kingdoms: New England Towns in the Eighteenth Century* (New York, 1970), 94–95, 105–6, 272–73.

16. Theophilus Parsons, *Memoir of Theophilus Parsons* (Boston, 1859), 359–63, 384–89; Handlin and Handlin, *Massachusetts Constitution of 1780*, 324–65.

17. See the responses of Greenwich, Hardwick, Charlemont, Belchertown, Rochester, Chesterfield, Williamstown, Sutton, New Salem, Lenox, Upton, Mendon, Blandford, Shelburne, Spencer, and Pelham, in Handlin and Handlin, *Massachusetts Constitution of 1780*, 212–13, 215–21, 226–28, 230–38, 244, 253–58, 262–64, 266–68, 281–82, 285–86, 301–3, 321–22.

18. Samuel Eliot Morison, "The Struggle over the Adoption of the Constitution

of Massachusetts, 1780," *Proceedings of the Massachusetts Historical Society* 50 (May 1917): 356–58; *Journal of the Convention for Framing a Constitution for the State of Massachusetts Bay, September 1, 1779, to June 16, 1780* (Boston, 1832).

19. Handlin and Handlin, *Massachusetts Constitution of 1780*, 334–35, 441–72; Main, *The Sovereign States, 1775–1783*, 181–83.

20. Morison, "Struggle over the Adoption of the Constitution of Massachusetts, 1780," 360–63, 396–400; Douglas, *Rebels and Democrats*, 209–10; Handlin and Handlin, *Massachusetts Constitution of 1780*, 693–700; MA 276:59; *Manual for the Constitutional Convention of 1917* (Boston, 1917), 22–23.

21. Handlin and Handlin, *Massachusetts Constitution of 1780*, 475–506, 533–626, 807–901. See also "A Lover of American Independence," in *Massachusetts Gazette* (Springfield), October 15, 1782.

22. MA 45:276; Handlin and Handlin, *Massachusetts Constitution of 1780*, 550.

23. Handlin and Handlin, *Massachusetts Constitution of 1780*, 538, 561–62, 483, 860.

24. Handlin and Handlin, *Massachusetts Constitution of 1780*, 475–506, 533–626, 807–901.

25. Zuckerman, *Peaceable Kingdoms*, 10–45; J. R. Pole, *Political Representation in England and the Origins of the American Republic* (New York, 1966), 38–75; Samuel Eliot Morison, *The Maritime History of Massachusetts, 1783–1860* (Boston, 1921), 28–29; Samuel Eliot Morison, "Comments on Ralph V. Harlow, 'Economic Conditions in Massachusetts, 1775–1783,'" in *Colonial Society of Massachusetts, Publications* 20 (1920): 192–93.

26. Whitney K. Bates, "The State Finances of Massachusetts, 1780–1789" (M.A. thesis, University of Wisconsin, 1948), 166; E. James Ferguson, *The Power of the Purse* (Chapel Hill, N.C., 1961), 245.

27. Bates, "Finances of Massachusetts," 91; Ferguson, *The Power of the Purse*, 245.

28. Ferguson, *The Power of the Purse*, 273–75. For information about individual creditors, two sources are especially valuable: William H. Dumont, "A Short Census of Massachusetts–1779," *National Genealogical Society Quarterly* 49–50 (1966–67) and the Subscription Register, Loan of 1790, Massachusetts, National Archives, University of Maryland branch. In recent years, the National Archives has been unable to locate the key document from these "Old Loan" records that lists the state creditors in 1790, their holdings, and how they obtained their holdings. I was able to obtain a microfilm copy, thanks to George Kennedy of Amherst, from the Church of Jesus Christ of Latter Day Saints. Some of these documents list holdings in pounds, others in dollars. To minimize confusion, I have converted the dollar figures to pounds, which was the Massachusetts currency at the time.

29. Hamilton Andrews Hill, "William Phillips and William Phillips, Father and Son, 1722–1837," *New England Historical and Genealogical Register* 39 (April 1885): 109–17; N. S. B. Gras, *The Massachusetts First National Bank of Boston, 1784–1934* (Cambridge, Mass., 1937), 17–18.

30. Benjamin Lincoln to George Washington, December 4, 1786 to March 4, 1787, in W. W. Abbot et al., *The Papers of George Washington: Confederation Series*, 6 vols. (Charlottesville, Va., 1995), 4:422.

31. Computed from data assembled primarily from List of Subscribers, MA 189:66,

217–18; "To the Forty Thousand Pound Loan established by the Act of the General Court, passed the 6th February 1787," Treasurer's Office, Journal B, 1786–1787, p. 477, MA; Gras, *First National Bank of Boston*, 530; *Boston Directory*, 1787; *Fleets Pocket Almanac . . . 1791* (Boston, 1790), 57.

32. J. S. Davis, *Essays in the Early History of American Corporations* (Cambridge, Mass., 1917), 2:179–83, 199.

33. *Hampshire Herald* (Springfield), March 7, 1786; *Massachusetts Gazette*, April 3, 1786.

34. *Hampshire Herald* (Springfield), December 7, 1786.

35. Joseph Hawley to Ephraim Wright, April 16, 1782, "Document," *American Historical Review* 36 (July 1931): 776–77; Richard D. Brown, "Shays Rebellion and Its Aftermath: A View from Springfield, Massachusetts, 1787," *WMQ* 40 (October 1983): 603, 599; David P. Szatmary, "Shays' Rebellion in Springfield," in Martin Kaufman, ed., *Shays' Rebellion: Selected Essays* (Westfield, Mass., 1987), 8.

36. *Massachusetts Centinel* (Boston), February 18, 1786; "Public Faith," *Massachusetts Centinel*, February 8, 1786; "Plain Truth," *Massachusetts Centinel*, February 18, 1786; "Objections Against Reducing the Public Debt Examined," *Massachusetts Centinel*, March 1, 1786; *Worcester Magazine* (April 1786): 32–33; "A Member of the Hatfield Convention," *Hampshire Gazette*, November 1, 1786.

37. Noah Webster to His Excellency Governor Bowdoin, March 15, 1787, in *The Bowdoin and Temple Papers, Collections of the Massachusetts Historical Society* (Boston, 1907), 66:173, 178–79.

38. Parmenter, *History of Pelham*, 367–70; E. P. Conklin, *Middlesex County and Its People* (New York, 1927), 2:99; Sidney Kaplan, "Veteran Officers and Politics in Massachusetts, 1783–1787," *WMQ* 9 (January 1952): 49.

39. Whiting, "Some Brief Remarks on the Present State of Publick Affairs," 133.

40. Oliver Dickinson's account book, 1783–93, Jones Library, Special Collections, Amherst, Mass.

41. Van Beck Hall, *Politics Without Parties: Massachusetts, 1780–1791* (Pittsburgh, 1972), 111.

42. Massachusetts Tax Evaluation List, 1785, MA. The town assessors of every Massachusetts town filled out one of these documents. So the information demanded by the state, as well as a town's response to it, can also be found in many town archives.

43. Bates, "Finances of Massachusetts," 96, 99; Harold Hitchings Burbank, "The General Property Tax in Massachusetts, 1775 to 1792" (Ph.D. diss., Harvard, 1915), 96–98; Franklin Russell Mullaly, "The Massachusetts Insurrection of 1786–1787" (M.A. thesis, Smith College, 1947), 10–11; Charles J. Bullock, *Historical Sketch of the Finances and Financial Policy of Massachusetts from 1780 to 1905* (New York, 1907), 5f.

44. Kaminski, "Democracy Run Rampant," 249–61; Polishook, *Rhode Island and the Union*, 133–42.

45. William G. Anderson, *The Price of Liberty: The Public Debt of the American Revolution* (Charlottesville, Va., 1983), 31; Polishook, *Rhode Island and the Union*, 115.

46. Anderson, *The Price of Liberty*, 31–32; B. U. Ratchford, *American State Debts* (Durham, N.C., 1941), 49; Polishook, *Rhode Island and the Union*, 115.

47. *United States Chronicle*, May 25, 1786; Francis Dana to Elbridge Gerry, September 2, 1787, Lloyd C. Stevens Collections, Morristown National Historical Park, Morristown, N.J., as cited in David P. Szatmary, *Shays' Rebellion* (Amherst, Mass., 1980), 51–52; Rufus King to Elbridge Gerry, August 26, 1786, in Charles R. King, ed., *The Life and Correspondence of Rufus King*, 6 vols. (New York, 1894), 1:189.

48. F. E. Oliver, ed., *The Diary of William Pynchon of Salem* (Boston, 1890), 54; Herbert S. Allan, *John Hancock: Patriot in Purple* (New York, 1948), 310; William M. Fowler, Jr., *The Baron of Beacon Hill* (Boston, 1980), 213–16, 259; Hall, *Politics Without Parties*, 133–36.

49. For Governor Bowdoin, a controversial figure, I have drawn together material from the following sources: Gordon E. Kershaw, *James Bowdoin II: Patriot and Man of the Enlightenment* (New York, 1991), chap. 3 and passim; Robert L. Volz, *Governor Bowdoin and His Family* (Brunswick, Maine, 1969); Hall, *Politics Without Parties*, 118–20; Forrest McDonald, *We the People* (Chicago, 1958), 200; Gras, *First National Bank of Boston*, 530; *Boston Directory*, 1787; Tingba Apidta, *The Hidden History of Massachusetts: A Guide for Black Folks* (Roxbury, Mass., 1995), 22–23; Gordon E. Kershaw, *The Kennebeck Proprietors* (Somerworth, N.H., 1975); Alan Taylor, *Liberty Men and Great Proprietors: The Revolutionary Settlement on the Maine Frontier, 1760–1820* (Chapel Hill, N.C., 1990), chaps. 1–3.

50. Rufus King to John Adams, October 3, 1786, in King, *Life and Correspondence*, 1:190; John Adams to Thomas Jefferson, November 30, 1786, in Lester J. Cappon, ed., *The Adams-Jefferson Letters*, 2 vols. (Chapel Hill, N.C., 1959), 1:156.

Chapter 5. Banner Towns and Core Families

1. Computed from data assembled from oaths of allegiance, town histories of Groton and Pepperell, the New England Genealogical Society's vital records of the towns of Groton and Pepperell to 1850, town tax assessments, local church and court records, and genealogical accounts of individual families. For help on the Groton area, I owe much to Thomas Keefe Callahan, who provided me with his excellent M.A. thesis "The Voice of the People of This County: The Birth of Popular Politics and Support for the Shaysite Insurrection in Groton, Massachusetts" (Harvard, 1992), and to Jeanne Palmer of the Lawrence Library, Pepperell, who spent an entire afternoon guiding me through local genealogical records.

2. Oaths of allegiance, MA; list of Amherst insurgents, Carpenter & Morehouse, *The History of the Town of Amherst, Massachusetts* (Amherst, Mass., 1896), 133; "Pay Roll of Capt. Moses Cook's Company in Colonel Elisha Porter's Regt., in Defense of the Government at Springfield, Sept. 1786," MA 191:173. For details on the Cooks and other Amherst families, I have relied on the resources of the Jones Library, Special Collections, Amherst. Especially valuable is the "Families of Amherst, Massachusetts," 4 vols., comp. James Avery Smith. On the Cooks's debt suits, see *Mary Ann Townsend v. Moses Cook, Jr.* (1785) and *Nathaniel Dickinson v. Clark Lawton and Moses Cook, Sr.* (1786), Court of Common Pleas, Hampshire County, vol. 18, MA, microfilm no. 00886429.

3. This is just an educated guess, based on tracking some fifteen hundred New England families.

4. Arthur W. Calhoun, *A Social History of the American Family*, 3 vols. (New York, 1945), vol. 2, passim; Bernard Bailyn, *The New England Merchants in the Seventeenth Century* (Cambridge, Mass., 1955); Bernard Farber, *Guardians of Virtue: Salem Families in 1800* (New York, 1972); Peter Dobkin Hall, "Marital Selection and Business in Massachusetts Merchant Families, 1700–1900," in Michael Gordon, ed., *The American Family in Social-Historical Perspective*, 2d ed. (New York, 1978), 101–14.

5. Computed from data on rebel families and Amherst Town List, August 1786, Jones Library, Special Collections, Amherst.

6. For a list of Amherst selectmen and other elected officials, see Carpenter & Morehouse, *History of the Town of Amherst*, Appendix A.

7. Hugh F. Bell and Andrew Raymond, "Early Amherst," in Theodore P. Greene, ed., *Essays on Amherst's History* (Amherst, Mass., 1978), 3–24; Kathleen Burns, "The Legacy of Rev. David Parsons in Light of the Shays' Rebellion" (seminar paper, University of Massachusetts, 1998); Laurence Emilio Rothenberg, "The History of Amherst during the American Revolution and Shays' Rebellion" (senior thesis, Amherst College, 1991), 63–64; Sylvester Judd, *History of Hadley* (Springfield, Mass., 1905), 407–8.

8. Bell and Raymond, "Early Amherst," 3–24; Burns, "Legacy of Rev. David Parsons"; Rothenberg, "History of Amherst," 63–64.

9. For the incorporators of the Second Church, see Carpenter & Morehouse, *History of the Town of Amherst*, 113.

10. *Simeon Strong and David Parsons (for the estate of David Parsons) v. Inhabitants of Amherst (1786)*, Court of Common Pleas, Hampshire County, vol. 18, MA, microfilm no. 00886429.

11. On military service, a handy guide is "Hampshire County Soldiers and Sailors in the War of the Revolution," Forbes Library, Northampton, Mass. (1939), an index to *Massachusetts Soldiers and Sailors of the Revolutionary War*, 17 vols. (Boston, 1896–1908). I have repeatedly relied on both sources throughout this chapter. For officers and men of the Massachusetts Line, some additional information can be gleaned from Francis B. Heitman, *Historical Register of Officers of the Continental Army* (Washington, D.C., 1914) and Fred Anderson Berg, *Encyclopedia of Continental Army Units* (Harrisburg, Pa., 1972).

12. Diary of Jonathan Judd, February 14, April 12, May 6, 17, 1782, Forbes Library, Northampton, Mass.; John Hancock, message of June 17, 1782, in E. M. Bacon, ed., *Supplement to Acts and Laws of Massachusetts* (Boston, 1896), 141; *Acts and Laws of Massachusetts, 1782–1783*, 2:6–7, 240–41, 248, 278–79, 81–82; John H. Lockwood, *Western Massachusetts: A History, 1636–1925*, 2 vols. (New York, 1926), 1:115–18; James M. Craft, *History of the Town of Whately, Mass, 1661–1899* (Conway, Mass., 1899), 233–34, 237.

13. Rothenberg, "History of Amherst," 46–47.

14. Black List County of Hampshire, Robert Treat Paine Papers, MHS; Suffolk County Court, File 160538; Report of General William Shepard, February 27, 1787, MA 190:379–81.

15. Mattoon to Thomas Cutler, May 6, 1787, MA 189:300–301. In this letter, Mattoon essentially argued that Henry McCulloch, the man facing the gallows, was just a dumb youth who had been misled by the leaders of Pelham. In fact, McCulloch was thirty-six years old and Mattoon's senior by four years. For further details about McCulloch and his pardon, see Gregory H. Nobles, "The Politics of Patriarchy in Shays's Rebellion: The Case of Henry McCulloch," *Dublin Seminar for New England Folklife, Annual Proceedings* (1985): 37–47.

16. For information on the Grays and other Pelhamites, I have relied primarily on C. O. Parmenter, *History of Pelham* (Amherst, Mass., 1898); Daniel W. Shelton, "'Elementary Feelings': Pelham, Massachusetts, in Rebellion" (honors thesis, Amherst College, 1981); the New England Genealogical Society's *Vital Records of Pelham to 1850*; Gregory H. Nobles, "Shays's Neighbors: The Context of Rebellion in Pelham, Massachusetts," in Robert A. Gross, ed., *In Debt to Shays: The Bicentennial of an Agrarian Rebellion* (Charlottesville, Va., 1993), 185–203; and the genealogical collection assembled by Robert Lord Keyes of the Pelham Historical Society. Subsequent to my using Keyes's collection, he published "Who Were the Pelham Shaysites?" *Historical Journal of Massachusetts* (Winter 2000): 23–55. His emphasis differs from mine. So do some of his findings. The main difference is that I began with a longer list of rebels, relying on jail records and indictments as well as the published list of oath takers in Parmenter's town history.

17. Computed from "Table on Ranked Evaluations, 1784," in Shelton, "'Elementary Feelings.'"

18. Of the many fine studies of the Scots-Irish and their cultural outlook, I have relied mainly on James G. Leyburn, *The Scotch-Irish: A Social History* (Chapel Hill, N.C., 1962); David Hackett Fisher, *Albion's Seed: Four British Folkways in America* (New York, 1989), 605ff; Carlton Jackson, *A Social History of the Scotch Irish* (New York, 1993), chap. 6.

19. Rory Fitzpatrick, *God's Frontiersmen: The Scots-Irish Epic* (London, 1989), 52–55; Kenneth W. Keller, "The Origins of Ulster Scot Emigration to America: A Survey of Recent Research," *American Presbyterian* 70 (1992); A. L. Perry, *Scotch-Irish in New England* (Boston, 1891), 8–21; Rich Angers, "The Scotch-Irish: From Scotland to Pelham" (seminar paper, University of Massachusetts, 1998).

20. Fisher, *Albion's Seed*, 662–68; Raymond Gillespie, *Colonial Ulster: The Settlement of East Ulster, 1600–1641* (Cork, 1985), 147–50. There is a long-standing debate over whether Lowland Scots in northern Ireland had intermarried with the Irish. See Leyburn, *The Scotch-Irish*, chap. 10.

21. Parmenter, *History of Pelham*, 410–11, 124–27.

22. James Russell Trumbull, *History of Northampton*, 2 vols. (Northampton, Mass., 1898–1902), 2:373–74.

23. Oscar Handlin and Mary Handlin, eds., *The Popular Sources of Political Authority: Documents on the Massachusetts Constitution of 1780* (Cambridge, Mass., 1966), 322, 591.

24. Stephen Burroughs, *Memoirs of Stephen Burroughs*, 2 vols. (Hanover, N.H., 1798), 50–54; Parmenter, *History of Pelham*, 320–40; Robert A. Gross, "The Confidence Man and the Preacher: The Cultural Politics of Shays's Rebellion," in Gross, *In Debt to Shays*, 299–301.

25. For information on the Days, Leonards, Elys, and other West Springfield families, I have relied on the New England Genealogical Society's *Vital Records of West Springfield to 1850* as well as on a wide assortment of town histories and town records. On the Day family, I also gleaned much from George Edward Day, *A Genealogical Record of the Descendants in the Male Line of Robert Day . . .* , 2d ed. (Northampton, Mass., 1848). On the Leonard family, I obtained much more from John Adams Vinton, *The Giles Memorial* (Boston, 1864), which traces not only the male line but also the female line. My most helpful source, however, was the town historian of West Springfield, Bernie Lally, who had collected a wealth of information which he was happy to share.

26. Computed from data: West Springfield Assessment, June 26, 1786, Connecticut Valley Historical Museum, Springfield, Mass.

27. William Buell Sprague, *Annals of the American Pulpit*, 9 vols. (New York, 1857–69), 1:530–31; Gross, "The Confidence Man and the Preacher," 308.

28. Joseph Lathrop, *A Sermon, Preached in the First Parish in West-Springfield, December 14, 1786 . . .* (Springfield, Mass., 1787), especially 5, 15, 23; Moses King, ed., *King's Handbook of Springfield* (Springfield, Mass., 1884), 52–53; Richard D. Brown, "Shays's Rebellion and the Ratification of the Federal Constitution in Massachusetts," in Richard Beeman, Stephen Botein, and Edward C. Carter II, eds., *Beyond Confederation: Origins of the Constitution and American National Identity* (Chapel Hill, N.C., 1987), 117–18.

29. For information on the Graves, Smith, and other Whately families, I have relied on the New England Genealogical Society's *Vital Records of Whately to 1850*, genealogical information in James M. Craft, *History of the Town of Whately, Mass., 1661–1899* (Conway, Mass., 1899), and other town histories, as well as documents assembled by Professors Paul Boyer and Stephen Nissenbaum in the DuBois Library, University of Massachusetts, Special Collections.

30. Computed from Whately Property Evaluations, 1784 (Whately, Mass.).

31. J. H. Temple, *History of the Town of Whately* (Boston, 1872), 158; diary of Elizabeth Porter, February 22, 1787, Porter-Phelps-Huntington Papers, Amherst College.

32. Temple, *History of the Town of Whately*, 158.

33. For Colrain, I have relied primarily on the New England Genealogical Society's *Vital Records of Colrain to 1850* and Lois McClellan Patrie's *History of Colrain, Massachusetts, with Genealogies of Early Families* (Troy, N.Y., 1974). In a few cases, I have also acquired information from gravestones in Colrain.

34. MA 276:45; Handlin and Handlin, *Massachusetts Constitution of 1780*, 550–51.

35. Computed from Colrain Tax List, May 1, 1783, Colrain Papers, Pocumtuck Valley Memorial Association Library, Old Deerfield, Mass.

36. Charles H. McClellan, *The Early Settlers of Colrain, Mass.* (Greenfield, Mass., 1885), 63–66; Patrie, *History of Colrain*, 89.

37. Henry Lee to Washington, October 1, 1786, Henry Knox to Washington, March 19, 1787, in W. W. Abbot et al., eds., *The Papers of George Washington: Confederation Series*, 6 vols. (Charlottesville, Va., 1995), 4:281; 5:97.

38. North Callahan, *Henry Knox: George Washington's General* (New York, 1958);

Alan Taylor, *Liberty Men and Great Proprietors: The Revolutionary Settlement on the Maine Frontier, 1760–1820* (Chapel Hill, N.C., 1990), 38–39, 47.

39. "List of Persons who the [Worcester] Grand Jurors found Bills against for Treason, April term, 1787," Ward Family Papers, AAS; warrant of arrest to Sheriff of Worcester County, January 19, 1787, MA 189:75; Indictments for Treason, Sedition, Worcester, 1787, Suffolk County Court, File 155325; Heitman, *Officers of the Continental Army*, 583; J. M. Stone, *History of the Town of Hubbardston* (Hubbardston, Mass., 1881), 367–68, 62; Sidney Kaplan, "Veteran Officers and Politics in Massachusetts, 1783–1787," *WMQ* 9 (January 1952): 51.

40. Adam Wheeler to the public, Hubbardston, November 7, 1786, in *Worcester Magazine*, fourth week in November 1786.

41. Computed from data: Captain Solomon Allen's payroll, September 1786, MA 192:474; Captain Russell's payroll, January 1787, MA 192:503; "Hampshire County Soldiers and Sailors in the War of the Revolution"; *Massachusetts Soldiers and Sailors of the Revolutionary War*.

42. Computed from data: John H. Lockwood, *Westfield and Its Historic Influences, 1669–1919*, 2 vols. (Springfield, Mass., 1922), 2:113–14, 494–99, and passim; *Massachusetts Soldiers and Sailors of the Revolutionary War*.

43. Computed from data: Oaths of allegiance, MA 190:70, 81, 84, 89, 112, 176, 177, 210; Black List County of Hampshire, Robert Treat Paine Papers, MHS; warrants of arrest to Sheriff of Hampshire County, January 19 and February 15, 1787, MA 189:81–82, 135; bills of indictment, Robert Treat Paine Papers, MHS; "Names of the Persons Before Supreme Judicial Court, Northampton, April 1787," Suffolk County Court, File 159008; "A Return of Prisoners now confined in Gaol in Northampton . . . 9 April 1787," Robert Treat Paine Papers, MHS; Lockwood, *Westfield and Its Historic Influences*, 2:113–14, 126–27, 494–99, and passim; *Massachusetts Soldiers and Sailors of the Revolutionary War*.

44. William Shepard to Benjamin Lincoln, February 19, 1787, in Frederick J. Allis, Jr., and Wayne A. Frederick, eds., *The Benjamin Lincoln Papers* (Cambridge, Mass., 1977), microfilm; Lockwood, *Westfield and Its Historic Influences*, 2:113–14, 127, and passim.

45. Elnathan Haskell to Colonel Pratt, January 31, February 1, 1787, Knox Papers, MHS.

46. Cf. diary of Samuel King, September 17, 1786, Pocumtuck Valley Memorial Association Library, Old Deerfield, Mass.; diary of Elizabeth Porter, December 14, 17, 1786, January 7, 28–29, 1787; Lathrop, *Sermon*; Timothy Newell to John Hancock, June 10, 1787, MA 190:16; Brown, "Shays Rebellion and Its Aftermath: A View from Springfield, Massachusetts, 1787," *WMQ* 40 (October 1983): 598–615; Emory Washburn, *Historical Sketches of the Town of Leicester . . .* (Boston, 1860), 331; Arthur Chase, *History of Ware, Massachusetts* (Boston, 1911), 93–97; comment of the Reverend Samuel Bigelow, August 31, 1787, in Isaac Backus, *A Church History of New England. . . with Reference to the Baptists*, 3 vols. (Philadelphia, 1839), 2:470; John Langton Sibley, *Biographical Sketches of the Graduates of Harvard University*, 17 vols. (Boston, 1933–75), 17:133, 246.

47. William Allen, "Thomas Allen," in Sprague, *Annals of the American Pulpit*,

1:607–12; Sibley, *Biographical Sketches of the Graduates of Harvard*, 15:159; J. E. A. Smith, *The History of Pittsfield, Mass., 1734–1800* (Boston, 1869), 399.

48. Thomas Robbins, *The Diary of Thomas Robbins*, ed. Increase N. Tarbox, 2 vols. (Boston, 1886), 1:33; Franklin Dexter Bowditch, *Biographical Sketches of the Graduates of Yale College*, 6 vols. (New York, 1885–1912), 2:772.

49. Chase, *History of Ware*, 95–97.

50. John L. Brooke, "A Deacon's Orthodoxy: Religion, Class, and the Moral Economy of Shays's Rebellion," in Gross, *In Debt to Shays*, 207; John L. Brooke, *The Heart of the Commonwealth: Society and Political Culture in Worcester County, Massachusetts, 1713–1861* (New York, 1989), 214–21; Stephen A. Marini, "The Religious World of Daniel Shays," in Gross, *In Debt to Shays*, 249–77; Harold Field Worthley, *An Inventory of the Records of the Particular (Congregational) Churches of Massachusetts Gathered 1620–1805* (Cambridge, Mass., 1970), passim.

Chapter 6. Reverberations

1. *The Diary of William Bentley, D.D.*, 4 vols. (Salem, Mass., 1905), 2:58.

2. Whitney K. Bates, "The State Finances of Massachusetts, 1780–1789" (M.A. thesis, University of Wisconsin, 1948), 131–33, Appendix 3.

3. Bates, "Finances of Massachusetts," 131–33, Appendix 3; E. James Ferguson, *The Power of the Purse* (Chapel Hill, N.C., 1961), 247–48; Van Beck Hall, *Politics Without Parties: Massachusetts, 1780–1791* (Pittsburgh, 1972), 41.

4. Bates, "Finances of Massachusetts," Appendix 3; Harold Hitchings Burbank, "The General Property Tax in Massachusetts, 1775 to 1792" (Ph.D diss., Harvard, 1915), 96–98; Hall, *Politics Without Parties*, 97.

5. Royall Tyler to Benjamin Lincoln, February 18, 1787, MA 318: 366; Royall Tyler Report to Lincoln, March 1787, Tyler Papers, Vermont Historical Society; Michael A. Bellesiles, *Revolutionary Outlaws: Ethan Allen and the Struggle for Independence on the Vermont Frontier* (Charlottesville, Va., 1993), 252; Robert E. Shalhope, *Bennington and the Green Mountain Boys: The Emergence of Liberal Democracy in Vermont, 1760–1850* (Baltimore, 1996), 191.

6. Harold C. Syrett and Jacob E. Cooke, eds., *The Papers of Alexander Hamilton*, 27 vols. (New York, 1961–87), 4:112–18, 126–41; John C. Miller, *Alexander Hamilton and the Growth of the New Nation* (New York, 1959), 131–33.

7. E. P. Walton, ed., *Records of the Governor and Council of the State of Vermont*, 8 vols. (Montpelier, 1783–80), 3:379–80, 423–38; Bellesiles, *Revolutionary Outlaws*, 253–54.

8. Miller, *Alexander Hamilton*, 133; Peter S. Onuf, *The Origins of the Federal Republic: Jurisdictional Controversies in the United States, 1775–1787* (Philadelphia, 1983), 103–45.

9. Report of William Shepard, February 27, 1787, MA 190:379–81; John H. Lockwood, *Western Massachusetts: A History, 1636–1925*, 2 vols. (New York, 1926), 1:189–90; Megan Breen, "Two Amherst Leaders: Reuben Dickinson and Joel Billings" (seminar paper, University of Massachusetts, 1998), 6; James Avery Smith, "Families of Amherst," entry 1584, Jones Library, Special Collections, Amherst.

10. "List of Persons who the [Worcester] Grand Jurors found Bills against for Treason, April term, 1787," Ward Family Papers, AAS; Indictments for Treason, Sedition, Worcester 1787, Suffolk County Court, File 155325; warrant of arrest to Sheriff of Worcester County, January 19, 1787, MA 189:75; Sidney Kaplan, "Veteran Officers and Politics in Massachusetts, 1783–1787," *WMQ* 9 (January 1952): 51; Francis B. Heitman, *Historical Register of Officers of the Continental Army* (Washington, D.C., 1914), 282; Lucius R. Paige, *History of Hardwick* (Boston, 1883), 161, 396.

11. J. S. Davis, *Essays in the Early History of American Corporations* (Cambridge, Mass., 1917) 2:179–183, 199; Ferguson, *The Power of the Purse*, 248, 256; William G. Anderson, *The Price of Liberty: The Public Debt of the American Revolution* (Charlottesville, Va., 1983), 41.

12. Hall, *Politics Without Parties*, 40; Robert A. East, *Business Enterprise in the American Revolutionary Era* (New York, 1938), 320–21; William G. Sumner, *The Financier and Finances of the Revolution*, 2 vols. (New York, 1891), 2:253ff; Orsamus Turner, *History of the Pioneer Settlement of the Phelps and Gorham's Purchase* (Rochester, N.Y., 1851).

13. Alexander Hamilton to Robert Morris, August 13, 1782; Hamilton to George Washington, April 8, 1783; Hamilton to John Dickinson, September 25–30, 1783, in Syrett and Cooke, *Papers of Alexander Hamilton*, 3:138–41, 318, 438–58.

14. Merchants and Traders of Boston to Governor Bowdoin, June 4, 1785; Committee of Tradesmen and Manufacturers to Governor Bowdoin, June 7, 1785, in *The Bowdoin and Temple Papers: Collections of the Massachusetts Historical Society* (Boston, 1907), 66:50–53.

15. Massachusetts Delegates to Governor Bowdoin, August 18 and September 3, 1785, Rufus King to Nathan Dane, September 17, 1785, Massachusetts Delegates to Governor Bowdoin, November 2, 1785, in Edmund C. Burnett, ed., *Letters of Members of the Continental Congress*, 8 vols. (Washington, D.C., 1936), 8:206–10, 218–19, 245–46; Nathan Dane to Rufus King, October 8, 1785 and King to Elbridge Gerry, May 1, 1786, in Charles R. King, ed., *The Life and Correspondence of Rufus King*, 6 vols. (New York, 1894), 1:67–69, 93.

16. Rufus King to Jonathan Jackson, June 11, 1786, Theodore Sedgwick to Caleb Strong, August 6, 1786, in Burnett, *Letters of Members of the Continental Congress*, 8:389–90, 415–16; *Acts and Laws of the Commonwealth of Massachusetts, 1786*, ed. E. M. Bacon (Boston, 1890–97), 4:286–87; Records of the Governors' Council, August 8–24, 1786, MA.

17. That Shays's Rebellion provided the spark for the Constitutional Convention has had a long and distinguished history. George Washington and James Madison, among others, saw it as the catalyst in 1787. Later, so did John Fiske and John Bach McMaster among prominent nineteenth-century historians; and Forrest McDonald, Jackson Turner Main, and Gordon Wood among prominent twentieth-century historians. (See Fiske, *The Critical Period of American History, 1783–1789* [Boston, 1888]; McMaster, *A History of the People of the United States from the Revolution to the Civil War*, 8 vols. [New York, 1883–1913]; McDonald, *We the People: The Economic Origins of the Constitution* [Chicago, 1958]; Main, *The Antifederalists: Critics of the Constitution, 1781–1787* [Chapel Hill, N.C., 1961]; Wood, *The Creation of the American Republic, 1776–1787* [Chapel Hill, N.C., 1969]). Robert A. Feer has challenged this interpre-

tation, but his challenge has barely made a dent in the literature. (See Feer, "Shays's Rebellion" [Ph.D. diss., Harvard, 1958] and Feer, "Shays's Rebellion and the Constitution: A Study in Causation," *New England Quarterly*, 42 [1969]: 388–410.) For a more recent survey of the literature, see Rock Brynner, "'Fire Beneath Our Feet': Shays' Rebellion and Its Constitutional Impact" (Ph.D. diss., Columbia, 1993), 264–93.

18. Stephen Higginson to John Adams, August 8, December 30, 1785, July 1786, Higginson to Henry Knox, November 12, 25, 1786, January 20, February 13, 1787, Higginson to Nathan Dane, March 3, 1787, in "Letters of Stephen Higginson," *Annual Report of the American Historical Association* (Washington, D.C., 1896), 1:724–25, 729, 741–45, 751–54; William Sullivan, *The Public Men of the Revolution* (Philadelphia, 1847), 391; Thomas W. Higginson, *Life of Stephen Higginson* (Boston, 1907), 90–95.

19. Brooks to Oliver Prescott, November 25, 1786, as quoted in Feer, "Shays's Rebellion," 328 n. 2. For biographical information on Brooks, see *Dictionary of American Biography*, 3:80; Heitman, *Historical Register of Officers of the Continental Army*, 123; Fred Anderson Berg, *Encyclopedia of Continental Army Units* (Harrisburg, Pa., 1972), 73, 149; Ronald P. Formisano, *The Transformation of Political Culture, Massachusetts Parties, 1790s–1840s* (New York, 1983), 63–65.

20. Mercy Warren to John Adams, December 1786, Mercy Warren Papers, MHS; Mercy Warren, *History of the Rise, Progress and Termination of the American Revolution* . . . (Boston, 1805), 3:346.

21. George Richards Minot to Nathan Dane, March 3, 1787, in *Proceedings of the Massachusetts Historical Society* 48 (June 1915): 430. See also George Richards Minot, *The History of the Insurrections in Massachusetts* (Worcester, Mass., 1788), 105.

22. Richard Krauel, "Prince Henry of Prussia and the Regency of the United States, 1786," *American Historical Review* 17 (October 1911): 44–51; Louise B. Dunbar, *A Study of "Monarchical" Tendencies in the United States from 1776 to 1801* (Urbana, Ill., 1922), chap. 4; Feer, "Shays's Rebellion," 474.

23. Washington to the Secretary for Foreign Affairs, August 1, 1786, in John C. Fitzpatrick, ed., *Writings of George Washington*, 39 vols. (Washington, D.C., 1931–44), 28:503–4.

24. Humphreys to Washington, November 1 and 9, 1786, in W. W. Abbot et al., eds., *The Papers of George Washington: Confederation Series*, 6 vols. (Charlottesville, Va., 1995), 4:324–25, 350–51.

25. Knox to Washington, October 23, 1786, in Abbot et al., *Papers of George Washington: Confederation Series*, 4:300.

26. Donald Jackson and Dorothy Twohig, eds., *The Diaries of George Washington*, 7 vols. (Charlottesville, Va., 1976), 1:18 and passim. Of the many books that deal with Washington and the backcountry, eye-opening are Bernard Knollenberg, *George Washington: The Virginia Period, 1732–1775* (Durham, N.C., 1964), chap. 14, and Thomas Slaughter, *The Whiskey Rebellion: Frontier Epilogue to the American Revolution* (New York, 1986), chap. 5.

27. Edward Carrington to Governor Edmund Randolph, December 8, 1786, in Burnett, *Letters of Members of the Continental Congress*, 8:516; James Madison to George

Mutter, January 7, 1787, in William T. Hutchinson et al., *The Papers of James Madison*, 17 vols. (Chicago, 1962–91), 9:321; George Washington to David Humphreys, December 26, 1786 in Abbot et al., *Papers of George Washington: Confederation Series*, 4:478.

28. Washington to Madison, November 5, 18, 1786, in Abbot et al., *Papers of George Washington: Confederation Series*, 4:331–32, 382–83.

29. Washington to Henry Knox, February 3, 1787, in Abbot et al., *Papers of George Washington: Confederation Series*, 5:9.

30. Washington to Henry Knox, December 26, 1786, February 3, 1787, in Abbot et al., *Papers of George Washington: Confederation Series*, 4:481–82; 5:9.

31. Madison to Washington, November 8, 1786, in Hutchinson et al., *Papers of James Madison*, 9:166.

32. Washington to Lafayette, June 6, 1787, in Abbot et al., *Papers of George Washington: Confederation Series*, 5:222.

33. Brynner, "'Fire Beneath our Feet,'" 180–217, 256. See also Paul M. Thompson, "The Reaction to Shays' Rebellion," *Massachusetts Legal History* 4 (1998): 37–61.

34. Max Farrand, ed., *The Records of the Federal Convention of 1787*, rev. ed., 4 vols. (New Haven, Conn., 1966), 1:318.

35. Farrand, *Records of the Federal Convention*, 1:48.

36. Farrand, *Records of the Federal Convention*, 1:406–7.

37. Farrand, *Records of the Federal Convention*, 2:332. For a recent analysis of Shays's Rebellion and the militia debate, see also Lawrence Delbert Cress, *Citizens in Arms: The Army and the Militia in American Society to the War of 1812* (Chapel Hill, N.C., 1982), 95–98, and Don Higginbotham, "The Federalized Militia Debate: A Neglected Aspect of Second Amendment Scholarship," *WMQ* 55 (January 1998): 43–44.

38. Farrand, *Records of the Federal Convention*, 2:317.

39. Farrand, *Records of the Federal Convention*, 2:326, 330–32.

40. Farrand, *Records of the Federal Convention*, 2:318, 386–87; 3:318–19.

41. For the details, see Leonard L. Richards, *The Slave Power: The Free North and Southern Domination, 1780–1860* (Baton Rouge, La., 2000), 32–36.

42. For further particulars on the "dirty compromise," see Paul Finkelman, *Slavery and the Founders: Race and Liberty in the Age of Jefferson* (Armonk, N.Y., 1996), 19–29.

Chapter 7. Climax

1. *Pennsylvania Gazette*, September 5, 12, 1787. Also quoted in Merrill Jensen, John P. Kaminski, and Gaspare J. Saladino, eds., *The Documentary History of the Ratification of the Constitution*, 16 vols. (Madison, Wis., 1976–88), 13:192.

2. *Pennsylvania Gazette*, September 26, 1787.

3. "Centinel [Samuel Bryan] to the Freemen of Pennsylvania," *Independent Gazetteer*, October 5, 1787, in Cecelia M. Kenyon, ed., *The Antifederalists* (Indianapolis, 1966), 13.

4. Pauline Maier, *The Old Revolutionaries: Political Lives in the Age of Samuel Adams*

(New York, 1980), 164–200; Jack N. Rakove, *Original Meanings: Politics and Ideas in the Making of the Constitution* (New York, 1996), 108–10; Washington to James Madison, October 10, 1787, in W. W. Abbot et al., eds., *The Papers of George Washington: Confederation Series*, 6 vols. (Charlottesville, Va., 1995), 5:366.

5. Richard Henry Lee, "Observation Leading to a Fair Examination of the System of Government, Proposed by the Late Convention . . . 1787, No. 5," in Paul Leicester Ford, ed., *Pamphlets on the Constitution of the United States* (New York, 1888), 321. For nearly two hundred years this pamphlet was attributed to Lee. In recent years, his authorship has been questioned. Cf. Kenyon, *The Antifederalists*, 197; Gordon S. Wood, "The Authorship of the *Letters from the Federal Farmer*," *WMQ* 31 (April 1974): 299–308, and Robert H. Webking, "Melancton Smith and the *Letters from the Federal Farmer*," *WMQ* 44 (July 1987): 510–28.

6. James Wilson, December 11, 1787, as quoted in Rock Brynner, "'Fire Beneath Our Feet': Shays' Rebellion and Its Constitutional Impact" (Ph.D. diss., Columbia, 1993), 226.

7. Knox to ———, January 3, 1788, Knox Papers, MHS; Knox to ———, February 10, 1788, in Francis S. Drake, *Life and Correspondence of Henry Knox* (Boston, 1873), 150.

8. Madison to Washington, January 20, 1788, in William T. Hutchinson et al., eds., *The Papers of James Madison*, 17 vols. (Chicago, 1962–91), 10:399.

9. Elbridge Gerry, "Hon. Mr. Gerry's Objections to Signing the National Constitution," *Massachusetts Centinel*, November 3, 1787.

10. Saul Cornell, *The Other Founders: Anti-Federalism and the Dissenting Tradition in America, 1788–1828* (Chapel Hill, N.C., 1999), 25, 28–30, 309.

11. Rufus King to James Madison, January 27, 1788, in William T. Hutchinson et al., *Papers of James Madison*, 10:436–37; Charles R. King, ed., *The Life and Correspondence of Rufus King*, 6 vols. (New York, 1894), 1:314, 317; Samuel Bannister Harding, *The Contest over the Ratification of the Federal Constitution in the State of Massachusetts* (New York, 1896), 78–79.

12. Samuel Adams to Richard Henry Lee, December 3, 1787, in William V. Wells, *The Life and Public Services of Samuel Adams*, 3 vols. (Boston, 1865), 3:251–53; *Massachusetts Centinel*, January 9, 1788; Stephanie Rodgers, "Samuel Adams and the Constitution" (seminar paper, University of Massachusetts, 2000).

13. Rufus King to James Madison, January 27, 1788, in Hutchinson et al., *Papers of James Madison*, 10:436–37; King, *Life and Correspondence*, 1:314, 317; Harding, *Contest over the Ratification*, 78–79.

14. Samuel Nasson to George Thacher, January 22, 1788, Thacher Papers, Boston Public Library.

15. Knox to ———, February 10, 1788, in Drake, *Life and Correspondence of Henry Knox*, 150; Henry Jackson to Henry Knox, February 3, 1788, Knox Papers, MHS; Benjamin Lincoln to George Washington, February 3, 1788, in Abbot et al., *Papers of George Washington: Confederation Series*, 6:82.

16. Richard Lebaron Bowen, *Early Rehoboth*, 2 vols. (Rehoboth, Mass., 1946), 2:87; D. Hamilton Hurd, *History of Bristol County* (Philadelphia, 1883), 477, 487; Senate Journal, June 8, 1787; Lisa Paulhus, "Phanuel Bishop and Bristol County's Role in

Shays' Rebellion and the Ratification of the Federal Constitution" (seminar paper, University of Massachusetts, 2000).

17. "List of Persons who the [Worcester] Grand Jurors found Bills against for Treason, April term, 1787," Ward Family Papers, Box 16, AAS; "A Register of the Names of Criminals in the Gaol in the County of Worcester," Suffolk County Court, File 155297; Arrests and Trials of Worcester (County) Insurgents, 1787, Shays Rebellion Collection, Folder 5, AAS; Indictments for Treason, Sedition, Worcester, 1787, Suffolk County Court, File 155325; Kenneth Campbell, "The Constitution From Big to Little: How the Bay State Helped Forge a Nation Despite Caleb Curtis' Best Efforts" (seminar paper, University of Massachusetts, 2000).

18. Oath of allegiance, MA, 190:170; Samuel Abbott Green, *Groton During the Revolution* (Groton, Mass., 1900), 185; Green, *Epitaphs from the Old Burying Ground in Groton, Massachusetts* (Boston, 1878).

19. Black List County of Hampshire, Robert Treat Paine Papers, MHS.

20. Black List County of Hampshire, Robert Treat Paine Papers, MHS; warrant of arrest to Sheriff of Hampshire County, January 19, 1787, MA 189: 81–82; bills of indictment, Robert Treat Paine Papers, MHS; "Names of the Persons Before Supreme Judicial Court, Northampton, April 1787," Suffolk County Court, File 159008; "List of Persons who the [Worcester] Grand Jurors found Bills against for Treason," April term, 1787, Ward Family Papers, AAS; "A Register of the Names of Criminals in the Gaol in the County of Worcester," Suffolk County Court, File 155297; Arrests and Trials of Worcester (County) Insurgents, 1787, Shays Rebellion Collection, Folder 5, AAS; Indictments for Treason, Sedition, Worcester 1787, Suffolk County Court, File 155325; warrant of arrest to Sheriff of Worcester County, January 19, and March 9, 1787, MA 189:75, 210.

21. Edward Pearson Pressy, *History of Montague: A Typical Puritan Town* (Montague, Mass., 1910), 167; Paul Jenkins, *The Conservative Rebel: A Social History of Greenfield, Massachusetts* (Greenfield, Mass., 1982), 44–45.

22. MA 190:25.

23. William Cushing et al. to James Bowdoin, Northampton, April 8, 1787, MA 190:417–19; Increase Sumner to Elizabeth Sumner, April 8, 1787, as quoted in *Berkshire Eagle*, September 30, 1946; MA 190:25.

24. MA 190:138.

25. Hugh F. Bell and Andrew Raymond, "Early Amherst," in Theodore P. Greene, ed., *Essays on Amherst's History* (Amherst, Mass., 1978), 27–28; Black List County of Hampshire, Robert Treat Paine Papers, MHS; oath of allegiance, MA 190:209.

26. Jonathan Elliot, ed., *Debates of the State Conventions on the Adoption of the Federal Constitution*, 5 vols. (New York, 1888), 2:182.

27. Computed from data in George Donald Melville, "Evidences of Economic and Social Influences at Work in the Massachusetts Convention which Ratified the Federal Constitution" (M.A. thesis, University of New Hampshire, 1920), 67, 71–89; and Elliot, *Debates of the State Conventions*, 2:178–81.

28. David P. Szatmary, *Shays' Rebellion* (Amherst, Mass., 1980), 133.

29. Quoted in Jackson Turner Main, *The Antifederalists: Critics of the Constitution, 1781–1788* (Chapel Hill, N.C., 1961), 202.

30. Benjamin Lincoln to George Washington, February 9, 1788, in Abbot et al., *Papers of George Washington: Confederation Series*, 6:104–5.

31. Elliot, *Debates of the State Conventions*, 2:23–24; *Massachusetts Gazette*, January 25, 1788; Harding, *Contest over the Ratification*, 77.

32. Diary of George Richards Minot, in Theodore Sedgwick Papers, MHS; Robert Feer, "George Richards Minot's *History of the Insurrections*: History, Propaganda, and Autobiography," *New England Quarterly* 35 (June 1962): 207.

33. Nathaniel Gorham to Henry Knox, January 30, 1788, Knox Papers, MHS.

34. Eben F. Stone, "Parsons and the Constitutional Convention of 1788," *Essex Historical Institute Collections* 35 (1899): 87–91. The nine amendments are in Elliot, *Debates of the State Conventions*, 2:177. Some sources erroneously list fourteen amendments.

35. *Debates and Proceedings in the Convention of the Commonwealth of Massachusetts ... 1788* (Boston, 1856), 80–86, 224–27.

36. Caleb Gibbs to George Washington, February 9, 1788, in Abbot et al., *Papers of George Washington: Confederation Series*, 6:103–4.

37. King to Henry Knox, February 3, 1788, Knox Papers, MHS.

38. *Boston Gazette*, January 21, 1788; Elliot, *Debates of the State Conventions*, 2:64, 150; *Historical Magazine* (November 1869): 268; Harding, *Contest over the Ratification*, 101.

39. For the vote, I have relied on two sources, which are especially helpful when analyzed side by side: Melville, "Economic and Social Influences at Work in the Massachusetts Convention," 67, 71–89; and Elliot, *Debates of the State Conventions*, 2:178–81.

40. Henry Jackson to Henry Knox, October 21, 1787, Knox Papers, MHS; E. James Ferguson, *The Power of the Purse: A History of American Public Finance, 1776–1790* (Chapel Hill, N.C., 1961), 256; William G. Anderson, *The Price of Liberty: The Public Debt of the American Revolution* (Charlottesville, Va., 1983), 41.

41. Van Beck Hall, *Politics Without Parties, Massachusetts, 1780–1791* (Pittsburgh, 1972), 40; Robert A. East, *Business Enterprise in the American Revolutionary Era* (New York, 1938), 320–21; William G. Sumner, *The Financier and Finances of the Revolution*, 2 vols. (New York, 1891), 2:253ff; *Acts and Resolves, 1789–1790*, 691–92; Orsamus Turner, *History of the Pioneer Settlement of Phelps and Gorham's Purchase* (Rochester, N.Y., 1851).

42. Max Farrand, ed., *The Records of the Federal Convention of 1787*, rev. ed., 4 vols. (New Haven, Conn., 1966), 1:299, 288–89, 309; Richard B. Morris, ed., *Alexander Hamilton and the Founding of the Nation* (New York, 1957), 335, 339. Of the many excellent studies of Hamilton's aspirations, I am particularly indebted to Gerald Stourzh, *Alexander Hamilton and the Idea of Republican Government* (Stanford, Calif., 1970) and Cecelia M. Kenyon, "Alexander Hamilton: Rousseau of the Right," *Political Science Quarterly* 73 (June 1958): 161–78.

43. *Annals of Congress*, 1st Congress, 2d Session (1790), 1191–96.

44. Alexander Hamilton to Provincial Congress of the Colony of New York, May 26, 1776, in Harold C. Syrett and Jacob E. Cooke, eds., *The Papers of Alexander Hamilton*, 27 vols. (New York, 1961–87), 1:184.

45. For a convenient summary, see tables in Hall, *Politics Without Parties*, 330, 332.

46. *Annals of Congress*, 1st Congress, 2d Session (1790), 1280–84, 1319–26, 1332–38, 1405–12, 1443–48, 1525–26; Winfred E. A. Bernhard, *Fisher Ames: Federalist and Statesman, 1785–1808* (Chapel Hill, N.C., 1965), 119–39; Ferguson, *Power of the Purse*, 289–305; Paul Goodman, *The Democratic-Republicans of Massachusetts* (Cambridge, Mass., 1964), 32–37; Hall, *Politics Without Parties*, 340, table 77.

47. *Annals of Congress*, 1st Congress, 2d Session (1790), 1622–23.

48. John Carnes to George Thacher, April 20, 1790, Nathaniel Wells to Thacher, April 27, 1790, Thomas B. Wait to Thacher, April 21, 1790, Thacher Papers, Boston Public Library.

49. Message of September 15, 1790 in *Acts and Resolves, 1790–1791*, 554–55; Whitney K. Bates, "The State Finances of Massachusetts, 1780–1789" (M.A. thesis, University of Wisconsin, 1948), 134.

50. Ferguson, *Power of the Purse*, 272; Andrew Craigie to Leonard Bleecker, December 19, 1789, in Craigie Papers, AAS.

51. Hall, *Politics Without Parties*, 42; *Massachusetts Magazine*, July 1789–June 1792.

52. Ferguson, *Power of the Purse*, 274.

53. Ferguson, *Power of the Purse*, 273–75. Information about individual creditors can be found in the Subscription Register, Loan of 1790, Massachusetts, National Archives, University of Maryland branch. The National Archives has the pertinent volumes of the "Old Loan" records that cover annual interest payments, but for some reason cannot locate the key document that lists the state creditors in 1790 and their holdings. I was able to obtain a microfilm copy, thanks to George Kennedy, from the Church of Jesus Christ of Latter Day Saints.

54. Anderson, *The Price of Liberty*, 37; Peter J. van Winter, *American Finance and Dutch Investment, 1780–1805 . . .* , 2 vols., rev. ed. (New York, 1977), 1:385.

55. Charles J. Bullock, *Historical Sketch of the Finances and Financial Policy of Massachusetts from 1780 to 1905* (New York, 1907), 15–16; Bates, "State Finances of Massachusetts," 134.

56. For details on Minot's life, I am indebted to Lemuel Shattuck, "The Minot Family," *New England Historical and Genealogical Register* 1 (1847), 171–78, 256–62, and Feer, "George Richards Minot's *History of the Insurrections*," 203–28.

57. Diary of Minot, June 9, 1787.

58. Diary of Minot, 1788.

59. George Richards Minot, *The History of the Insurrections in Massachusetts* (Worcester, Mass., 1788), 192.

60. Washington to Minot, August 28, 1788; Washington to Lincoln, 28 August 1788, in Abbot et al., *Papers of George Washington: Confederation Series*, 6:482–85.

61. Gore Vidal, *Homage to Daniel Shays: Collected Essays, 1952–1972* (New York, 1973); Ronald W. Reagan, Proclamation 5598, *Public Papers of the President of the United States* (Washington, D.C., 1987); *Valley Dollar Directory* (Winter 1996–97): 69, as cited in Thomas E. Conroy, "'Amongst the Disaffected in Massachusetts': History, Memory, and Shays' Rebellion" (seminar paper, University of Massachusetts, spring 1997), 3.

INDEX

Abercrombie, Reverend Robert, 101–2, 108

Abnakis, 45

Act of Indemnity, 17

Adams, James, 25

Adams, John, 70–72, 83, 87–88, 162

Adams, Samuel: and Massachusetts Constitution, 71, 78; and Massachusetts ratifying convention, 143, 149; and Shays's Rebellion, 11, 16–18, 21, 32, 34

African slave trade, 137–38

Alamance, Battle of, 65

Alford, Massachusetts, 146

Allen, Ethan, 34, 67, 120–21

Allen, Solomon, 112

Allen, Reverend Thomas, 114

American Revolution: in Amherst, 94, 97; betrayal of, 59, 73–74, 111, 131; in Colrain, 107–8; in Pelham, 98–101; support for, 111; in West Springfield, 44–45; in Westfield, 112–13; in Whately, 105. *See also* Veterans

Ames, Fisher, 155–56

Amherst, Massachusetts, 8–9, 25, 27, 54, 74, 82, 89–90, 100–101, 103, 107, 110, 119, 146, 150; as banner rebel town, 56–57, 91–98, 111, 116; church conflict in, 93–94, 116

Anderson, John, 107

Andover, Massachusetts, 77

Annapolis Convention, 126–27

Antifederalists, 140–41, 144, 155–56

Arnold, Benedict, 45–46

Articles of Confederation, 2, 124–29, 131, 151–52

Ashfield, Massachusetts, 57

Ashley, John, 35–36

Assumption of state debts, 152–59

Athol, Massachusetts, 31

Backcountry: clergy in, 26, 93–94, 101–5, 108, 113–16; debt in, 1–2, 58–62, 176n. 30; disdain for state government and legal system, 7–8, 10–11, 51, 63, 68–74, 101, 148–49; economy of, 4–7; lack of legal tender, 7–8, 82; political culture, 5, 146; and U.S. Constitution of 1787, 147–50

"Balanced government," 70–72, 83
Baldwin, Jeduthan, 54
Baldwin, Reverend Moses, 40
Bardwell, Perez, 53–54
Becket, Massachusetts, 36
Belchertown, Massachusetts, 52, 57, 61, 73
Belknap, Reverend Jeremy, 32
Bement, Asa, 35
Bemis, William, 17
Benning, William, 66
Bennington, Vermont, 66, 123
Bentley, Reverend William, 117
Berkshire County, Massachusetts, 8, 14–15, 30–31, 33–35, 39–41, 55, 59–62, 81, 115
Bernardston, Massachusetts, 40–41, 105, 146
"Big Dig," 162–63
Bill of Rights, 70, 140–42, 148–49
Billings, Joel, 9, 18
Billings, Sylvanus, 21
Bishop, Phanuel, 145, 148
"Black List," 33, 96–97, 145
Blacks, 25, 35, 43, 70
Blair, Timothy, 145
Blandford, Massachusetts, 145
Bleecker, Leonard, 157
Blood family (Groton), 80
Blue-Backed Speller, 80
Bly, John, 41–42, 119
Boltwood family (Amherst), 97
Boltwood, Solomon, 100–101
Boston, Massachusetts, 11–12, 25–26, 29–30, 55, 71, 74, 81, 96, 109, 122, 130, 143–44; bankers and speculators in, 75, 77–79, 107, 124; debt in, 58, 62; disdain for Rhode Island, 84–85; reaction to Daniel Shays, 117–19; resentment of, 7–8, 140, 143, 159–60, 162–63; support for assumption, 155–60; support for U.S. Constitution, 147–51
Bowdoin, James, 124, 128, 130; and

Articles of Confederation, 125–27; on backcountry, 130; and John Hancock, 85, 118; and Shays's Rebellion, 11, 18–19, 21–23, 26–27, 32–34, 38–40, 56, 68, 71, 160, 162–64; support for speculators, 85–88; and U.S. Constitution, 144, 147
Boyd, Samuel, 110, 115
Boylston, Massachusetts, 21
Braintree, Massachusetts, 70–71
Brant, Joseph, 34
Brattleborough, Vermont, 122
Breck, Samuel, 157
Brimfield, Massachusetts, 57
Bristol County, Massachusetts, 8, 12, 55, 145
Bromfield, Edward, 77–78
Brooke, John L., 115
Brookfield, Massachusetts, 54
Brooks, John, 128
Brown, Aaron, 21
Brown, John, 84
Bruce, John, 8
Brynner, Rock, 132
Bunker Hill, Battle of, 95
Burgoyne, John, 34, 96
Burke, Aedanus, 48
Burroughs, Stephen, 102–3
Burt, Gideon, 31

Cambridge, Massachusetts, 18, 127
Carrington, Edward, 130, 132
Carter, Aaron, 43
Castle Island, 41
Champney, Ebenezer, 21
Charleston, South Carolina, 23, 48, 65, 118
Charlton, Massachusetts, 145
Chenery, Isaac, 21
Cherokee War, 65
Chesterfield, Massachusetts, 57
Chicopee, Massachusetts, 28
Chittenden, Thomas, 120–21

Cincinnati, Society of the, 46–48, 53, 125, 128
Cincinnatus, 47
Clapp, Elizabeth, 97
Clapp, Oliver, 97
Clark, John, 107
Clark, Matthew, 110
Clark, Samuel, 9
Clergy: in Amherst, 93–94, 116; in Colrain, 108, 115; in Massachusetts ratifying convention, 147; in Pelham, 101–2, 115; in West Springfield, 103, 115; in Whately, 105; response to rebellion, 26, 103–4, 113–16
Clinton, George, 122
Clinton, Henry, 23
Cobb, David, 12
Collins, John, 83
Colrain, Massachusetts, 43, 73–74, 89, 91, 100, 119, 146, 150, 159, 175n. 21; as banner rebel town, 56–57, 61–62, 106–9, 111, 115–16
Colton, Elihu, 145
Common Sense, 69
Concord, Massachusetts, 11, 20, 39
Congress, Continental, 15–16, 48, 126–28, 130
Congress, U.S., 153–58
Confession Act of 1782, 51
Conkey Tavern, 5, 99
Connecticut, 5, 55–56, 58, 60, 62, 66, 134, 140–41
Consolidated debt, 75, 81–82, 156
Constitution of 1778 (Massachusetts), 70–72, 101
Constitution of 1780 (Massachusetts), 2, 59, 68, 114; backcountry attitude toward, 7, 10–11, 71–74, 101
Constitution of 1787 (U.S.): and domestic rebellion, 134–36; and economic needs of merchants, 135–38; impact of Shays's Rebellion on, 1–3, 134; impact on speculators, 150–52; opposition to, 140–44, 155; Philadel-

phia convention, 2–3, 12, 131–33, 140, 143–44; and slavery, 136–38; ratification, 139, 147–50
Continental Line. *See* Massachusetts Line
Conway, Massachusetts, 52
Cook, Levy, 90–91
Cook, Martin, 90–91
Cook, Moses, Jr., 90–91
Cook, Moses, Sr., 90–91
Cooley, Daniel, 146–47, 150
Cooley, Martin, 96
Cornwallis, Lord, 23, 46
Cortlandts, 65–66
Country Party (Rhode Island), 83–84
County Conventions, 8–9
Court closings, 1–2, 8–10, 13–14, 20–22, 58–60
Cowls, Oliver, 92
Creditors, rebels, 54
Crown Point, 95
Curtis, Reverend Caleb, 145
Cushing, William, 12

Dana, Francis, 84–85
Davis, Abijah, 114–15
Davis, Josiah, 105
Day family (West Springfield), 102–4
Day, Luke, 18–29, 34, 58, 89, 96, 103–4, 112, 116; as stereotypical rebel, 44–55, 63
Day, Thomas, 49
Death sentences, 39–43
Debt: consolidation of, 74–76, 152–58; debt suits, 58–62, 176n. 30; imprisonment for, 50–54; insurgents and, ix–x, 1–2, 16–17, 54, 58, 116; merchants and, 58, 62; "recognizance cases," 60–61
Declaration of Independence, 67–68
Declaration of martial law, 32
Dedham, Massachusetts, 75
Deerfield, Massachusetts, 117
Delaware, 140–41

Democracy, fear of, 128, 133–34
Dickinson, Elijah, 92
Dickinson, Emily, 92
Dickinson family (Amherst), 9, 91–98, 106
Dickinson, Medad, 92
Dickinson, Moses, 92–93, 97
Dickinson, Nathan, 93
Dickinson, Nathan, Jr., 92–93
Dickinson, Nathaniel, Jr., 94
Dickinson, Oliver, 82
Dickinson, Reuben, 26, 54, 60, 95–97, 101, 116, 122–23
"Dirty Compromise," 137–38
Disqualification Act, 33–34, 36–37
Dorchester, Lord (Guy Carleton), 34
Draper, Reverend Ichabod, 94–95

Eddy family (Colrain), 146
Eddy, Samuel, 146, 150
Edinburgh University, 101–2
Edson, Jonathan, 105
Egalitarianism, 101, 108
Egremont, Massachusetts, 146
Elections and officeholding: in back-country, 5, 144–47; under Massachusetts law, 5, 72
Ellsworth, Oliver, 134
Ely, Benjamin, 8, 102–4, 145, 150
Ely family (West Springfield), 102–4
Ely Rebellion, 54, 60, 96
Ely, Reverend Samuel, 60, 96
Essex County, Massachusetts, 39, 71, 155–56
"Essex Result," 70–72, 147
Exeter, New Hampshire, 13

Family, importance of, 89–91. See also names of individual families
"Family reconstitution," 166n. 1
Faneuil Hall, 11
Farmers. See Yeomen
Federalists, 139–41, 148–49, 152, 160
Fisk, Asa, 145
Fitch, Ephraim, 146

Fowler, Silas, 145
Freeman, Elizabeth, 35
French and Indian War, 95
Funding of national debt, 152–58

George III (king of England), 8, 16, 59, 97, 128, 145
Georgetown, 155
Georgia, 139–41, 154
Gerry, Elbridge, 15, 134, 141–44, 147, 155–56
Gibbs, Caleb, 149–50
Gilbert, Daniel, 54
Goodhue, Benjamin, 155–56
Gorham, Nathaniel, 124, 128–29, 147–49, 150–51
Goshen, Massachusetts, 57
Gracchus, Tiberius and Gaius, 14–15
Granby, Massachusetts, 30
Granville, Massachusetts, 56–57, 61–62
Graves, Electa, 105
Graves family (Whately), 104–6
Graves, Israel, 104
Graves, Oliver, 104–5
Graves, Rebecca, 105
Graves, Ruth, 105
Graves, Selah, 104
Gray, Daniel, 98
Gray, Ebenezer, 98, 102
Gray family (Pelham), 98–102
Great Barrington, Massachusetts, 12, 14, 35–36, 39–40, 59
Great Britain: alleged ties with rebels, 26, 130; empire, 120; hatred of, 98–100
Green Dragon Resolution, 143
"Green Mountain Boys," 34, 66–67, 69, 120–21
Green, Peter, 43
Green, Tobias, 43
Greenleaf, William, 11
Greenwich, Massachusetts, 6, 9, 54, 56–57, 73, 113, 163
Groton, Massachusetts, 11, 19–20, 41, 55, 81, 90, 116, 145

Grover, Thomas, 80

Habeas corpus. *See* Writ of habeas corpus
Hadley, Massachusetts, 9, 30–32, 57, 59, 89, 94, 101, 113–14
Hall, Van Beck, 60–61
Hamilton, Alexander, 120–23, 125, 127, 132–33, 152–58
Hamlin, Perez, 35–36
Hampshire County, Massachusetts, 8, 14, 25, 34, 39–41, 95, 115, 162; as most rebellious county, 55–57, 59–62
Hampshire Herald, 79–80
Hancock, John, 39–41, 78, 85–87, 118, 149–50, 156, 160, 162
Hapsgood, John, 21
Hard money, 7, 82
Hardwick, Massachusetts, 123
Hartford, Connecticut, 48, 67, 72
Harvard College, 70, 77, 94, 114–15, 159
Harvard, Massachusetts, 145
Harvey, Moses, 14, 39–40, 119
Hastings, John, 8
Hatfield, Massachusetts, 8, 80–81, 101, 105–6
Hawley, Joseph, 80
"Hay Mow Sermon," 102
Hazelton, Simeon, 63, 123–24
Heath, Massachusetts, 56–57, 89
Heath, William, 111, 147
Henry (prince of Prussia), 128
Henshaw, Joseph, 38
Hichborn, Benjamin, 20–21
Higginson, Stephen, 11, 16, 33, 125, 127–28
Hines, Joseph, 9, 18, 163
Hines, Nehemiah, 4–6, 26, 42, 54, 98, 163
Hines, Timothy, 54
Historical Magazine, 150
History of the Insurrections in Massachusetts, 161
Holden, Massachusetts, 21

Hopkins, Henry, 35–36
Hopkins, Reverend Samuel, 114
Howard, Reverend Bezaleel, 33, 80
Hubbardston, Massachusetts, 111
Humphreys, David, 2, 129
Hunt, Joshua, 61–62
Hurlburt, John, 146
Hutchinson family, 91

Imprisonment for debt, 50–54
Indians, 15, 70
Ingersoll, Jonathan, 35
Insurrections: in New Hampshire, 13–14; in New York, 65–66; in North Carolina, 64–65; in South Carolina, 64–65; in Vermont, 13–14, 66–67
Intolerable Acts, 101

Jackson, Henry, 16, 144
Jackson, Jonathan, 11
Jefferson, Thomas, 155
Johnson, John, 54
Johnston, Isaiah, 52
Josselyn, Benjamin, 145
Judd, Reverend Benjamin, 114–15
Judd, Sylvester, 8, 94

Kelsey, John, 19–21
Kemp, John, 67
Kennebec River, 45
King, Rufus, 85, 88, 126–27, 132, 142–44, 147–51
Kingsley, Nathaniel, 36
Kirkland, John, 50
Knox, Henry, 16, 28, 68, 113, 152–53; characterization of rebels, 2, 109–11, 144; in favor of new constitution, 125, 127–31, 141; and Society of the Cincinnati, 46–48
Knox, Lucy, 2, 109–10

Laborers, 4, 53
Lafayette, Marquis de, 26–27, 54, 111, 131–32
Lake Champlain, 95

Land speculation. *See* Speculators

Lanesboro, Massachusetts, 36

Langdon, John, 135

Lathrop, Reverend Joseph, 103–4

Lee, Henry, 132

Lee, "Lighthorse" Henry, 109

Lee, Massachusetts, 35

Lee, Nathaniel, 49–50

Lee, Richard Henry, 140–41, 190n. 5

Lenox, Massachusetts, 41

Leonard family (West Springfield), 102–4

Leonard, Reuben, Jr., 103–4

Leverett, Massachusetts, 36

Lexington and Concord, Battles of, 10, 26, 44, 53, 95, 111–12

Lincoln, Benjamin: 27, 106, 113, 127; and Boston speculators, 78–79; and later career, 118, 162–63; and punishment of rebels, 36, 38, 120; and ratification of Constitution, 144, 147; and Society of the Cincinnati, 46–48; and state army, 23–24, 26, 30–35, 56, 160

Livingstons, 65–66

Localism, appeal of, 122–24

Longmeadow, Massachusetts, 57, 145

Loyalists. *See* Tories

Madison, James, 2–3, 130–37, 143–44, 153–55

Maine, 16, 85, 109–10, 130, 139, 141, 144, 156

Manning, William, 41

Marblehead, Massachusetts, 134, 141, 155

Maryland, 70, 140–41

Mason, George, 135

Mason, Jonathan, 76–79, 155, 157–58

Mason, Jonathan, Jr., 77

Massachusetts Bank, 78–79

Massachusetts Centinel, 29, 80, 142

Massachusetts congressional delegation, 155–56

Massachusetts Constitution of 1778. *See* Constitution of 1778 (Massachusetts)

Massachusetts Constitution of 1780. *See* Constitution of 1780 (Massachusetts)

Massachusetts Gazette, 79

Massachusetts government: colonial charter, 72, 74; debt consolidation, 74–76; hiring an army, 23–25, 32, 34–35, 106; legal system, 8, 10; George Richards Minot and, 160–62; qualifications for voting and holding office, 5, 72–73; tax collection, 85, 87–88; viewed as tyranny, 7–8, 10–11, 63, 68–74. *See also* Constitution of 1778 (Massachusetts); Constitution of 1780 (Massachusetts)

Massachusetts Line, 1, 6, 8, 19–20, 44–48, 53–54, 75, 96, 111

Mattoon, Ebenezer, Jr., 94, 97–98, 110–11, 116

McClellan, Hugh, 109–11, 115

McCulloch, Henry, 183n. 15

McGee, Thomas, 62

Mercantile Party (Rhode Island), 83–84

Merchants: and Articles of Confederation, 125–26; debt of, 58, 62; and Hamilton's fiscal program, 153–56; and Lincoln's army, 23–24, 78–79; and state debt, 74–77; and U.S. Constitution of 1787, 135–38, 147–51. *See also* Boston, Massachusetts; Speculators

Middlesex County, Massachusetts, 8, 11, 18, 20–21, 39, 55, 115, 145

Militia, 65–66, 123; and American Revolution, 10; and Shays's Rebellion, 11–15, 18, 42, 146; and U.S. Constitution of 1787, 134–36

Ministers. *See* Clergy

Minot, George Richards, 128, 147–48, 159–62, 164

Monson, Massachusetts, 57

Montague, Massachusetts, 14, 80
Morgan, John, 52
Morris, Gouverneur, 137
Morris, Robert, 126
Morse, Benjamin, 145
Murray, Seth, 8, 81

Nash, John, 97
Nasson, Samuel, 144
Nationalists, 1–3, 125–28, 132–34
Nation's capital, location of, 155–56
New Braintree, Massachusetts, 25, 39, 145
New England Regulation. *See* Shays's Rebellion
New Hampshire, 31, 38, 55, 58–59, 66, 102, 135
New Haven, Connecticut, 129
New Jersey, 140–41
New Lebanon, New York, 36
New Salem, Massachusetts, 57, 73
New York, 35–36, 48, 70, 125, 130, 141, 163; anti–rent war, 65–66; and Green Mountain Boys, 66–67, 120–22; and Massachusetts ratifying convention, 150–51
New York City, as nation's capital, 152, 155–56
Newburyport, Massachusetts, 49, 71
Newell, Josiah, 61
Newell, Oliver, 61
Newport, Rhode Island, 48, 84
North Carolina, 58, 64–65, 154, 162
North Carolina Regulators, 64–65
North End Caucus, 78
North, William, 15
Northampton, Massachusetts, 8–10, 18–19, 39–40, 44, 50, 52–54, 57–58, 60, 80, 96, 112–13, 163
Norwich, Connecticut, 78
Note speculation. *See* Speculators

Oaths of allegiance, ix–x, 36–37, 43–44, 144

Officeholding: in backcountry, 5; in Massachusetts, 72–73
Old State House, Boston, 149
Orange County Court (North Carolina), 65
Owens, Daniel, 83

Page, Benjamin, 19–21, 127
Paine, Robert Treat, 33
Paine, Thomas, 68–70
Palmer, Massachusetts, 28, 57
Pardons, 17, 39–40
Parker family (Groton), 90
Parker, Oliver, 19–20, 90, 127
Parmenter, Jason, 40–41, 105–6
Parsons, Reverend David, Jr., 8, 93–95, 116
Parsons, Reverend David, Sr., 93–95, 97
Parsons, Eli, 28–29, 33–34, 122
Parsons, Theophilus, 70–71, 147, 149
Paterson, John, 12, 30–31
Patterson, Joseph, 52
Payner, Edward, 11, 16
Peck, John, 75
Pelham, Massachusetts, 4–6, 9, 25, 30, 35, 52, 54, 91, 107, 113, 119, 159, 162–63; as banner rebel town, 56–57, 98–103, 111, 115–16
Pennsylvania, 51, 68, 141, 159; western, 135–36
Pennsylvania Constitution of 1776, 68–70
Pennsylvania Gazette, 139
Pennsylvania Packet, 132
Penobscots, 45
Pepper, Isaac, 145
Pepperell, Massachusetts, 55, 90
Perry, Mrs., 35
Petersham, Massachusetts, 31–33, 73, 105
Petitions to Massachusetts legislature, 6–8
Phelps, Oliver, 124, 151

Philadelphia, 48, 100, 127, 130–33, 140, 156

Philipses, 65–66

Phillips, William, 11, 23, 32, 62, 77–79, 124, 126, 155, 157–58

Phillips, William, Jr., 77

Pinckney, Charles, 137–38

Pinckney, Charles Coatesworth, 134–36

Pittsfield, Massachusetts, 34–35, 81, 114

Plainfield, Massachusetts, 43

Politics Without Parties, 60–61

Poll taxes, 82–83

Poor Debtor's Oath, 50–51

Popular protests. *See* Insurrections

Porter, Elisha, 40, 96

Pratt, Micah, 52, 54

Pratt, Sylvanus, 54

Prendergast, William, 66

Prescott, Oliver, 19–20

Prime, Nathaniel, 157

Princeton, Massachusetts, 116

Providence, Rhode Island, 84

Pynchon, William, 8

Quabbin Reservoir, 162–63

Quebec, 34

Quebec Expedition, 45–46

Rand, John, 21

Randolph, Edmund, 132

Ratification of U.S. Constitution of 1787: battle in Congress, 139–40; impact on speculators, 150–52; in Massachusetts, 140–41, 144–51, 159–60; in other states, 139–41

Reagan, Ronald, 164

Rebellion, agrarian. *See* Insurrections

Regulators, 63–65

Republicanism, endangered, 14–16, 21, 33–34, 38, 81, 131

Revere, Paul, 143

Rhode Island, 69–70, 134; "virus," 83–85, 124

Riot Act, 17, 32

"River Gods," 91, 101

Rockingham, New Hampshire, 13

Rose, Charles, 41–42, 119

Rowe, Massachusetts, 56–57

Russell, Hezekiah, 112

Rutland, Vermont, 13

Salem, Massachusetts, 81, 117, 127

Sandgate, Vermont, 123–24

Sandisfield, Massachusetts, 114

Saratoga, Battle of, 10, 23, 96

Sash, Moses, 43

Scots-Irish, 98–101, 107–8, 115

Securities, Boston market in, 119, 124, 150, 157–58

Sedgwick, Theodore, 14–16, 35, 132, 136–37, 147, 156, 160

Selectmen, 5–6, 9, 19, 41–42

Senate (Massachusetts), 7, 8

Shattuck family (Groton and Pepperell), 90

Shattuck, Job, 11, 19–21, 39–42, 89–90, 127

Shays, Abigail, 5–7, 26, 54, 89, 162

Shays, Daniel: background, 5–7, 26–27, 54, 89–90, 95, 97; as historical figure after rebellion, 117–18, 120, 160, 162–64; impact on U.S. Constitution and its ratification, 135, 139–40, 143–44; as rebel leader, 9, 26–34, 39, 41–42, 98, 111

ShaysNet.com, 164

Shays's Rebellion: history of, 159–62; impact on Constitution, 2–3, 134–35, 187n. 17; naming of, 26, 137, 162; as Regulator movement, 63, 67–68; standard explanation, ix–x, 1–2, 58–62

Sheffield, Massachusetts, 32, 35–37

Shepard, William, 12, 28–30, 33, 56–58, 110, 112–13, 117

Shirley, Massachusetts, 19–20, 55

Shrewsbury, Massachusetts, 10, 38

Shutesbury, Massachusetts, 6, 26, 54, 57, 95, 116

Sidney, Lord, 34
Singletary, Amos, 148–49
Slaveowners, 147–48
Slavery, impact on Constitution,
    136–38
Smith family (Whately), 104–6
Smith, Gad, 106
Smith, Hezekiah, 107
Smith, Maverick, 114–15
Smith, Nathan, 19–21
Smith, Nathaniel, 96
Society of the Cincinnati. See Cincin-
    nati, Society of the
South Brimfield, Massachusetts, 57,
    145
South Carolina, 48, 58–59, 64–65,
    134–35, 137–38, 140–41, 154, 157,
    162
South Carolina Regulators, 64–65
South Hadley, Massachusetts, 57, 113
Southampton, Massachusetts, 8
Southwick, Massachusetts, 145
Specie. See Hard money
Speculators, 76, 119, 124, 154; contri-
    butions to state army, 78–79; in land,
    85, 107, 120–22, 124, 128, 130,
    150–51; in notes, 75–79, 124,
    141–42, 151–52, 154–58; resentment
    of, 79–81, 84
Spencer, Massachusetts, 17
Springfield arsenal, 1, 2, 15, 24, 27–30,
    39, 44, 57, 110, 112
Springfield, Massachusetts, 8, 12,
    21–22, 25, 32–33, 52, 57–59, 80, 91,
    96, 117
St. Lawrence River, 45
Stamp Act (1765), 158
Starkweather, John, 36
Steuben, Baron Friedrich Wilhelm von,
    15–16, 48
Stevens, William, 109–10
Stockbridge, Massachusetts, 12, 35–36,
    147
Storrs, Reverend Eleazar, 114
Strong, Caleb, 147

Stuart, Archibald, 132
Sullivan, James, 38, 41
Sullivan, John, 13–14, 38
Sunderland, Massachusetts, 96
Supreme Judicial Court, 33–34, 39–40,
    112
Sutton, Massachusetts, 148
Swift River, 162
Szatmary, David, 147

Taunton, Massachusetts, 8, 12
Taxes: as cause of Shays's Rebellion, 7,
    81–82, 129–30, 156; direct, 119, 137,
    147–48, 155–56, 158–59; excise,
    82–83, 119, 159; import, 82–83, 119;
    land, 119, 158–59; poll, 82–83, 119,
    158–59
Thacher, George, 156
Thetford, Vermont, 96, 122–23
Thompson, John, 9
"Three–fifths compromise," 137,
    147–48
Ticonderoga, Battle of, 96
Tillotsons, 62
Tories, 90, 94, 96–97, 101, 116
Townsend, Massachusetts, 55
Tracy, Jonathan, 49–50
Trade: between Boston and western
    Massachusetts, 58, 62; between Hart-
    ford and western Massachusetts, 62;
    with West Indies, 58
Trevett, John, 84
Tyler, Royall, 25

United States Constitution of 1787. See
    Constitution of 1787 (U.S.)
Uxbridge, Massachusetts, 145

Vermont, 31, 33–34, 40, 42, 55–56, 58,
    66–67, 96; Constitution of 1777,
    68–70; as haven for rebels, 120–24;
    and New York land speculators,
    120–22
Veterans, 6, 18–20, 43–44, 60–61, 75,
    79–81, 84, 90, 95, 101, 107–9, 128;

Veterans (*continued*)
  failure to support state, 25, 111–13,
    160; resentment of speculators,
    79–80, 84; support for rebellion, 27,
    109–13
"Vices of the Political System of the
  United States," 133
Vidal, Gore, 164
Virginia, 49, 126, 135, 141, 148,
  154–55, 162; reaction to Shays's
  Rebellion, 2–3, 131–33

Wait, Thomas, 156
Waldo Patent, Maine, 109–10
Walker, Jacob, 105–6
Ward, Artemas, 10–11
Ware, Massachusetts, 52, 56–57,
  114–15
Warner, Jonathan, 11, 18, 145
Warner, Seth, 66–67
Warren, John, 20–21
Warren, Mercy Otis, 128
Warwick, Massachusetts, 57
Washington, D.C., 155
Washington, George, 6, 10, 23, 29, 68,
  109–11, 118, 135–36, 150, 152, 162;
  at Constitutional Convention,
  131–33; and ratification of Constitu-
  tion, 139–41; reaction to Shays's
  Rebellion, 1–4, 129–31; and the Soci-
  ety of the Cincinnati, 46–49
Watkins, John, 103
Wealth, of rebels, 6, 19–20, 92–93, 98,
  102–3, 105–6, 108
Webster, Noah, 80–81
Weeden, John, 84
Wells, Agrippa, 146
Wells, Reverend Rufus, 105–6
Wendell, Massachusetts, 56–57
West Indies (British), 58, 91

West Springfield, Massachusetts, 8–9,
  28, 44–45, 49, 52–53, 61, 91, 107,
  112, 145, 150; as banner rebel town,
  55–57, 102–4, 111, 115–16
Westchester County, New York, 66
Westfield, Massachusetts, 27, 56–58,
  112–13, 117
Whately, Massachusetts, 57, 74, 104–7,
  111
Wheeler, Adam, 111, 123
Wheeler, Joseph, 145
Whipple, Joseph, 25
Whiskey Rebellion, 135–36, 159
Whiting, William, 12, 14–15, 39–40,
  68, 81, 119, 160
Whitney, Josiah, 145
Wilbraham, Massachusetts, 57
Wilcox, Molly, 40
Wilcox, Peter, Jr., 35
Willard, Samuel, 145
Williams, Elisha, 35–36
Williams, Israel, 101
Williamsburg, Massachusetts, 53
Wilson, James, 141
Windsor County, Vermont, 13
Winthrop family, 91
Woodbridge, Jahleel, 12, 35
Worcester County, Massachusetts, 11,
  25, 39, 55, 60–62, 81, 100, 115, 123,
  145, 148
Worcester, Massachusetts, 8, 10, 39
Worthington, Massachusetts, 43
Wright, Silas, 52
Writ of habeas corpus, suspension of,
  17–19, 21

Yale College, 60, 114, 146
Yeomen, 4, 19, 53, 159
Yorktown, Battle of, 128
Young, David, 39